MAXED OUT

AMERICAN MOMS ON THE BRINK

KATRINA ALCORN

SEAL PR

D0018721

MAXED OUT
AMERICAN MOMS ON THE BRINK
Copyright © 2013 Katrina Alcorn

Author's Note: To respect the privacy of my friends and former coworkers, I have changed their names and the name of the company where I worked. In some cases, I changed identifying details as well. As is common in creative nonfiction, some scenes and conversations are composites (so as not to bore you with meaningless specifics).

SEAL PRESS
A Member of the Perseus Books Group
1700 Fourth Street
Berkeley, California 94710

Library of Congress Cataloging-in-Publication Data

Alcorn, Katrina.
  Maxed out : American moms on the brink / by Katrina Alcorn.
    pages cm

  ISBN 978-1-58005-523-9
1. Alcorn, Katrina. 2. Working mothers--United States. 3. Stress (Psychology)--United States. I. Title.
  HQ759.48.A43 2013
  306.874'30973--dc23
                              2013016150
10 9 8 7 6 5 4 3 2 1

Cover design by Elke Barter
Interior design by Tabitha Lahr and Erin Seaward-Hiatt

Printed in the United States of America

Distributed by Publishers Group West

For my grandmothers, Sally Van Schaick and Barbara Fisher

INTRODUCTION

MUCH INK HAS BEEN SPILLED instructing women how to have it all—thriving careers, happy children, and satisfying marriages. You will find no shortage of magazines and self-help books bursting with snappy, upbeat directives like "Lose the guilt!" "Lean forward!" and "Don't let yourself go!" Taken together, their message is this: *Work smart, keep a positive attitude, and everything will be just fine.*

Years ago, when I was first coping with the competing demands of a new baby and a new job, I reached for those books with both hands. With their help, I learned how to "Stay ahead of my schedule!" "Make dinner in ten minutes or less!" and "Succeed at staying fit!"

I was so pleased with myself back then. No one was more organized, more efficient. When other working moms complained about how hard their lives were, I listened sympathetically, but secretly I thought, *She's just not trying hard enough.*

But after my second child was born, the limits of positive thinking became clear. No four-week Power Program or Efficiency Work Flow or other Jedi mind trick could resolve the ridiculous demands on my time.

One day, I went home sick from work and never went back. I never even cleaned off my desk. I fell into a profound despair, plagued by panic attacks, insomnia, shame, and dread. After almost six years of "successfully" balancing a job and family, I had completely maxed out. A yearlong journey through medication, meditation, and therapy began. As I learned over the months to heal my body and my mind, I sought the answer to one question: *What the hell happened?*

My collapse didn't make any sense. I was a smart, capable, healthy person. I had a loving husband, a supportive boss, healthy kids, great day care, a good income. If I couldn't manage a career and a family, then how were other working moms doing it, women who didn't have those advantages?

When I first attempted to write this book, a few months after I stopped working, I did so in a kind of feverish delirium, writing every moment I was not with my children. That first draft was what I thought of as a typical memoir—it was an intensely personal story about my life as a working mom, my attempt to "have it all," and my miserable failure.

It was my story, but it didn't tell the *whole* story. I knew I was not alone in my "failure." All around me, I saw women staggering through their days, trying to make the best of their own difficult circumstances. At work or at the park they made self-deprecating jokes about exhaustion, but once you scratched the surface, it stopped being funny. They suffered from panic attacks and depression, heart palpitations and hives, migraines and mysterious coughs that wouldn't go away. Many had tried antidepressants, antianxiety medications, or both. Most fantasized about quitting their jobs. Some actually did, trading their chronic time deficit for regular ol' debt.

It seemed gauche—selfish, really—to complain. After all, we were all living the lives we'd chosen. We had what we thought we wanted—wonderful children and a level of financial independence that our mothers never knew. And yet, most days, it felt as if our lives were being held together by Band-Aids and Elmer's glue. None of us could make sense of the wretched state we found ourselves in. What were we doing wrong?

I started researching the topic of women and work in earnest. In 2010 I launched a blog called *Working Moms Break* to share my thoughts about what I was learning. It was my own personal con- sciousness-raising period. Over the next couple of years, I heard from thousands of women and men around the world. Their stories helped me make sense of my own. So I rewrote the book. It's still a deeply personal story, but in each relevant chapter, I include a short essay about something I learned in my research, often backed with quotations or stories that women shared with me on my blog.

It is time we realized just how maxed out this generation of women has become. It does not have to be this way. And frankly, we deserve better. My deepest hope is that if we can see this problem for what it really is, perhaps together we can do something about it.

If you feel profoundly, inexplicably alone in shouldering the triple burden of work, school/day care, and family, this book is for you. If you wonder whether ticking off all the items on a daily to-do list is really the apex of human achievement, this book is for you. If you're working as hard as you can and it doesn't feel like enough, this book is for you. And if you suspect that there is a better way to live, then this book is most certainly for you.

CHAPTER 1.

MARCH 2009

I was driving down an empty frontage road, alone, in our dusty Subaru Outback, near the I-80 freeway in Berkeley, California. It was Saturday. I had just dropped off our junk electronics at the eco-recycling place. The irony was not lost on me that my next stop was Target, to buy a jumbo box of very non-eco diapers. After that, the grocery store, to stock up on party supplies.

My husband, Brian, was home with our one-year-old, Jake, our six-year-old, Ruby, and our eight-year-old, Martha (my stepdaughter). We often divided up the weekends this way, with one parent hunting and gathering and the other being, well, the parent. Our family was part of a relatively new tribe in America, one that sociologists call "dual-earner, multiple-child, middle-class families." In layperson's terms, we had kids and we both worked. Like so many members of this massive and growing tribe (which now numbers a little under half of all American households with children), our weekdays were devoted to work and basic kid care, while our weekends revolved around the time-honored ritual known as Getting Shit Done.

But on this particular weekend, we were planning to break out of that routine. We were going to host a big brunch on Sunday to celebrate my and Brian's birthdays, which were only four days apart. Brian had just completed a particularly grueling design project, one that had required him to work so many nights and weekends that his rare appearance at the dinner table caused the kids to gasp and leap out of their chairs, as if a real-life SpongeBob SquarePants had just strolled into the kitchen.

Now that Brian's project was over, we wanted to celebrate the return to normal life. There was only one problem. I didn't actually feel normal. I didn't want to see anyone, not even our friends. Years ago, I had been a person with lots of friends. The phone rang regularly with invitations to parties and dinners and plays. But little by little, work and family obligations had squeezed out just about any social event that didn't exist primarily for our children. At some point I had silently come to the conclusion it was too much effort to have friends.

I passed one gray warehouse after another on my way to Target. The black leather steering wheel grew sticky under my sweaty grip. I rolled down the window to let in some air, and sounds of freeway traffic rushed into the car, like the roar of a waterfall.

Suddenly, I knew the whole thing was wrong. The party was wrong. My attitude was wrong. Everything was wrong. The last few months had been a carnival ride of constant motion that left me dizzy and sick to my stomach. I wanted off. I wanted someone to pull the brake. I wanted to make it stop, but I didn't know how to make it stop. I didn't even know what stopping meant.

That's when I got the feeling that something horrible was about to happen. It was a feeling I knew all too well, a ghost pressing down on my chest. I pulled off the road onto the shoulder, kicking up pebbles and dust. Adrenaline shot through my body like an electric jolt. The thing I'd been dreading was happening now. At least this time the kids weren't in the car.

My heart pounded in my chest. My head hurt. My hands shook. I heard a familiar sound in my head, the electric drone of cicadas.

This will be over soon, I thought. *This feeling will pass and you'll still be here.*

I took several slow, deep breaths.

The sun pounded through the windshield. A truck rumbled down the frontage road, piled high with stacks of cardboard held together with twine. I watched a crow the size of a large cat alight on a telephone wire. The drone in my ears slowly died to a faint hum.

I fumbled for my phone inside my purse. There was only one person I wanted to talk to in that moment. Brian picked up on the second ring.

"Honey," I said. "Something's wrong with me." The voice that said these words didn't sound like mine. It was a woman I barely knew.

"Where are you?"

I could hear the concern in his voice. I could also hear his tiredness. I closed my eyes and saw him, unshaven, leaning heavily on his elbows at the kitchen table, the phone pressed tightly to his ear, while our son Jake toddled after his sisters, whose squeals I could hear in the background.

"I'm in the car. I just had a panic attack. I'm sitting on the side of the road."

"Oh, sweetheart . . ."

"I can't do this anymore," I said, my voice cracking. And even though Brian could take that statement a million different ways, he immediately knew what I meant.

"It's time to quit," he said. "It's over."

For a brief moment, I felt relief wash over me like a cool rain.

"It's over," he said again. "Just come home."

CHAPTER 2.

BACK WHEN RUBY WAS A BABY, combining work and motherhood was relatively easy. Brian and I both worked as freelance web designers then. We set up our office in an upstairs bedroom in our Oakland home, a sweet two-story Victorian we'd bought when I was eight months pregnant. We had no family in the area, so I paid a friend to come to the house a few afternoons a week and hold the baby while I worked. When Ruby was hungry, I'd zip downstairs, nurse her, then zip back upstairs. This cozy arrangement allowed me to make a little money without having to be away from my baby. On my days off, Ruby and I did leisurely errands, took naps together on the couch, or met up with the other women from my birth class for tea and walks around Lake Merritt. All in all, it was a Mommy-Baby Love Fest.

These halcyon days of early motherhood were something I'd just stumbled into. I'd never planned to work from home. Actually, I'd never planned to be a web designer, either. I'd dabbled in various jobs, including magazine reporter and campaign fundraiser, before going back to school when I was twenty-five to get a master's in journalism. My first job out of graduate school was working as an associate producer on a PBS documentary series based in Oakland. Although I was there for only a year, I thought I'd found my calling. I loved interviewing people and debating story ideas with my producer. I loved jetting around the country scouting locations and staying in fancy hotels on my company's dime. But I had no health insurance and barely made enough money to pay my rent.

This was in the late '90s, when the Bay Area was at the peak of the dot-com craze. It was a time of absurd excess. Salaries for kids just out of college were four times what I made for the PBS show. Everywhere you looked, start-ups sprouted like mushrooms. Not only did they offer health insurance, but they also beckoned to one and all with stock options and foosball tables. It didn't take too many narrow escapes at rent time before I decided to take one of those start-up jobs, even though I had no Internet experience.

Six months later, I took a better job at a web design agency in San Francisco. With six whole months of experience under my belt, I demanded a signing bonus. I officially became a dot-commer.

At my new job, employees were given orange jumpsuits with the company logo as their "uniform," a weird insider joke that I never did get. Free PowerBars and organic fruit lined up neatly in the company fridge next to the microbrews. It was common for companies like ours to sponsor team-building cruises, mountain-climbing trips, and lavish launch parties with open bars. I didn't play foosball and I looked terrible in orange. I was pretty sure my stock options would never be worth the paper they were printed on (they weren't).

But I didn't care. The work was challenging, the pay was great, and it was a relief to finally have health insurance.

BRIAN AND I MET AT THAT agency in San Francisco. He, too, had been a journalist, working at newspapers for more than a decade before joining the dot-com party. I knew right away Brian wasn't my type. He was a country-music-listening, whiskey-drinking, football-watching kind of guy. I was more of a samba-yoga-tofu gal myself. But we enjoyed working together, and gradually, against our better judgment, we fell in love. By then it was 2001, and our company, along with hundreds of others across the Bay Area, spiraled down into the recession. Like contestants on a reality show, we survived a round of layoffs, then another, and another—eight in less than a year. Over and over we watched our stricken, twentysomething coworkers tearfully gather up their things.

"They look like those Galapagos Island birds," Brian muttered to me, both sympathetic and scornful. "They had no idea there was such a thing as a predator."

Our day finally came that fall when the president of the company announced we'd run out of money. We would be closing our doors that very day. After months of trying to hide our blossoming romance from our coworkers, it was a relief not to work at the same company anymore. Of course, now we had a new problem—neither of us had a job. We started freelancing, because that was the only option. There wasn't a job to be had from Portland to Bakersfield. Luckily, we soon landed freelance gigs and found the lifestyle suited us well.

When Ruby was born, in 2003, Brian managed to do most of his work from home. He often took midday breaks to hold the baby, change her diaper, or carry her to the corner store to buy himself a Coke. Like all new parents, we were tired—okay, we were more than tired; we were exhausted—but since neither of us had a commute we could take turns letting each other sleep an extra hour, which took the edge off our sleep deprivation. Working from home also gave us time to adjust to being new parents together, and revel in the experience.

BRIAN'S DAUGHTER, MARTHA, was barely a year old when we got together. She was a thoughtful child with round cheeks, chocolate-brown eyes, and a mop of thick dark hair. She spent weekdays at her mother's in San Francisco and weekends with us in Oakland.

Martha was two and a half when Ruby was born, and the presence of a new baby seemed to knit our little family securely together. Martha fawned over her baby sister, and about as soon as Ruby's eyes could focus, they gazed at Martha with pure adoration. We took the girls on trips to the beach, to the zoo, to a children's museum in Berkeley where Brian carried Ruby in the Björn while I helped Martha paint cat whiskers on her face. We delighted in each new milestone—Ruby learning to laugh and make raspberry sounds, Martha learning all the words to "Raindrops Keep Falling on My Head," which she sang in her delightful Elmer Fudd accent ("Dooooose . . . waindwops keep faaah-wing on my head!").

Really, everything was perfect. Except for one thing: We weren't making enough from our freelance work to cover our basic expenses.

My entrée into freelancing had seemed relatively easy before Ruby was born, but now it was harder to find gigs that fit the hours I had available, and I had to turn down clients who wanted me at their offices in San Francisco or farther down the Peninsula. Brian was available for full-time gigs, but we were still in a recession, and there were often harrowing gaps between his projects when no money was coming in. Each month our credit card balance showed us going deeper into debt.

I obsessively added and re-added our budget, hoping we could find ways to cut back. We didn't eat out or go to movies, for reasons that anyone with an infant can readily understand. There were no fancy vacations, unless you count visiting my folks once every two years. (*Woo hoo! Schenectady!*) Our cars were more than ten years old, but since they drove fine, we had no intention of replacing them.

Our mortgage was about average for the Bay Area, not much more than we'd been paying in rent if you factored in the tax break for homeowners. But still . . . When you added in the cost of covering our own health insurance, plus car insurance, child support to Martha's mom, the payments on my student loans, groceries, diapers, utilities . . . it added up to *a lot*. There was no way around it: We had to make more money.

All the women from my birth class struggled with the same predicament—how to work enough (to pay the bills, to keep a foot in the door at their companies, to keep their careers alive) but not too much. I suppose "too much" was subjective, but we all seemed to agree that working five full days a week plus commuting was too much.

What I needed—what we *all* needed—was a decent-paying, stable, part-time job. Unfortunately, getting a good part-time job, even in a booming economy, would have been about as easy as a new parent getting a good night's sleep.

This, by the way, is a distinctly American phenomenon. In case you hadn't heard, we have the highest percentage of women who work full-time of any country in the world. Research shows 62 percent of working moms would prefer to work part-time but many don't have that option. Those who do (26 percent) are seen as "time deviants" by their coworkers and take a big hit in pay. Consider this staggering fact: People who work part-time earn as little as *58 cents on the dollar* for each hour worked. That's on top of the prorated cut in pay and benefits.

One of the moms I knew was thrilled when she talked her boss into letting her work a "reduced schedule." Later she told me she ended up doing more work on nights and weekends to make up for her day "off." In the end, she did the same amount of work but made less money.

So what's a girl to do—sacrifice her earnings and career status to have a little more time with her child (if she's lucky enough to have that option) or suck it up and go full-time?

Back when Ruby was a baby, I didn't think either was an option. No one was hiring.

MY FAVORITE DAY WITH RUBY was Friday. That's when we went to our mommy-baby yoga class.

To some people, this class, which combined regular "grown-up" yoga postures with baby massage, might sound like a Privileged White Mommy Thing, like aromatherapy bubble bath or playing classical music to your baby in utero. *Do babies really need massage?*

But there was nothing pretentious about the class, which was located on a busy street near our house, in a converted apartment with simple wood floors and bare white walls. It smelled pleasantly of apricots and cedar. The first time we tried it, I fell in love with the peaceful atmosphere, the quiet acceptance of life on Baby Time. The yoga poses helped relieve my postpartum aches and pains, and the baby massage seemed to help Ruby sleep better at night.

One Friday morning, I rested on my hands and knees on a yoga mat in a neutral cat/cow pose, alternately arching my back, then crouching, like a cat. Ruby, who was six months old, lay on her back on a towel beside me, fast asleep. Today, like most Fridays, the class was crowded with moms and their babies. Some of the moms stretched while their babies slept beside them. Other moms lay on their sides to nurse, or cooed softly as they changed a baby's diaper. The morning sun glowed through gauzy white curtains.

A voice beside me cut through the gentle murmur of the room: "I want you to come work for me."

It was Stella, slumped against the wall in a very un-yoga-like posture. Stella was one of my favorite clients—the only one, in fact, who paid on time—and I'd invited her to the class. She owned a small up-and-coming web design firm in San Francisco called Dogstar, where I had done several freelance jobs. We had worked with each other for a few months when we realized, giddily, that we were both pregnant with due dates only a week apart. She was about ten years older than I. I was thirty-one; she was about forty and had another child, a boy Martha's age, about three years old. Although Stella was, as Brian would say, a "strong flavor," with her loud voice and sometimes off-color jokes, I looked up to her in a shy, little sister kind of way.

"Joan is leaving in the fall," Stella continued a little too loudly, in her Staten Island accent. She had pulled her black tank top up on one side almost to her collarbone so she could nurse Claire, the infant daughter who nestled against her, naked except for a diaper.

I sat up quickly. "Joan is leaving?"

A woman with long blond dreadlocks looked at me sharply from her own yoga mat. Now I was the one being too loud.

Stella lowered her voice a notch. "She's getting married and moving to the Peninsula. We've started interviewing, but we haven't found the right person yet . . ."

She had my attention. Joan was the director of the user experience department, the group that did all the research, strategy, and interaction design for Dogstar's web projects. It was Joan who'd first hired me as a freelancer. Her job was so glamorous. She was always organizing industry events or jetting to New York or Las Vegas to speak at conferences. Everyone in the web design world knew her. Her job was demanding, but I knew it had to pay well.

". . . It could be a fantastic opportunity for you, Katrina." Stella, sensing my interest, leaned in as if we were conspirators. ". . . The next step in your career. You know everyone loves working with you. We'd be lucky to get you."

I was a sucker for this kind of flattery. Surely, in this job market Stella could find someone far more qualified. I had zero management or public speaking experience. She just happened to like working with me.

"It's intriguing," I said, not wanting to appear too eager. "I'll talk it over with Brian."

I returned to the cat/cow pose, which was working wonders for the lower back ache that had started during pregnancy and continued as I lugged Ruby around in her car seat.

"Think about it," Stella said. She leaned back and inspected a stray hair between her finger and thumb. "Whoever takes the job is going to hire a whole team. I can't guarantee we'll have freelance work forever . . ."

Bull's-eye. My biggest fear was that the little freelance work I had would dry up. I lifted my knees into a downward dog position, feeling the stretch spread from my hamstrings to my upper back. I took a deep breath in and then slowly out.

"All right, moms. Let's take off those diapers!" said the teacher, a tall woman with a long white braid, who gracefully threaded her way between the crowded yoga mats the way a long-legged bird might pick its way through a marsh. "If your babies are sleeping and you don't want to wake them, moms, by all means, keep doing your poses . . ."

I glanced at Ruby, who was still fast asleep. Her little fists were pulled up to her ears. Every once in a while she puckered her lips a few times, as if she was nursing in her dreams. I hated to wake her, even though she loved the baby massage. If I took a job, this class would be one of the first things to go out the window.

". . . and now rub a few drops of oil into the palms of your hands to warm them . . ."

I ignored the teacher's instruction. Still in downward dog, I lifted my right leg to intensify the stretch, and peered sideways at Stella under my right armpit.

"Damn, girl. You're so stretchy," she said to me as she stripped off Claire's diaper and set her gently on a towel. I took a moment to consider Stella. She was striking, with high cheekbones and a wide mouth. Her thick hair hung to her shoulders in bold contrasting stripes of red, blond, and dark brown. It gave her a kind of Corporate Punk look when she was at the office, and a Mommy Punk look when she was hanging out with her baby.

I admired the way Stella ran her business. All dozen or so employees in her office were friendly and down-to-earth, without a trace of the aggressive, adolescent-boy energy that permeated so many web design companies in San Francisco. Dogstar employees ("Doggies" as they called themselves jokingly) were always bringing in homemade muffins to share and Anne Lamott books to swap. People kicked off their shoes and walked around the office in socks when there were no clients around, and there were free tampons in the bathroom, the signature mark of a woman-owned company. I had no doubt that Stella would make a great boss.

". . . Now rub the oil gently in a clockwise motion on their bellies," the teacher said in a soothing voice. "This is very good for digestion . . ."

Stella turned to me, as if she could hear my thoughts, and with all her big-sisterly charm she said, "Katrina, I'm a working mom, too. If you took a job at Dogstar, we'd give you the flexibility you need."

I flashed her an upside-down smile and then switched legs. Ruby had just begun to stir. Her milky skin was so delicate I could see the razor-thin red vessels just beneath the skin of her eyelids. With her eyes still closed, she puckered her lips and let out a delicate squeak. I settled into a cross-legged position, then lifted her up high on my chest so I could rub my lips against the delicate peach fuzz of her hair, soft as baby chick feathers. With her eyes still closed she started tapping her face against my neck, rooting for milk.

She's so little, I thought as I lifted my shirt and unsnapped my nursing bra. *How could I possibly take a full-time job now?*

A FEW DAYS LATER, THE PROJECT Brian was working on was abruptly canceled. The client had decided to take its business elsewhere without paying for the work that had been done. We'd heard of things like this happening to other people. It was one of the risks you took when you worked for yourself. Now it had happened to us.

We had barely enough in the bank to cover two months' expenses, no income coming in, and we owed a small fortune in credit card debt.

The more I thought about the job with Dogstar, the more I realized Stella was throwing us a life preserver. Finally, one of us would have a steady paycheck, health care benefits and paid sick time. No one was offering jobs like this, not in the wake of the dot-com bust. What's more, it would be a big step up in my career.

I saw myself in my new life, thirty-one years old, happy, confident, large and in charge. I'd hire a big team and learn how to be the best manager they'd ever had. I'd perfect the art of public speaking and jet around the country lecturing about design. I'd wear shiny leather boots and designer glasses. I would be a real grown-up, with a 401(k) and college savings accounts for the girls. Most evenings I'd make it home in time to have dinner with my family.

It would be hard at first, sure, but we'd work it out. Lots of mothers with young children worked full-time, some of them with babies even younger than Ruby and bosses far less understanding than Stella. If they could do it, I could, too.

The next day, I called Stella and told her I wanted the job.

Unfortunately, the job wasn't mine yet. Hiring at Dogstar was a democratic process. Even though I had Stella's vote, I still had to convince the project managers and the creative director who managed the visual design department that the job should go to me.

Brian watched Ruby and Martha all weekend while I put together my portfolio, a half dozen case studies with screen shots of web projects I had led. I spent a small fortune getting it bound at Kinkos. The following week, I donned my most grown-up black skirt, squeezed into my most uncomfortable shoes, and tucked extra-thick breast milk pads into my bra to keep from leaking through my shirt. Then I rode the BART train to San Francisco to interview with four other "Doggies" and try to convince them that I was the best-qualified candidate.

For two anxious weeks, I bit my fingernails and waited for an offer. Nothing came.

The longer I waited, the more I wanted this job, and the more certain I was I'd screwed it up. Why hadn't I acted more interested when Stella brought it up in yoga class? If I didn't get this job, we'd be back where we started, hustling for freelance gigs, hoping we had enough to pay the mortgage, and going deeper into debt.

Now that I had the prospect of this new job, I couldn't stand the thought of not getting it. Money had been a constant source of stress for my parents when I was growing up. I didn't want Ruby to grow up the way I had.

My parents had been very young when they had me—nineteen and twenty-two. When I was little, they worked minimum-wage jobs in Upstate New York—Dad was a gas station attendant, Mom a cocktail waitress in a downtown bar.

There were no vacations or dinners out. Instead, there were long waits for the bus in the dead of winter when we couldn't afford to fix the car, long walks to the laundromat because our apartment didn't have a washing machine. Later, when my friends wore designer jeans and Nike sneakers to school, my clothes came from the Next to New on Jay Street and never fit right. We moved about once a year, from one apartment to the next, as we tried to climb our way out of bad neighborhoods and into something that resembled middle-class status.

Our money problems were more than a source of instability; they were a source of embarrassment, too. My mother once told me about going to the local department store to buy a toy. She wanted to get me something special, something new—most of my toys were hand-me-downs—and she'd been saving up for it. We rode the bus to Two Guys and selected a doll. Mom was planning to pay with change she'd saved from her waitressing tips, but she hadn't accounted for the tax. As she urgently searched through her pockets for that last quarter, a man in line behind us grew impatient and threw a crumpled dollar bill at her. She was mortified. The cashier picked up the dollar and handed the man his change.

I vowed I'd never live the way my parents did. Which was why I'd waited until I was thirty to have Ruby, and why I'd been so intent on buying a house before she was born, so my child wouldn't have to know what it was like to move every year. And yet, here I was, a new parent, going deeper into debt each month.

Finally, Stella called.

"We all agree. We want to offer you the job." She sounded as relieved as I felt. I could hear her wide smile through the phone.

The offer came with three weeks' vacation and a six-figure salary—both firsts for me. She said I could even hire my own husband as a freelancer when there was a good fit, so not only was I going to have a steady paycheck, but I would also be able to help Brian get steady work.

We closed the deal with a drink at an upscale bar next to the Dogstar office.

"To you," Stella said, lifting her wineglass.

"To Dogstar," I said.

We brought our glasses together with a clink. I felt instantly lighter, as if the weight of my money troubles and freelance worries had been cast off, a hunk of useless metal thrown over the rail of a ship.

I was lucky. So very, very lucky. I couldn't wait to start.

THE LACK OF PART-TIME OPTIONS

What if we didn't *have* to choose between having a career and having enough time with our children? As I mentioned earlier, this lack of good part-time jobs is a distinctly American problem. The Dutch, for example, have already figured it out. They've made it possible for almost any worker to tailor her job to a part-time schedule and keep her benefits.

Seventy-five percent of Dutch women work part-time (as opposed to less than a quarter of American women). The trend is not limited to female-dominated sectors like customer service and education. Today in the Netherlands there are part-time surgeons, part-time managers, and part-time engineers, and about a quarter of Dutch men work reduced schedules. These part-time workers earn less than full-timers, of course, but they earn the same per hour—there's no penalty for having a sane schedule. This solution has a nice side effect of helping to lower the unemployment rate.

➤

I know what you're thinking. This sounds like a huge hassle for businesses. Why would they agree to this if they didn't have to? Actually, there's something in it for them, too. Study after study shows companies that accommodate flexible schedules benefit in lower turnover, increased productivity, and higher workplace morale, and according to the U.S. Office of Personnel Management, working part-time may actually "increase employee effectiveness."

So why don't we do that here? Why does part-time work have such a cultural stigma, not to mention the brutal pay penalties? We're told over and over that Americans are the most productive workers in the world. Are we really as proud of that as our political leaders say we are? Or are we just afraid of losing our jobs?

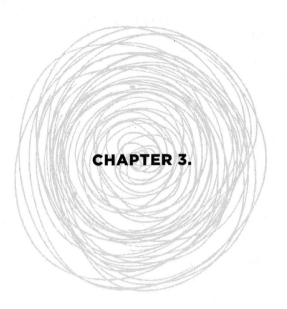

CHAPTER 3.

I WOKE UP TO THE SENSATION of someone tapping at my chest. I had a vision of a chicken pecking at grain in the dirt, but it was just my baby girl telling me she was hungry. Without opening my eyes, I pulled my T-shirt up so Ruby could nurse, then tried to enjoy the last precious minutes of shut-eye. When she was done, I nudged Brian awake.

"It's almost six o'clock, sweetie. Can you take her so I can shower?"

"Just set her down next to me," he groaned.

"She has to burp," I said. "*Sit. Up.*"

It was Day 5 of my new job and we were still adjusting to the new morning hustle. Before the job, we took turns letting each other sleep in most mornings. But now we both got up with the baby so I could be out the door in time to catch the 7:35 train.

Brian sat up against the headboard. I set Ruby in his arms.

"Mornin', Little Wonder," he mumbled. Eyes still closed, he sleepily thumped her back. Ruby let out a loud burp.

Suddenly, Brian was wide awake.

"Damn it! Can you get me a cloth?" He scowled at the spit-up dribbling down the front of his pajama top. "Why does she only do that to me?"

"Because you thump her too hard," I giggled. I took off my T-shirt and handed it to him.

Brian wiped himself off, then took Ruby downstairs. Soon I could hear the muffled clang of dishes as he unloaded the dishwasher.

I quickly showered and dressed, stuffing extra-thick nursing pads into my bra. They made me look like Jessica Rabbit but kept my shirts dry. Usually a B cup, nursing made me swell to a D, even without the pads. I didn't have many work shirts that fit. That hadn't been a problem when I worked in my pajamas. I made a mental note to go clothes shopping that weekend, then remembered with glee that I could afford to go to a nice place like Anthropologie instead of digging around the racks at the used-clothes store near the university.

By the time I got downstairs, Brian was assembling Ruby's lunch (a colorful assortment of mashed things in small glass jars) while she sat in her high chair, trying to stuff fistfuls of Cheerios in her mouth, most of which wound up on the floor. Later, after I left, he would play with Ruby or read one of her Maisy books. Around 8:00 AM he would dress her and take her to day care so he could start his own workday.

It had been a near thing, getting Ruby into a full-time day care. I hadn't expected it to be so hard.

I had set off on my search (with the naïveté of someone who has never had to directly confront the abysmal lack of quality child care in America) by calling two day care centers I'd heard moms at the park rave about. Both had good child-to-adult ratios and low staff turnover. They were pricey but less expensive than hiring a private Mary Poppins. One of them boasted a bilingual Spanish-English program. The other served hot, home-cooked, organic meals so parents didn't have to pack lunch. I imagined some kind of serene baby spa with pristine, brain-building toys lining the shelves, classical music playing softly in the background, the aroma of bread baking in the oven, and a backyard garden bursting with flowers. I left messages, but a week went by with no return call. When I tried again a few days later, one of them picked up.

"I'm sorry, we have sixty-seven children on the waiting list," said the woman who answered the phone.

I was incredulous. She went on to explain that some of the children on the waiting list hadn't even been born yet. Apparently, getting into a baby spa was like getting a table at a hot new restaurant. You had to know someone.

Eventually, at the bottom of my list, was a brand-new day care. A woman named Thania picked up on the second ring. She was from Honduras and had worked as a nanny for several years. She had two school-age kids of her own. She was licensed and CPR-certified. I was in luck—she had one space open. When I visited her modest, two-bedroom bungalow the next day, Thania opened the door. She was heavyset with a kind, dimpled smile. When I walked into her home I was enveloped not in the aroma of baking bread like my fantasy, but in the equally pleasant aroma of beans and tortillas.

Before we enrolled Ruby in her day care, Thania watched her

one morning, as a trial run, and quickly determined that Ruby liked her bottles extra-warm, thus solving a mystery that had confounded us for months: why Ruby was always so fussy when Brian tried to feed her. After that, Ruby knocked back her bottles like a Viking with a mug of mead, and I suspected we'd found our very own Mary Poppins after all.

"Whatcha got goin' today?" I asked as I shoved two pieces of bread into the toaster. While we'd been waiting for my new job to start, Brian had snagged a freelance contract with a medical device company on the Peninsula.

"The usual. Meetings in San Carlos." Like a lot of men, Brian had two modes of conversation about work—Ahab-level obsession and slacker-level indifference. This morning he was in Slacker Mode. "You?"

"Meetings and more meetings. Deliverable due to my bank client next week—might need to finish it over the weekend." I restrained myself from delving into the details. Work was suddenly front and center in my life and I could talk about it all day. Brian was a good listener, but even he had his limits.

Brian handed me a mug of coffee. I took a long sip, then caught sight of the clock above the dishwasher. "Shit! It's 7:20?" I slathered butter on my half-toasted toast. "Love you guys." I pecked Brian and Ruby and darted out the door to catch the BART train, carrying a breast pump in one hand, a laptop bag in the other, and the toast between my teeth.

I drove ten blocks to the BART station, parked in the lot, and raced down the stairs. A San Francisco train had just arrived on the platform, packed with office-bound men and women reading newspapers or tapping out email on their BlackBerrys, and I got on.

Part of me was jealous that Brian had a more leisurely morning with Ruby, but another part of me felt liberated standing on the train alone as it thundered along under the bay. I gripped the metal commuter rail, wearing grown-up clothes and eyeliner and dangly earrings, the kind I could never wear around little grasping hands.

In my first week at the new job, I was surprised how much easier it was to be at an office than working at home. The go-go Internet world was a walk in the park compared to bouncing a baby on my knee while trying to sketch a wireframe and keep an eye on chicken soup as it bubbled on the stove.

At 7:50 AM, I emerged from the Powell Street Station and jog-walked eight short, foggy blocks south of Market Street, past men in business-casual blue button-down shirts, past chic women in their swanky leather boots, past homeless people nestled under dirty sleeping bags or piles of discarded newspapers, sidestepping litter and the occasional bit of dog poo, finally arriving at the Dogstar office on Folsom Street. I unlocked the metal gate, then the glass door, punched the code to quiet the beeping alarm, and climbed the creaky stairs.

I was the first one in, as usual. Official hours were nine thirty to six, but Stella let me work an early shift—eight to four thirty—so I could pick up Ruby on my way home before Thania's day care closed at six. This was the best time of the day to catch up on email, read new proposals, or dig into anything else that required focused attention.

I left the lights off, preferring the gray light that filtered in the high windows and bounced off the white painted-brick walls. The office was a large, mostly open space with desks for a dozen people, although it could easily have fit twenty. It had a funky, artist-loft feel, with large rusty skylights, floors that sloped slightly toward the bay, and thin gray carpeting inexpertly applied, so that it bunched up from the floor in a few spots. The office wasn't properly heated or insulated—I knew from my freelance days that it could be a sweat lodge in the summer, a meat locker in the winter—but Stella had a sweetheart deal on the rent. What we sacrificed in comfort we gained in job security. The wreckage of the dot-com bust was still fresh on our minds. Everyone had come down in the world. Once we might have complained if the refrigerator wasn't stocked with the right microbrew. Now we shut up and dressed in layers.

WITHIN THE HOUR, my coworkers started arriving. By nine thirty, I was hustling from one meeting to the next. I built in discreet breaks at three-hour intervals to pump breast milk in the bathroom. Each day flew by until, suddenly, it was four thirty, at which point I'd excuse myself from whatever meeting I was in, pack up my pump and laptop bag, and speed-walk back to BART. Most days I managed to pick up Ruby by five thirty and get home by six. I was still expected to answer random emails or phone calls after I left the office, but my coworkers (even though most didn't have children) were uniformly respectful; they contacted me only if they needed a response right away.

At home, the next two hours was the usual routine of *B*'s—Breast-feed, Bath, Book, Brush teeth, Bounce the baby (Ruby liked to lie flat on her tummy on a pillow that I bounced on my knees until she fell asleep), then—blessedly—Bedtime. Somewhere between the second and the fourth *B*, I'd give Ruby rice cereal and more mashed veggies for dinner, and I'd make do with whatever I scrounged out of the refrigerator for me—cheese and crackers or leftover soup, anything that could be eaten one-handed. On the occasional weeknight that we had Martha, Brian entertained the girls while I cooked pasta or a stir-fry or some other Big Kid dinner that required a full set of teeth to chew.

It would have been nice if Brian could eat with us more often, but since he started his day later than I did, he usually ended later, too. Most evenings he joined us around seven or seven thirty, made himself a sandwich, then ate at the sink while he washed dishes. So much for the lauded Family Dinner. Oh well, it didn't start with a *B* anyway.

Once Ruby was asleep, I'd check email for the last time, respond to anything urgent, and go back downstairs where Brian and I would catch up on our day (or, if he was in Slacker Mode, he'd give me the two-sentence summary of his day, and I'd give him the blow-by-blow of mine). If we had the energy, we might watch an episode of *The Sopranos* while we folded laundry together. By ten thirty, we were two lumps in the bed.

A few hours later, I'd wake from a deep sleep to the sound of Ruby crying in the next room. I'd carry her back to our bed to nurse, where she'd stay until morning. One of the things I loved about motherhood was cuddling up in a warm bed with a drowsy baby. The only catch was that neither Brian nor I slept well with Ruby in our bed—she was a wiggly little piglet in her sleep. If I put her back in her crib, she cried, and at 2:00 AM, I couldn't stand to hear her cry. Which meant most nights we got two or three hours of real sleep. After that we dozed in a strange fugue state that was neither complete rest nor complete wakefulness.

Every new parent becomes intimately acquainted with sleep deprivation. Whether it's something they've experienced before or not, it's always a fresh torment. Our friend Tim once complained to his twin babies' pediatrician about how little sleep he was getting.

"Yep," said the doctor with a knowing nod. "Sleep deprivation's a bitch. That's why they use it for torture."

When we don't get enough sleep, our brains start to malfunction in all sorts of bizarre ways—we lose our emotional resilience, our tempers, and our ability to sustain logical thought. I once read that parents of very young children incur a "sleep debt"—an accumulated amount of lost sleep—of five months or more, just in the first two years of parenting. Which means the vast majority of parents with children under the age of two are the emotional equivalent of stumbling, bleary-eyed drunks looking for a fight or a warm place to take a nap.

At this point of our adventure as Ruby's parents, Brian and I were no exception. We had not experienced a full, unbroken night of sleep for more than eight months. Between the nighttime nursing and soothing and diaper changing, our lack of sleep had been piling up like snow outside the door, threatening to trap us inside. Until my new job started, we'd managed by taking turns letting each other sleep in. But now there was no sleeping in, and it wasn't long before the lack of sleep would start to take its toll.

THE REALITY OF BEING A full-time working mom was like diving into a cold pool. You can't prepare for it. The exhilaration of that first week quickly gave way to a deep, numbing ache for the former days with my baby. Leisurely midday grocery-shopping trips were replaced by harried evening trips with a cranky baby in the cart. No more baby yoga, peaceful afternoons at the park, reading

The New Yorker while Ruby napped on my chest, or walks around the lake with the moms from my birth class.

I missed my baby.

I was also worried about her. Although she seemed to be doing well, it didn't seem right that she spent the better part of each waking day with someone other than me. Maybe I would have felt differently if she'd been home with her dad, or a grandparent, but that wasn't an option. Brian's parents lived in Detroit, thousands of miles away. My parents were even farther away—my mother in Upstate New York, my dad and stepmother in Connecticut. I was still getting to know Thania, and while I trusted her, she wasn't family. When I added up the hours that Ruby was at Thania's, the number shocked me. I half expected a social worker to knock on my door. *Ma'am, we hear your baby is in day care forty-five hours a week . . .*

"Keep in mind, hon, you and I are amateurs," Brian said. "Thania's a professional."

He was right. Thania had more experience with children than I did—she'd read more books, she'd taken more classes, and she had two kids of her own—but that wasn't the point. *Mothers are supposed to be with their babies,* I thought. How could I be sure that Ruby was bonding with me the way she was supposed to? What if she didn't know how much I loved her? Was it really okay to be away from her so much?

I searched the Internet at night, when Ruby was asleep in her crib, looking for answers. What I read only made me more confused.

Some studies said that full-time day care could lead to psychological problems for a small percentage of children later in life, while other studies found that the effects of day care were negligible. Around the time I started the job at Dogstar, CBS ran a story called "The Negative Effects of Child Care?" about new research that showed longer stays in day care led to aggressive behavior later for some children. This could happen even if they were in high-quality care. The key to avoiding these behavior problems, one study concluded, was the mother: "The sensitivity of the mother could offset those negative effects."

In other words, it was up to me—and only me—to make it all right that Ruby was in day care all day. No mention of the father's role. I had already suspected this; now I had scientific proof. It was as if someone had just squirted an entire can of lighter fluid over the flames of my guilt.

So I did what I assumed any good mother would do in my situation: I tried to compensate for the time I was at work by devoting every extra moment to my daughter. I gave up exercise. I gave up seeing friends on the weekends. I continued to sacrifice sleep. At night, after Ruby was safely tucked in her crib, and before I started in on the laundry, I steamed and mashed and jarred fresh organic vegetables for her lunch the next day.

"You know they sell organic baby food now," Brian chided me one evening as I scraped puréed carrots from the blender with a tablespoon. "You don't have to do all this."

"I want to do it," I said stubbornly.

This was not entirely true. The truth was, my back ached from sitting at the computer and bending over a nursing baby, and I longed to collapse into bed. But the food I made—more nutritious than anything I could buy—was a way to care for Ruby when I wasn't with her.

When Ruby woke up to nurse at 1:00 or 2:00 AM, I continued to bring her to bed and keep her with us until morning. I wanted to squeeze in every extra opportunity for togetherness.

"WHEN DO YOU WANT TO TALK ABOUT sleep training?" Brian asked groggily one morning as he filled the kettle from the kitchen sink.

I felt myself tense up immediately. Sleep training, in my mind, was a nice, clinical term for "Let your baby cry alone in her crib." It was bad enough that I had abandoned my baby during the day. Now I was supposed to be away from her at night, too? I dismissed the idea with a frown and a vigorous shake of my head. "She's too little still."

Technically, this wasn't entirely true. According to a book some friends had given us, Ruby had surpassed the "magic weight" of eleven pounds, which meant her body didn't need a nighttime feeding. Physically she was capable of sleeping through the night. Brian knew this. After all, he told me that Martha was only four months old when she started sleeping through the night in her own crib. But Brian knew how bad I felt about being away from Ruby. Out of kindness, he let the subject drop. For a week.

"Hon, you can't keep bringing her to bed," Brian rubbed his eyes and slumped against the kitchen counter one morning. "We've got to start sleeping better."

I poured boiling water into the coffee filter over my mug, too tired to respond.

"Katrina, are you listening to me?"

"Yes, but I don't want to," I sighed. "Stop bringing her to bed, I mean." I breathed in the steamy aroma of Italian roast, willing the caffeine to enter my nose and go directly to my brain.

If I'd been thinking clearly, I would have seen that Brian and I both desperately needed to sleep, by any means necessary. If I'd been thinking clearly, I would have seen that the only way to function was to give up the thing I cherished. But sleep deprivation is a circular problem. I wasn't thinking clearly because I desperately needed to sleep.

"Look at you!" Brian snapped.

I jumped, startled at the abrupt anger in his voice.

"You have circles under your eyes. You've only been at this job for a month and you're running yourself ragged!"

"Thanks." I narrowed my eyes at him. "I really needed to hear how shitty I look."

"You know what I mean," Brian said, his voice softening. "I'm just worried about you." He put his hand on my arm, but I shrugged it away.

I had a feeling he was right—we had to do something—but I was so tightly cocooned in my own guilt, I had no room for compassion or understanding, neither his nor my own. The only other feeling I had room for was rage. *How could Brian possibly understand what this was like?* I fumed silently. He was the *dad.* The bar was so low for dads. Dads were like clowns at the party. Show up, make everyone laugh, take a bow, then disappear before the mess had to be cleaned up.

This wasn't fair, of course. Brian worked hard, too. He just knew his limits, and he didn't obsess over what he couldn't do. Once a week, he took a night off to see a movie or hang out at a sports bar with a friend. He didn't feel bad about it. And maybe that's what pissed me off. Because while I could have done those things, I couldn't have *enjoyed* them. Meanwhile, no matter what I did or didn't do, it seemed as if every day I was failing my child.

Brian rubbed his bald spot for a moment, then tucked a thumb in the waistband of his pajamas and tried again.

"Sugar, you're not taking any time for yourself. You need to take care of yourself . . . Go to a yoga class tonight. I'll watch Ruby."

"I don't want to be away from my baby." My voice came out low and quiet, almost a growl. To my own ears I sounded like some wild woodland creature.

"Listen, I know it's different for me . . . I have Martha . . ." Brian continued in his conciliatory voice. ". . . Ruby's your first. You worry more with the first one. But you don't have to do everything perf—"

Yep. He had already *been through this before*. And that was part of what I was pissed about. He wasn't worried about Ruby. I was alone.

"Shut up!" I snarled. "I don't need your fucking advice."

I looked straight into his eyes as I said that, and immediately wished I could take it back. Brian has the kindest brown Croatian eyes, which turn down at the outer corners. He stands a good six inches taller than me, and most of the time, he's like a big, strong, warm teddy bear. But when he's angry, he resembles something closer to a big, strong, actual bear, and although he has never inflicted harm on a creature larger than a house spider, the physical display of his anger always takes me aback. It took about a millisecond for this transformation to take place. Suddenly, I was staring up into hard, cold eyes.

"Fine. Fuck you, too!" Brian roared, slamming his mug down and sloshing coffee on the counter.

Ruby, propped up in her high chair, started to cry. Brian stalked out of the kitchen.

And so, in the fine tradition of exhausted, guilt-ridden mothers everywhere, I had alienated the person I most depended on—my husband—and upset the person I most wanted to protect—my child. And all it took was one stupid remark. I was becoming quite efficient.

DOES DAY CARE HURT BABIES?

In her parenting book, *Raising Happiness,* Christine Carter points out that while mothers are very important to the development and well-being of their children, we tend to go a bit overboard. She says our belief that it's only *natural* for mothers to be with their babies all the time is not, well, natural.

"Indeed, most of the world's children are *not* cared for exclusively or even primarily by the mother. Our sense that children will be best-served when cared for exclusively by their moms is a product of Western industrialization. Mothers serve as the exclusive caregiver in only 3 percent of nonindustrial societies."

She points out that children are just as likely to develop secure emotional attachments with fathers as they are with mothers, and day care, particularly for preschool-age children, can improve academic performance later in life. But that doesn't mean all child care is good or that the amount of child care doesn't matter. There have been many new studies about the effects of child care since my daughter was born in 2003. Higher-quality care (with low child-to-adult ratios and warm, attentive caregivers) is, not surprisingly, better for children than lower-quality care, and less child care (especially for infants) is better for children. But most effects, whether negative or positive, disappear by the time children are in sixth grade.

One thing we absolutely, positively know affects children is the well-being of their parents. Yet, studies show that mothers who take shorter maternity leaves or work more than forty hours a week are at higher risk for depression than those who don't. Perhaps instead of fretting about whether our children are being damaged by too much child care, we should ask ourselves this: "Are parents being damaged by too much time away from their children, and a lack of time to themselves?"

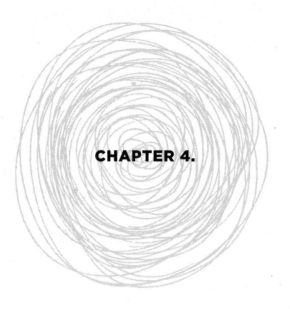

CHAPTER 4.

ONE COOL MORNING IN OCTOBER, I took Ruby to day care so Brian could make an early-morning meeting. I dressed her in a white onesie and her red stretchy pants with the heart patch just below her left hip. She cooed at me and kicked her feet in the air as I slipped on her socks. I was in the usual rush to get to work, but I took a moment to appreciate her succulent chubbiness. She wasn't old enough to walk yet, and her unused feet were like tiny bread loaves, unflattened by gravity. Her thighs looked like a kind of high-end pastry dough meant to be baked into cookies. Her wrists were so chubby it looked as if she had rubber bands pinching a deep crease where she bent her hand.

I tickled her through the hole in the onesie above her belly button, and she squealed. I had cut that hole and identical ones in most of her other onesies, too, to accommodate her new quirk. While other babies sucked their thumbs when they were tired or upset, Ruby fondled her belly button. If she couldn't reach it, she howled in frustration.

I gulped down my usual Breakfast of Champions—a piece of buttered toast—strapped Ruby in her car seat, and drove twelve blocks, past the liquor store, the senior center, another liquor store, and the apartments on Sacramento Street, then turned right onto Thania's street.

Thania watched us park from her picture window. She met us on the porch as I climbed the steps, Ruby in one arm, and in the other, a paper bag of accoutrements, which included a set of clean cloth diapers for the day and three small bags of frozen breast milk.

"Oh good, you brought more," Thania said, reaching for the bag. "She's going through the milk fast. Do you want to come in for a minute?"

I hesitated. I didn't want to rush the drop-off, but I had a meeting at 10:00 AM at a client's office, and I had to print a document at the Dogstar office first. If I sat down, Ruby would want to nurse again, and I'd be late.

"No, it's okay," I said. "I should go now."

I gave Ruby a kiss on her cheek and then, because I couldn't resist the soft warmth of her pearly skin, another one on her neck.

"You have a good day with Thania," I said as I passed her to Thania's outstretched arms.

Back when I had my first start-up job as a web writer, before I had a child, I wrote a story about mothers who feel guilty about leaving their children in day care. According to the experts, these guilt-prone mothers had to be careful not to transfer their anxiety to their babies. Little gestures were important, the experts said. For instance, you were supposed to hand your baby to the caregiver, rather than wait for the caregiver to take the baby, thus signaling that you trusted this person, and your baby could trust her, too.

Apparently, the experts had never seen the likes of my daughter, because as soon as I passed her to Thania, Ruby's face broke like a pane of glass through which I'd just thrown a rock.

"NOOOOOO! MAMAAAAAAA—" she wailed, making excellent use of her two favorite words.

"It's okay. She'll be okay," Thania assured me over Ruby's howls. She bent her head to Ruby's ear, bouncing her gently on her hip. "Come on, mamacita . . . You're okay. Mommy will come back . . ."

"MAMMMMMMMMMAAAAAAAAA—" Ruby continued at top decibel, as if I was putting her on a ship about to set sail for the New World or giving her up for adoption. For all I knew, that's what she thought I was doing.

"It's okay," Thania said, now trying to soothe both of us. "It happens sometimes. She'll be okay once you leave."

I stood looking at them for a moment, not knowing what to do. Then I remembered another thing the experts said. This type of separation anxiety is normal. Once it's time to go, it's important to go. Don't drag it out. Leaving Ruby crying in someone else's arms went against every instinct I had. But staying would just make it harder for her.

I turned around, and walked numbly down the front steps.

"Do you want to wave to Mommy?" I heard Thania say from the doorway. I wiped a tear off my nose, composed my face in what I hoped was a smile, and turned around to wave, but Ruby, still sobbing, had her face buried in Thania's chest. She couldn't see me. Thania gave what I thought was a brave smile and shut the door.

AN HOUR LATER, JOAN AND I crossed bustling Market Street and clomped our way past several blocks of giant concrete buildings in our nice (read: uncomfortable) shoes. Our meeting was with our largest client, a financial services company, to discuss redesigning a small section of their website. This was supposed to be a low-key meeting, an informal review of early sketches.

We signed in at the front desk and flashed our contractor badges. Everything about the lobby was shiny and marbled and new and perfect, so different from my messy, milk-stained real life. Important people worked in this building. Magicians. People who knew how to make money from money.

"I'm so glad you're coming today," I said to Joan as we stepped into the elevator. Technically, I had Joan's job now, but she had stayed on for an extra month, at Stella's insistence, to help with the transition.

"Oh, you'd be fine without me," she said, and pushed the button for the seventeenth floor.

"Yeah, but you've been working with Brenda for what . . . five years?" I said. "She loves you. And anyway, I barely know the difference between a stock and a bond."

"I told you to get *The Only Investment Guide You'll Ever Need*," she chided.

"Still reading it," I sighed, blowing the air out my cheeks. "I *hope* it's the only one I'll ever need. I can't get through two pages without falling asleep."

Joan picked a piece of lint off my shirt. "You need to start a retirement account. Then you'll have to learn."

"Right, just as soon as I pay off my student loans. And the credit card," I said.

The doors opened and we stepped into the lobby. Joan led the way through a maze of cubicles until we found the right office.

Brenda, the client, sat at her desk thumbing through some files. A clean-cut young guy whose name I had forgotten sat beside her, reading over her shoulder. Brenda, probably in her early forties, wore a crisp, white button-down shirt. Her long dark hair was ironed flat against her head. Her eyebrows were waxed to perfection. Everything about her was meticulously put together. I could smell her perfume, a subtle, expensive, flowery scent.

I always felt like such a hippie around people like Brenda, even in my corporate disguise: a red button-down blouse, black Banana Republic pants, and remarkably stiff flats that bit into my ankles. I hoped I didn't smell like milk. I suspected that breast-feeding had made me oblivious to the smell of milk, the way smokers can't smell tobacco on their hands. I made a mental note: *To fit in, must wax eyebrows.*

"We'll be right with you guys. Help yourselves to coffee in the kitchen if you want," Brenda said without looking up.

I removed the light fall coat I'd worn, carefully folded it, and set it on my lap. Joan gave her curly hair an unselfconscious shake, removed her cardigan sweater, and hung it on the back of her chair. She seemed perfectly at home here.

On Brenda's desk sat one framed photo, a black-and-white candid shot of three little girls at the beach. The youngest looked about Martha's age. The oldest looked as if she was in third or fourth grade. They were grinning widely, speckled with sand, and shivering under big towels. I wondered how old they were when Brenda went back to work, and how she felt about it. How did she manage to work full-time and raise three kids? I searched for some sign—a flaw, a crack, a scratch on her glossy, well-coiffed surface—but saw none. She looked perfectly content to be here in this office, seventeen floors above the street, flipping through her papers. I had only one child plus another one on the weekends, and I was dying after only one month. Maybe she was one of those women who had a live-in nanny, or helpful in-laws, or both. But even if she had all that help, if she was working full-time and commuting, she was away from them at least as much as I was away from Ruby—more if she worked the long hours some of her coworkers did. Was she Wonder Woman? Was she a *machine*? Did she miss her kids as I missed mine?

I looked around the room for something to distract myself. The top half of the wall behind Brenda's desk was glass. Beyond her and the clean-cut guy a forest of tall gray buildings stood side by side, like strangers in an elevator.

The John Hartford song "In Tall Buildings" started playing in my head.

Someday, my baby, when I am a man,
and others have taught me the best that they can
they'll sell me a suit and cut off my hair
and send me to work in tall buildings . . .

Brenda looked up from her papers. "Okay!" she said brightly, as if she'd been waiting for us. "Let's get going!"

Joan pulled out our wireframes, black-and-white line drawings of specific pages on the website. Like the blueprints of a house, wireframes show how things will be organized—navigation goes here, a pull-down menu goes there . . . Often I find it satisfying to review wireframes, with every element of the design neatly lined up in the right place. Sketching wireframes is a little like organizing a closet—there is something reassuring about the gridlike order. But that day, I wasn't feeling it—I just wanted to get the meeting over with.

Brenda and the preppy guy, whose name turned out to be Rob, started pointing at pages, asking questions.

"If users want to go to 'Mutual Funds' from the landing page, how would they get there?" Brenda asked.

"We can use the 'Related Links' box for that, can't we?" Joan answered her question with a question. Joan often affected a bright, cheerful manner with clients, like an especially chirpy dental hygienist.

"But aren't those links supposed to rotate?" asked Rob. "Or are you thinking they would be *perma*links?"

Brenda gave out a delicate little snort. "*Perma*links! Is that your own word, Rob?"

"We can do a mix of rotating links and permalinks," Joan said.

Both Brenda and Rob thought that was hysterical.

I suddenly realized I was having trouble focusing. I was lightheaded and a little shaky. Breast-feeding made me get hungry so quickly. One minute I was fine; the next minute I was ravenous. The toast I'd gulped down for breakfast wasn't cutting it. Normally I'd grab a midmorning snack when hunger struck, but I'd gone in late after dropping off Ruby and I was out of my regular routine. I hadn't even had time to pump before we left the office. I casually brushed the edge of my forearm against one breast as if I were scratching a rib. Yup, full. Very full. That meant Ruby was probably getting hungry. I wondered if Thania had fed her a midmorning snack yet. I hoped my milk wouldn't let down in the middle of this meeting.

"You're not proposing any changes to the sub-nav, right?" Brenda said.

"Just a few teensy changes," Joan said. "We're probably going to take another look at the way we're categorizing the areas under 'Bonds.' We think it's a little confusing for users." Joan was very good with the pronouns. *We* could mean "we, the design agency." Or it could mean "we, the design agency, plus you, the client, working as a team." Avoid using the words *you* and *I*. Those words sounded rude. Divisive. I felt like a faker when I talked this way, but it was the type of consulting technique that Joan carried off with ease.

I looked out the window, wanting to rest my eyes on anything other than concrete and glass. Was that a rooftop garden?

"What about the promo space on the landing area? I know Marsha is going to fight to have her stuff there, so we'll need another box," I heard Brenda say.

"Hmmm," Joan turned to me. "What do you think, Katrina?"

Sure, I thought, *why not?* What's another box? In the end, it's all just boxes, isn't it? Pixels are tiny boxes we use to make web pages, which are shaped like boxes. People look at these boxes on their computer boxes, while they sit in their cubicle boxes in their tall building boxes. Meanwhile, Ruby was on the other side of the San Francisco Bay, staring up at Thania with her big blue eyes, playing with her belly button, and drinking my breast milk from a bottle.

"We can take a look at that in the next round of schematics," I said, but my voice sounded strange in my ears, like someone else. In my mind, I saw myself standing and putting on my jacket. *I'm sorry. I have to go. I have to see my daughter . . .*

Instead, I remained in my chair and looked out the window. A seagull flew past. I needed to leave. I couldn't leave. How would I explain it to these people, to Dogstar's biggest client, that I suddenly had to leave?

Brenda and Rob gazed intently at the next sketch, thinking.

And that's when it hit. I felt myself float, as if I were no longer safely tethered to my material body. I had an unbearable realization that I was fully capable of saying or doing any crazy thing that came to my mind. I imagined hurling myself against Brenda's giant window over and over, like a mad, frightened bird, until I broke through the glass and flew through the air, over all those tall buildings.

I have to get out of here.

My heart fluttered madly. My hands shook. I heard the machine buzz of cicadas in my ears. I continued to float up until I stopped occupying the space in my fingers and toes, my head and arms and legs and heart. It was too hard to be there. So I rose up above myself, as if I'd become my own puppeteer. No one suspected anything was wrong.

"What about Jeremiah's links?" someone said. "Can we put them in Marsha's box?"

I pulled the string. The puppet nodded.

DO YOU COMPARE YOUR INSIDES TO OTHER PEOPLE'S OUTSIDES?

Most of us do, even though we know better. We're social creatures. It's natural to make comparisons. But, we inevitably wind up comparing how we *feel* to how other people *seem*.

This may in part explain why so many mothers feel so much guilt. We look around at the women we know from the office or the kids' school and see patient parents, happy marriages, and well-adjusted children. And we think, *Why can't I be more like her?*

Recently, I asked several friends—all women I deeply admire—to send me a paragraph or two about the things you can't see about their lives from the outside.

Here are a few examples of what real-life, enviable, put-together-on-the-outside women are really thinking. Think of them the next time you feel as though you're doing everything wrong:

"Anneke"—Mom of one with coveted job in high-profile nonprofit

What people don't see about me (or maybe they do!) is how anxious and cranky my commute and job make me. Ever since I went back to work (and stopped breast-feeding), when I have a day of nonstop, back-to-back meetings, followed by the inevitable email backup, followed by the mad rush to the train to do day care pickup for my toddler, followed by her not wanting to get into the car seat and screaming and crying in the parking lot at the top of her lungs, I find myself hyperventilating in the car and I have to take an Ativan by the time we get home so that I can literally breathe. I'm cranky toward my husband when he gets home, annoyed with our dog. I manage to hold it together all day and be professional, upbeat, and on the ball (I even manage to work out at lunchtime a few days a week), but by the time evening comes around and I'm trying to cook, I'm a mess!

"Jenny"—Pioneering mom of two in the world of high-tech

What people don't see about me is that I've been on the edge of a panic attack for the past six to eight months—just started seeing a therapist. Worst time of the day is 5:35 PM, when I get home from picking up my twenty-one-month-old and three-and-a-half-year-old from day care/preschool and we're all starving, grumpy, and don't know what's for dinner.

I'm sick of being the main breadwinner and fantasize about moving to a little town where we can live on a farm and I can be with my kids all day and raise chickens.

"Alexa"—Glamorous mom freelancing in the music industry; her house looks like a movie set

Each day that goes by where I am not fully employed in my industry, I feel as if my career slips further and further out of reach. When I am ready to jump back in full-time, who is going to want to hire a forty-two-year-old mom, when there are twenty-somethings chomping at the bit to do my job for longer hours and less pay?

My mind swirls with this thought and others:

"I need to volunteer more at his school."

"I need to start running again in the mornings."

"How come my son can't memorize his Tae Kwon Do student creed?"

"Maybe we shouldn't have done private school so we could save money for college."

"Fuck, I have no 401(k)."

"I have to remember to water my zucchini garden when I get home; how do I get the tree rats to stop eating them?"

"I need to make more friends outside my marriage."

"Do the other moms think I am weird because I am gay?"

"Do the other moms think I'm hot?"

All of this could take place in my head in the same five minutes. I smile on the outside because to describe what's going on inside would make me seem off my rocker. I cry in my car on the way to pick up my son and then turn on the air-conditioning full blast to cool down my face and unpuff my eyes. It doesn't really work, but I say I have bad allergies.

"Gillian"—Creative stay-at-home mom whose talent could give Martha Stewart a run for her money
I never know what to say when people ask me, "Are you a stay-at-home mom?" To me, that implies that one parent works (and is able to support the entire family) and one parent agreed to not work and happily does all the home stuff . . . which I guess is me, but I don't remember "agreeing" to this arrangement at any time. I have a small business I

am trying to start and I teach a couple of classes a week, on top of all the housework, all the pickups/ drop-offs, all the shopping, all the bill paying, all the everything.

Most of the time I am crushed with the weight of the financial debt. I feel helpless and angry that I can't make more money myself to pay it down. I feel stupid and childish that I am thirty-three and have no savings, no investments, no 401(k), nothing. I have ideas, goals, dreams that seem so unrealistic in my day-to-day life that it feels as if they will never happen.

"Samantha"—Nurse with clear priorities around work and home and the perfect part-time schedule
What people don't know about me is that being a mother isn't satisfying the way I expected it to be. I tried so hard to become a mama, and sometimes I think that I lost sight of why I wanted to have a child, what my motivations and expectations were. My daughter is amazing—healthy, happy, energetic. It's just that spending time with her is often not as gratifying as I once believed it would be.

Sometimes I feel guilty about not wanting to have another child—as if people think I'm cheating my daughter, or I'm not truly part of the two-kids' "Mommy Club." I'm content with the kind of work that I do, but the daily grind of parenting and work-ing outside of the home often overwhelms and bores me at the same time. Career advancement is on hold since I only work part-time. I thought I would be fine with this, but I feel torn between spending enough time with my daughter and put-ting enough energy into work.

CHAPTER 5.

NO ONE SEEMED TO NOTICE a thing. The meeting in Brenda's office ended. I calmly walked back to Dogstar with Joan as if nothing had happened. *I just need to eat a better breakfast,* I told myself. After that, I started getting up earlier so I could eat an egg in the morning, and I started carrying a small bag of roasted almonds in my purse, to ward off future attacks.

But two weeks later, it happened again. Brian was squirreled away in his office at home, catching up on work. I zipped down busy MLK, headed for the freeway in our grubby Subaru Outback, while Martha sang "Jingle Bells" too loudly in the backseat and Ruby tried to hum along beside her. I wanted to do something fun with them, so we were on our way to the Oakland Zoo. But already my mind was racing, trying to figure out how to see the sun bears, the bats, and the elephants (all at different corners of the zoo) and still get home by noon so I could catch up on bills, finish a Power-Point presentation for Monday morning, and somehow get the oil changed. I glanced down at the gas gauge, which was almost on empty . . . And get gas.

Suddenly, I couldn't take a full breath. My heart was pounding, my hands gripped the steering wheel, and I had the same eerie feeling that I wasn't completely in my body anymore. I pulled over to the curb as cars whipped past us on MLK, headed for the freeway. I waited for my heart to stop pounding in my chest.

"Where are we?" asked Martha from the backseat. "Why are we stopping?"

"I'm sorry, girls," I said when I was calm. I pulled the car away from the curb and took a right on the first side street. "Mommy's sick. We have to go home."

"Aw!" said Martha. "I want to see the elephants!"

"El-phans!" Ruby protested. Then she started to cry. Then Martha started to cry. I wanted to cry.

WHY WAS THIS HAPPENING? I couldn't explain it away this time. I wasn't hungry—I'd eaten scrambled eggs an hour earlier. If I couldn't explain it, then I couldn't prevent it. The what-ifs began to flood in. What if next time I blacked out like Tony Soprano, only I did it while driving the kids? What if it happened while I was giving a presentation at work? What if I humiliated myself? What if I got fired?

That afternoon, I looked up "panic attacks" on my computer while the girls napped in their room. I was pretty certain I was having panic attacks—I'd had them when I was a teenager during a particularly tumultuous time—but I wanted confirmation.

Panic attacks are episodes of intense fear or apprehension that are of sudden onset and brief duration, I read. *Sufferers often report feeling nauseated, a numb sensation throughout the body, and a fear of dying, "going crazy," or losing control of themselves.*

Could they really make you faint, or was that just a TV show thing? It said that although panic attacks were said to be one of the most frightening things a person could experience, they were unlikely to cause fainting. The cause? Many things, but most commonly stress.

My stress was out of control.

In moments of crisis, some women reach for the Bible. Others reach for a bottle of whiskey or a box of chocolates. Many times I've wished that were me. I'm too high-strung to be so easily soothed. When in crisis, I reach for knowledge. Perhaps this explains why I've always been a good student, or why I pursued a career in journalism, which gave me formal practice finding answers to obscure questions. I find it deeply reassuring to know there are people in the world— experts, pundits, gurus, savants—who have already solved every problem I can possibly come up against.

Millions upon millions of women were juggling careers and family before I joined their ranks. Surely some had already come up with their own solutions for managing this kind of stress. I just had to apply myself to learning what they already knew.

With the power of Google at my fingertips, it didn't take long to find dozens of articles full of self-help advice for working-mom basket cases like me. They had aggressively positive titles like "Steal Back Your Time," "Grab Your Oxygen Mask First," and "Beat Back the Working Mom Blues." I pored over them, looking for clues.

Most of these articles were loaded with time-management tricks, admonishments to surrender guilt, and reasons why it was so important to make more time for ourselves.

How was this supposed to help? I was great at managing my time—too good, according to my husband, who didn't understand why I couldn't just relax with him and watch an episode of *The Daily Show* without folding the laundry. And while it was indisputable that I felt guilty about being away from Ruby, how was I supposed to let go of that feeling? It was like telling a dog to surrender a bone—not in my nature. But when it came to making more time for myself, I had to admit, there was probably something for me to learn there.

According to the working-mom gurus, I needed more sleep (lack of sleep could make you cranky, difficult to be around, and fat), more exercise (lack of exercise could also make you cranky, difficult to be around, and fat), and more sex (a great way to connect with your partner and zero calories!). But where was that time supposed to come from?

Briefly, I imagined how I would fit the missing ingredients into my new routine. The kids went to bed at eight o'clock and were usually asleep within a half hour. If I dragged Brian into the bedroom at eight thirty, we could fit in a quickie and still have time to do dishes and make the kids' lunches before collapsing into bed at ten. How romantic . . .

Then, if I fell into an instant swoon at ten, I could squeeze in four hours of sleep before Ruby woke up to nurse at 2:00 AM. But who was I kidding? I never fell instantly asleep. It took me a while to wind down from the day. Besides, it was impossible to predict when Ruby would really wake up to nurse—sometimes it was as early as midnight or one.

What if I ditched the cleaning, ditched the sex, and went to bed when the kids were asleep? If I could fall asleep by nine, I could sleep until Ruby woke up to nurse and then—then what? I certainly wasn't going to have sex or do calisthenics at 2:00 AM. And anyway, I didn't see how any of this was going to make me feel less stressed out. In fact, I was getting more stressed out just thinking about it.

I needed something with a little more substance than the magazines could offer. On Amazon, I found books for mothers about how to work from home, how to start your own business, and how to cook "fast and easy" dinners. There was a book called *Prayers for the Working Mom* and, inevitably, a *Chicken Soup for the Working Woman's Soul* (which claims in its introduction that "even the rough spots in a working woman's day have the power to become memories that later strengthen the spirit").

I ordered the most substantial, credible tome of working-mother advice I could find: *The Working Mother's Guide to Life*. It promised 450 pages of "Strategies, Secrets, and Solutions." Luckily, I was a speed-reader. The back cover had a picture of the author, Linda Mason, a perky young blond woman who had founded a large child care company and been named one of the "25 Most Influential Working Mothers in America" by *Working Mother* magazine.

The book arrived three days later. I eagerly ripped open the cardboard mailer and plunked myself down on the bathroom floor to scan through it while Ruby splashed in her bath.

Mason's book was less flippant than the articles I'd read. She said some women "grieve deeply" about returning to work. When she was interviewing mothers for her book, she kept a box of tissues handy because the mothers usually ended up crying, and she often ended up crying with them. I was relieved she was taking this seriously, and eager to get her diagnosis.

Mason said the key to thriving as a working mother was to rely on the "three pillars" of success. I flipped ahead. More than a hundred pages were devoted to this concept. Now we were getting somewhere. I needed pillars!

But first, Ruby needed dinner. I lifted her out of the bath and quickly patted her dry, dressed her in a plastic diaper (we'd given up on the cloth diapers soon after I started my new job) and her rosebud footie pajamas (with a hole cut in the belly button area). Then I plopped her into the high chair and snuck glances at the book while spooning puréed spinach into her mouth.

The first pillar was a "partner in parenting," someone to "share the joys and daily responsibilities" who would "help make your parenting journey easier and more meaningful."

I had that covered. Brian was surely the best partner in parenting I could ever ask for. He was a wonderful dad, loving, playful, and attentive. He was a fan of the kids the way other dads are fans of sports teams. On the weekends, while Martha and Ruby napped, we sprawled together on the couch, my feet resting on his lap, and replayed the day's highlights the way fans replay a good game. Sure, he was moody when he wasn't getting enough sleep, but hell, isn't everyone? He also hated making the bed and couldn't balance a checkbook to save his life, and it never would have occurred to him to trim the kids' nails, but who's perfect? He folded laundry, changed diapers, put away dishes, picked up toys, and washed the girls' hair. He bought groceries, packed lunches, and could assemble a mean chicken stir-fry that even Martha would eat.

"I'm a guy," he said, "so if I feel like I'm doing most of the housework, I'm probably pretty close to holding up my half."

Meanwhile, one friend complained that her husband worked most weekends and didn't help at all with the housework. Another friend hadn't slept past six thirty in two years because her husband never got up with the kids. Really. *Never.* Another said every time she worked late, her husband gave her the cold shoulder the next day. A friend from work complained how emotionally absent her husband was.

"Let me put it this way," she told me. "I didn't marry my 'Brian.' You got lucky, girl."

Partner in parenting? Check.

By now, Ruby had smeared green goopy purée like a facial mask from her chin to her eyebrows. I'm pretty sure one of those magazine articles had a tip about giving your child a bath *after* dinner, never before. I wiped her off, removed her messy bib, changed her diaper and pajamas for the second time that evening, brushed her (seven!) teeth, read her book of colors and *Olivia*, and then settled her on my lap with a pillow for her evening "bounce."

I held the two-pound book above my vibrating baby and continued to read.

The second pillar was having a "supportive employer."

"Most of us spend many hours and days in the workplace," Mason began ominously. "An unhealthy, unsupportive work environment is just as toxic for our family life as living in a home with asbestos and lead paint." This was followed by stories from women with bad bosses, like the one whose supervisor called when she was in labor to tell her he needed her help firing his secretary, and the woman who was denied a promotion because she worked an early schedule so she could pick up her kids from day care.

On a brighter note, Mason said, a supportive supervisor could "help you to succeed both as a worker and as a parent by offering you support, flexibility, and respect."

No doubt, I had support, flexibility, and respect. I left work early every day to get Ruby, and I was allowed to work from home on Fridays. Stella trusted me; she knew why I needed this schedule, and she knew I was giving everything I had to my job. Despite the limitations on my time, she'd given me a leadership role in her growing company. She had my back, all the way.

Yes, my job could be stressful at times. But if I had the same job at a different design agency, chances are I'd be expected to work ten- to twelve-hour days instead of eight. I'd be expected to travel more. I'd have to work with people, mostly men, who wouldn't understand why I couldn't fly to New York at a moment's notice. My career was demanding, but Stella was doing her best to ensure that everyone, including me, had time to have a life outside work.

"Supportive employer?" Check.

Pillar three was "excellent child care." By now, Ruby was asleep in her crib. Brian had cleaned up the kitchen and was back at his desk, working late on a deadline. I lay in bed alone, propped up against the headboard with the heavy book resting on my knees.

"Without confidence in her children's care, no mother can thrive at work," Mason wrote. Excellent child care was "essential to you in your journey through working parenthood."

I had serious reservations about the amount of time Ruby was away from me. But I had no reason to worry about the *quality* of her care. Thania provided a safe, loving environment. Ruby had bonded with her. She followed Thania around the house as if she were a second mother. Surprisingly, I wasn't jealous. I was relieved to know my baby felt loved and safe when I wasn't there.

I, too, had become attached to Thania. I looked forward to hearing her reports about Ruby's day when I arrived at five thirty or comparing notes about a cough we'd both noticed or the way Ruby was starting to pull herself up to standing. Thania had given me friendly pep talks about continuing with breast-feeding and counseled me about how to get Ruby to sleep through the night. Thania was more than Ruby's babysitter; she was a Baby Whisperer. Already she knew more about my child than Ruby's own grandparents, (who lived thousands of miles away), did. Thania was my ally in helping raise my daughter.

"Excellent child care?" Check.

I closed the book, set it on the floor with a *thunk*, and leaned back against the headboard, more depressed than ever. I had all the pillars. The right guy, the right boss, the right help.

The problem was obviously me.

MY PARENTS DIVORCED WHEN I was seven and my sister was two. This was in 1979, the decade when divorce rates in the United States nearly doubled. Everyone was splitting up, it seemed, and no one knew what it meant.

Around this same time, colleges began to lift caps on the numbers of female students, and women began to graduate with degrees in medicine and law and entered the workforce in droves. Attitudes were changing, in part because women had more opportunities to be financially independent.

Financial independence and divorce. Although I would never, *ever* wish for a return to a time when women were forced to depend on men for their livelihood, the connection is undeniable. As women like my mother saw they could bring home their own bacon, they had less reason to cling to a man who didn't even help with the dishes.

When I was ten my mother married her second husband, a college professor, and we moved to Chicago, where he had just received a teaching offer. My sister and I spent summers in New York visiting our father and grandparents and the rest of the year living with our mother and stepfather. When I was twelve, our stepfather got a new teaching job at the University of Hawaii, and we moved again.

These were not happy years.

My sister and I missed our family in New York terribly. It was hard to adjust to new schools again and then again. To make matters worse, my stepfather was a resentful and jealous man, and tension floated through our house like a thick fog.

Meanwhile, my mother was scrambling to earn a living as a research assistant and to go to school at night to earn her bachelor's and, eventually, her master's degree. It seemed that all she did was go to work, go to school, clean the house, and go back to work. I saw her life transform into a modern-day Cinderella story, only with no fairy godmother and no prince to save her (the good professor insisted she pay three-quarters of the rent and groceries since we were her children, not his).

In my memories from that time, she is always in motion, rushing from one room to another, looking a little too bony and birdlike, blue eyes framed by worried, knitted brows as she puts in her gold hoop earrings or sticks a bobby pin in her dark unruly hair, no time for makeup, frantically looking for the yellow legal pad with her notes so she can pack up her briefcase.

I felt sorry for her and wanted desperately to make things easier for her. By middle school, I was the model latchkey kid, riding a public bus home each day to meet my sister as she arrived home from elementary school. I learned to make tuna noodle casserole with egg noodles and a can of cream of mushroom soup. I folded laundry, mopped floors, raked leaves, scrubbed toilets, and wrestled my cranky sister into her bath. But nothing I did made my mother less hurried or less worried.

Once in a while, I felt a white flash of resentment, like a rare desert breeze on my neck. Why couldn't I play Atari at my friends' houses, join a tennis team, indulge in things other middle school kids took for granted? But I couldn't stay angry—my mother's physical and emotional exhaustion was too palpable. Getting angry about what we didn't have was counterproductive.

MEANWHILE, OUR BLENDED FAMILY was not blending well. When I hit puberty, I started talking back to my stepfather, and the fog of tension in our house grew so thick it sometimes felt hard to breathe. There was a lot of yelling—between the professor and my mother, between the professor and me, and then even between my mother and me—interspersed between days of stony silences.

When I turned thirteen, I announced to my mother that I couldn't live this way any longer. A month later, I moved back to New York to live with my father and his second wife. I took my sister with me. This was not an easy decision to make. I loved my mother more than anyone on earth. The idea of living without her seemed impossible, but I couldn't see any other way out.

It seems strange to think of this now. I was the *child*. Why was I making these grown-up decisions? But that's how it was for us then. My parents, who were practically children when they'd had me, didn't know what to do. We were growing up together. What's more, divorce was a relatively new social phenomenon. The rules were not clear.

I had my first panic attack soon after I moved back to New York.

I was sitting next to my grandmother in a plush velvet chair in Proctors Theater in downtown Schenectady. I think she'd bought us tickets to see *Oliver Twist,* but I never saw the play. What I do remember is that when the lights went down and the curtains parted, I suddenly became aware of the oppressive silence of the audience, the fraught expectations of the room. I felt certain that I was about to shatter the silence with a bloodcurdling scream.

I leaned toward my grandmother. "I feel sick," I whispered, and then bolted up the aisle for the bathroom.

When she reached me, I was locked in the stall.

"I think I have the stomach flu," I moaned weakly. I was afraid to tell her, or anyone, what had really happened, for fear they would think I was crazy.

After a few more of these episodes, my father sent me to a child psychologist, a petite woman with a kind smile who wore skirts that fell well below her knees. She explained that I wasn't crazy at all, just anxious. Over the next year, we dissected the many reasons for my anxiety—the moves, the new schools, the fighting with my stepfather, but more than all of it, the overwhelming responsibility I felt as the oldest child to make things right for my mother and sister. I was in over my head.

Once I understood where the panic came from, the attacks began to subside. By the time I graduated high school in 1990, I felt I'd overcome a rough start—I had a scholarship for college, and I was eager for adventure. Panic attacks seemed a long way behind me.

Fast-forward to 2003. Maybe being responsible for a new baby, combined with being away from her for work, brought up all those old feelings from when I was thirteen, when I was responsible for my little sister, when it felt as if there was no one to take care of me.

Maybe, once again, I was in over my head. It was time to call in the professionals.

DR. LITE LED ME TO HER cramped office, then sat behind a desk piled with manila folders and paperwork.

"What brings you here today?" she asked in a low, confident voice. She was a psychiatrist on my health maintenance plan. This was our first appointment.

I sat on a small couch that backed up against the window.

"I need help." I kept my voice even as I dug the fingernails of my right hand into my left palm. "Maybe medication." I told her about my two panic attacks.

"I'm sorry to hear that. Is something causing you stress?" She said this in a way that was neither friendly nor off-putting. She had a no-nonsense look, short curly brown and gray hair, no makeup. Something about her was pleasantly asymmetrical, like a sailboat that listed slightly. She seemed smart and curious.

"I work full-time. I have a baby." This sounded wholly inadequate in my ears. Lots of people worked full-time. Lots of people had babies.

Dr. Lite's expression didn't change. "Tell me more about the anxiety."

I told her everything. How things had been going along fine until I started the new job. Putting Ruby in day care. The guilt about being away from her. How tired I was. The arguments with Brian. My new snappish self. When I was done, she folded her hands on her desk and leaned toward me.

"I have good news for you. Anxiety is the most curable of all the mental disorders."

I tried to ignore the word *disorder*, which did not at all sound like good news.

"What do I need to do?" I asked.

"Well, I can write you a prescription for Xanax, that will help in the short term." She paused to make a note on the computer, then turned back to me. "The Xanax is just for occasional use. You don't want to take it every day; it's addictive. What I want you to do is join the anxiety group. It meets every Wednesday evening here in the behavioral medicine department."

I was grateful for the prescription, and I wouldn't have been surprised if she said I should see a therapist one-on-one, as I had as a teenager. But a *group?* I had just told her my main problem was that I had too much to do, and her answer was to give me another thing to do?

"Have you heard of cognitive behavioral therapy?" she asked. "CBT?"

I shook my head.

"CBT is a set of techniques for retraining your mind. It's incredibly powerful for anxiety, more powerful than any pill you can take."

I bit the inside of my right cheek and pretended I was seriously considering her suggestion. "I don't know," I said. I wasn't a joiner. I was a studier. I was a stand-back-and-assess-er. I would read any book she said I should read. I would do my homework. But even if I had all the time in the world, I was not going to join a "group."

"Katrina, listen to me," she said, as if she'd known me for years. "I know you've done talk therapy before. Talking about your feelings doesn't make them go away. CBT is different. I've been to the group myself to observe, and it's incredibly effective. Studies show that CBT can actually change your brain chemistry. It's only ten weeks. You need to take the class."

That's how she got me. *You need to take the class . . .* It wasn't a *group.* It was a *class.* That changed everything. We were in my sweet spot.

Good student that I am, I signed up for class.

HOW ANXIOUS ARE WE?

One-third of adults in the United States will have an anxiety problem within their lifetime, according to the World Health Organization. To quell our fears, we received forty-six million prescriptions for Xanax (a leading antianxiety medication) in 2010.

These numbers seem staggering to me. They also make me wonder: How would these statistics look for women with young kids, particularly those who work full-time?

According to the National Institutes of Health, women are 60 percent more likely to suffer an anxiety disorder than men. The age group who are most likely to suffer anxiety are those from thirty to forty-four years old—in other words, the years when we are raising young kids and still slogging through our workaday lives.

I conducted a poll on my own site, asking parents if they take Xanax.

Out of the 181 people who answered the poll,

about a third said they take Xanax or another drug for anxiety. Here are a few of their comments:

I began taking medication for combined anxiety and depression twelve years ago, when I was twenty-five . . . However, being a working mother has made the anxiety more intense—especially since the arrival of my second child coincided with the economic meltdown and the loss of several large clients at my employer. Working more and earning less with little sense of security is a surefire recipe for rampant anxiety.

I get depression and anxiety, and although it was present before I had children, it was nothing like it was after I had them. That is when medication ceased to be a choice and became a matter of survival.

I had a massive anxiety episode when I was pregnant with our third . . . Then I went back to work. Five years later with the demands of my sixteen-, fourteen-, and seven-year-old, full-time job, husband, home, pets, and extended family, I started having some pretty bad moments. Got a script for Xanax but when it got worse I ended up on Celexa . . . I hate having to take something but being in constant adrenaline mode is much worse.

Is this evidence of some type of *Working Mom Syndrome?*

CHAPTER 6.

MY NEW CLASS CONVENED in a cavernous room under flo-
rescent lights in the behavioral medicine department of my HMO.
We sat in a half circle, ten men and women, in old-fashioned school
chairs, the kind with the built-in desk on the right side. We looked
like the Sweathogs in *Welcome Back, Kotter,* except instead of snapping gum and cracking jokes, we stared down at our hands or out the
window at the half-dead roses in the courtyard. And instead of the
Afro-wearing, charismatic Kotter, we had Glen. He was probably in
his midforties, about five eight, and very thin. His hair was wavy, just
a little too long at the collar, and prematurely gray. His cheeks were
hollow, giving him a hungry, deprived look. He stood at the mouth
of our little bay of misery, next to a card table stacked high with papers and a tall white dry-erase board.

"I want to congratulate you all for coming today," Glen said. "For some of you, it may be difficult just leaving the house. But over time, it will get easier.

"We're going to do a lot of things over the next ten weeks," he continued. "Some things may be uncomfortable, but stay with it. This class is designed to help you get better."

There was nothing wrong with what Glen said; it was the way he said it. He talked without any inflection, as if he were reciting a script he'd memorized a long time ago. Everything in his manner announced there was nothing special about what we were going through—he'd seen it all before. My cheeks burned with humiliation. How could this guy possibly help me? Had it really come to this?

"Let's take a few minutes to go around the room and introduce ourselves," Glen said. "Say your name and why you're here."

There was an awkward pause.

"I'll go first," boomed a red-faced, barrel-shaped man in a white button-down shirt. He uncrossed his short, stubby legs and sat up straight. "Hi, everybody! I'm Roy. I have this really shitty job—" he quickly put his hand to his mouth and looked up at Glen, who was frowning. "Whoops! Sorry, Chief. Pardon my French." He turned back to our circle. "Anyways, I run IT for an insurance company. I'm always on call and, well, to say it's *stressful* is an *understatement*. One mistake can cost millions of dollars. So I don't make mistakes . . ." Roy's voice dropped a few decibels. ". . . I guess the stress is getting to me because I started having panic attacks when I drive to work so . . . so anyway, that's me. Next!" He finished brightly and looked at the woman next to him.

Okay, I thought. *Roy is goofy.* Still, I admired him for being brave enough to go first.

"I'm Camille," said a hip-looking young woman. She wore thick black eyeliner and had her stringy blond hair cut shorter in the back than in the front. "Why I'm here?" She paused and looked at Glen for reassurance. "Oh boy. Well. I've been having panic attacks for a while. Pretty much every time I leave the house. It started when my daughter was born. She's six months . . ." Her voice just sort of trailed off. She turned to the next person, as if passing a baton.

A mousy woman in a fitted wool jacket spoke next. "I'm Ivy." Her voice was so quiet I had to lean forward to hear her. "I had my first panic attack a few weeks ago when I was hosting a dinner party. I had to go upstairs and lie down on my bed until I could calm down. It just came out of the blue."

"What work do you do?" asked Roy.

I wasn't sure if he was breaking protocol. Were we allowed to ask each other questions? I looked over at Glen, who kept his gaze neutral.

"I lead a forensic crime team in Oakland," said Ivy.

Roy let out a low whistle. "Dang. I thought my job was tough."

Ivy folded her hands on her lap to indicate she was done.

"I'm Jesús. I do landscaping," said the man next to her, in a thick Mexican accent. Dark blue dragon tattoos spat fire along his thick, tan forearms. "I'm a, what you call, a single dad. I don't know what is my problem, but I'm always worry worry worry!" His lips trembled when he spoke, as if he were fighting back tears. "Worry about my son and gangs. Worry about if I lose my job. Worry about what we gonna do for health insurance. Then, a couple weeks ago, I think I was having a heart attack and I call 9-1-1. They take me to ER, but then they say it's not my heart. It's just anxiety. It happen again at the gym, so I stop going there. I just work and go home."

I felt myself choke up a little listening to Jesús. He had some of the same kinds of fears as I did—worry about his kid, worry about his job—but his situation sounded much worse, and he was doing it alone.

We continued around the room this way. By the time we got to me, there was a warm, intimate feeling in the room, as if we were toasting marshmallows around a campfire.

"Hi, guys. I'm Katrina," I said. "I started having panic attacks a month ago, after I started a new job. I have a baby, too," I looked at Camille. "I don't really know why it's happening. I just want them to go away."

Everyone smiled and nodded sympathetically. The woman next to me, Estelle, who wore a purple scarf and had a deathly fear of heights, patted my shoulder, as if we were old friends.

"Okay, thanks everyone. Let's get started." Glen began to pass around the handouts stacked on the card table.

The door opened and a middle-aged woman in a brown dress rushed in.

"I'm sorry I'm late," she said. "Is this Life Skills for Chronic Mental Health Problems?"

"No, this is the Panic Group," Glen said. "You want room 305A."

"Oh, sorry!" She glanced around the room quickly, then ducked back out.

"*Dios mío*," said Jesús. "I thought we got it bad."

Several people let out a small, suppressed laugh. Glen pretended not to notice.

One of the first exercises we did was to go around the room and describe how panic manifested for each of us. "Who would like to start?" Glen asked.

Jesús spoke first. "It's something that happens in your mind."

"Okay, good. Something that happens in your mind. It also happens in your body. Can anyone describe the symptoms they experience when they have a panic attack?"

About half the room raised their hands, as if we were in first grade. Glen called on us one by one and wrote our answers on the whiteboard in green marker.

"My heart beats real fast."

"I start shaking all over."

"I can't breathe right. It feels like there's a lead weight on my chest."

"I get dizzy."

"I feel like I'm going to throw up."

"I don't know how to explain it," said Camille, "but it feels like I'm not in control of my body. Almost like I'm not even in my body. It's surreal."

"Right!" said Glen. "We call that *depersonalization*." He wrote DEPERSONALIZATION on the board. That was the feeling I'd had in Brenda's office. At least it had a name.

Then Glen asked us to describe what went on in our minds during a panic attack. People talked about how they thought they were going crazy or about to lose control. Others thought they were about to pass out, or even die.

Roy said it was the worst feeling he'd ever felt. "It's like I'm being buried alive."

I knew just what he meant.

I've never been a hypochondriac, but just talking about panic attacks made me feel a little shaky. I reached under my chair for the bottle of water I brought and took a sip.

Later, Glen explained panic attacks were quite common—about one in five people experienced them at one time or another. They were usually the result of cumulative stress, although certain things, including childhood experiences, what you eat, and the workings of your particular nervous system, could make you more prone to having them.

Having one panic attack didn't mean you had an anxiety disorder, but if you started worrying about having another panic attack—and who wouldn't worry about being buried alive?—and you started avoiding certain situations to prevent them, you could easily develop an anxiety disorder. In other words, you could go from someone who has anxious thoughts on occasion to someone whose life is defined by these anxious thoughts. He said anxiety disorders were the number one mental health problem for women and the second most common one for men, after substance abuse.

Then he repeated what Dr. Lite had told me: *We could make them go away.* By the end of the ten weeks, we would know all kinds of techniques for calming our nervous system and we would be able to manage our stress better. Despite my misgivings, I felt a little surge of hope.

I CONTINUED TO GO TO THE ANXIETY group once a week. Brian and I rearranged our schedules so he could pick up Ruby on those nights. She was always asleep by the time I got home, and it hurt to give up those evenings with her, but I tried to remember it was only ten weeks, and I was determined to make my situation better.

Sometimes we meditated in our uncomfortable little chairs in silence.

"When thoughts come up, just let them float away, like soap bubbles," Glen would say.

That was my cue to scroll through all the things I hadn't had time to do. I thought about how I was behind on paying the bills. I put that thought in a soap bubble and let it float away. I felt approximately half a second of calm before a new thought appeared. The house was a mess. I should just hire a housekeeper. Oh, but it was so *bourgeois* to have a housekeeper. And besides, when was I going to find time to look for one? I let that thought float away, too. On and on, it went, this silent meditation, while my to-do list screamed in my head. But as the weeks wore on, it began to get easier. I learned to slow my breathing, until my body grew heavy and warm, and I could feel my heartbeat pulse through my hands.

Glen also led us through various writing exercises.

"Mistaken Beliefs are like scripts that play in our head," he explained one evening. "These beliefs can be so basic that we don't even recognize them. 'I'm powerless,' 'Life is a struggle,' or 'I always have to act nice no matter what.' These are Mistaken Beliefs. They are at the root of anxiety. What Mistaken Beliefs play in your head?"

"You mean something like 'Driving is dangerous'?" Roy asked.

"But it is dangerous," Camille said. "That's not a Mistaken Belief. It's true."

"I'm talking about a more universal belief," Glen said. "Maybe you grew up thinking that the world is a dangerous place, and that's at the root of your outlook."

"But the world *is* a dangerous place," Camille muttered.

I could see she had a point, but what good did it do to think about it?

Glen ignored her and looked at Roy. "Ask yourself, 'Is this belief helping me to live my life, or is it hurting me? Is there another way of looking at this?'"

I stared at my blank piece of paper for a long time. I thought about how much I wanted to be a good mother, to be good at my new job, and how certain I was that I was screwing everything up. Finally I wrote a Mistaken Belief: "I have to do everything right."

"Now rewrite your negative beliefs to make them positive," Glen continued as he paced around the room. "'Life is a struggle,' for example, could be written as 'Life is one great adventure.'"

"Does the new belief have to be true?" asked Roy.

"Yes," said Glen. "It has to be something you can believe in."

I wrote, "It's okay to make mistakes." Then I looked at the words for a long time, until I could see them in my mind when I closed my eyes, white letters on a black background.

AS THE WEEKS WENT ON, I began to root for my fellow panickers. When Ivy, the forensic scientist, said she had a good week, I felt as I did the first time Martha counted all the way to twenty. When Jesús had a setback—a panic attack at the gym—we took turns urging him to go back and reminded him of all the things he could tell himself before it happened again. When Camille said she made it to the grocery store by herself, we all cheered, and I raised my fist in the air, as if I were leading a group of farmworkers on strike. When goofy Roy said he drove over the Bay Bridge without panicking, I had to refrain from jumping out of my seat to give him a big bear hug.

I quit coffee, and even avoided sugar, as Glen suggested. (Unless someone brought a box of Krispy Kreme donuts into the office, and then I abandoned all self-control.) I did every exercise, including the ones Glen told us to do at home. I taped my daily affirmations on a little digital voice recorder I kept in my underwear drawer. For two months, I listened to them every evening in bed as I leaned against the headboard, while Brian lay beside me, reading *The New Yorker*.

"It's okay to make mistakes," my voice came out low and quiet from the recorder. I wondered if Brian could hear, the way I could sometimes hear the other person's voice when he talked on his cell phone. There was a long pause while I repeated the words silently in my head. It was so odd, listening to my own voice this way. I sounded very serious and younger than I felt. Like a little girl pretending to be a teacher.

"I don't have to be perfect . . ." the voice on the recorder continued. It was discomfiting to listen to myself this way, and yet, I could feel the words working their magic. I wanted to believe them. I could believe them.

"I'm fully whole and healthy in body and mind . . ." the voice continued.

Brian patted my knee when I was done. "Good girl," he said, without looking up from his magazine.

After several more rounds of affirmations, it dawned on me—I was brainwashing myself. It was simple as that. I was training my brain to behave the way I might train a dog to pee outdoors. It was weird and awesome and scary to realize I had the ability to control my own thoughts. We assume our thoughts are involuntary, but they're not. With practice and concentration, I was learning to choose my thoughts, reject the ones that were anxious or petty or angry, and replace them with thoughts that were hopeful and happy and peaceful. This was at the core of all self-help advice, even the stuff I'd disregarded as superficial. When the working-mom experts said "Stand up straight!" or "Lose the guilt!" I'd dismissed it. What they meant was, *You have to change your attitude.* That had seemed impossible to me, but now, through cognitive behavioral therapy, I was learning to do just that.

WHEN RUBY TURNED ONE, I got a chance to road-test the new serene me. We threw a big party at our house and invited our oldest, prekid friends, as well as new friends we'd met in our birth class and in postpartum yoga.

Although it was January, the sky was clear, and warm sunshine poured in through the French doors in the kitchen. I baked a chocolate cake, showing Martha how to stir the flour and hold the beater to mix the frosting, while Ruby, perched in the back carrier, watched over my shoulder. Brian fired up the barbecue on the deck and grilled platefuls of sausage, burgers, ribs, and vegetables. By noon, the kitchen was packed with people.

The last time I'd seen my new mom friends was before I'd started the job at Dogstar, when most of the babies were so small they could barely hold up their heads. It was a shock to see how much they'd changed in just a few months. Now they were alert, giggling, eating solid food, confidently scooting around on chubby knees.

The moms looked different, too. The last time we'd met, we peered at each other through puffy eyes, covered our zaftig, postpartum physiques with baggy shirts and sweatpants, and wore glazed, Mona Lisa half smiles, stoned on oxytocin and sleep deprivation from around-the-clock breast-feeding. Now, everyone looked younger, thinner, and, like our babies, more alert. A few of the moms had stopped breast-feeding (including me) and all but two had returned to work. When we first had our babies, the dominant topic of conversation was their schedules (*When does he sleep? How often does she eat?*). Now everyone wanted to talk about their *own* schedules.

"How much are you guys working now?" Jessica asked a few of us gathered around the chip bowl. Jessica looked like a petite version of Wonder Woman, with thick eyelashes and long dark hair.

"I'm back four days a week," said Dawn, a short, pale woman in baggy overalls. Dawn was a researcher for a large foundation in San Francisco where she probably wore crisp skirts and fitted sweaters, but whenever I saw her she looked as if she'd just come from pulling weeds in the garden. "I'd rather work three days, but my boss didn't go for it. Marcus is staying home with Ava while he works on his dissertation, so it's okay. I never worry about her."

"Does Marcus like being the stay-at-home dad?" I felt a small stab of jealousy but hoped it didn't show.

"Oh, he *loves* his Daddy Time," Dawn said, as she dropped a handful of tortilla chips on her plate. "The only problem is his dissertation is going slower, now that Ava's getting mobile. How 'bout you guys?"

"I'm back full-time," Jessica sighed, and ran a hand through her thick hair. "I hate it." Jessica had been one of those women who blossomed in pregnancy. But now I realized that she looked a bit, well, wilted. A little too thin, with more lines on her face than I remembered. I liked Jessica, and I felt a twinge of sadness for her.

"You work from home, right?" I asked.

"One day a week. The rest of the week I'm in the office. I work my ass off, skip lunch, and then the other attorneys give me dirty looks when I have to leave at five to get Henry. I go back to work after he's asleep . . ."

"That sucks," Dawn said. Then she excused herself to feed her daughter. I said a silent prayer of thanks that I worked for a family-friendly company.

"How's your nanny working out?" I asked Jessica.

"Esmeralda's great. Henry loves her. But she's with him so much . . . Sometimes, when he reaches for her in the morning, I get kind of jealous . . ."

Jessica paused, but before she could complete her thought, one of the yoga moms, Re-Ann, planted herself next to us.

Re-Ann was a few inches taller than me—about five nine—with light brown hair tied in two cute, girlish braids. She had wrapped herself in one of those complicated cloth sacks so that her ten-month-old son could sleep curled up against her back. There were a lot of women like Re-Ann in Berkeley—Earth Mother types who tended lush vegetable gardens in their backyards and devoted themselves to the latest attachment-parenting trends: natural birth, co-sleeping, toilet training at age one, and breast-feeding until age three. I admired their convictions and felt uneasy around them at the same time. Even before we had our babies, I sensed I would never live up to Re-Ann's standards.

"How's the new job?" she asked me brightly.

"Great! I love it!" I said. My voice sounded unusually high.

"It's four days a week, right?" Re-Ann took a bite from a drumstick.

"No. It's five."

Her drumstick froze in the air. "Five days? Where does she go when you're at work?" She set her chicken back on her plate and wiped her mouth with a balled-up paper napkin. I turned to Jessica for backup—but she had wandered off to change Henry's diaper.

I felt my jaw tighten. "She goes to that great family day care I told you guys about. Remember?"

"I thought that was only part-time! It's *every day* now? Brian can't stay with her?" She stuck her neck out so I could see the taut cords under the skin. She gave me a searching look. "Oh, it must be so hard on you."

"We're fine," I said flatly.

There was an awkward pause.

I imagined what I looked like to Re-Ann, with my newly waxed eyebrows and my big corporate job and my overgrown, produce-free backyard. I had weaned Ruby at ten months, and under her fancy party dress she wore plastic diapers. I had abandoned the cloth diapers three months before because I would rather destroy the planet than lug them back and forth from day care. I was selfish and impatient and my values were all out of order.

"What about you guys?" I said with my Nice Voice. "You're working now, aren't you?" Re-Ann was a nurse before she had her baby, and her husband did construction work.

"Javier and I work opposite shifts," she said. This was another trend I was aware of—it was called "tag team parenting." Some parents did this to avoid the "dangers" of day care, while others were just trying to avoid the outrageous cost.

"Isn't that hard? When do you see each other?"

"We see each other for a half day on Saturday. It's not easy, but it's all right. It's what's best for Manu right now." She stole a peek over her shoulder at her baby and bounced a little on the balls of her feet, which were clad in thick leather sandals. "I guess we're just lucky we don't need day care. That must be really hard—you know, on all of you." She shook her head in sympathy.

"Katrina, is it time to eat Ruby's cake?" I heard Martha's tiny voice by my hip.

"Great idea, sweetie. Do you want to help me put the candles in?" Her eyes opened wide. "Yeah!"

I excused myself from Re-Ann and fumed silently as I pulled the cake off the top of the fridge and set it on the kitchen island. I didn't need her pity! I'd read that couples who worked opposite schedules were *six times* more likely to divorce than those who did not. So who was the better mother—the one who put her kid in day care or the one who put her marriage at risk?

You don't have to engage in these emotions, I remembered. *Put that thought in a bubble and let it float away.*

I held Martha on my hip and leaned over the cake so she could plant the big number *1* candle in the center.

"Now we sing!" Martha said, clapping her hands.

Everyone formed a loose circle around us and I lit the candle. Brian held Ruby up to her cake while we sang "Happy Birthday." Ruby smiled her toothy smile and looked at all the adoring faces, mildly perplexed.

"Like this, honey," I said. I blew softly. The flame flickered.

"Make a wish, Ruby!" Martha said.

Ruby looked at me and tilted her chin up, as if she were waiting for me to do it again.

I smiled a tight smile at Brian and he gave me a questioning look. I shook my head almost imperceptibly.

"Like this, Ruby!" Martha said. "Ready, Katrina? One, two, three . . ." We blew together and the flame went out. Ruby looked around startled at all the people clapping, then she clapped, too. Brian set her in her high chair while I cut Ruby a sliver of cake and then offered her a forkful.

It was her first-ever taste of sugar. She took it into her mouth, then paused, squinting, unprepared for the avalanche of sweetness. For a moment I thought she would spit it out, but then she gulped it down, the way a seagull might swallow the soft flesh of a mussel.

Within five minutes, Ruby looked as if a cake bomb had detonated on her tray. Chocolate frosting hung from one eyebrow and both ears, and she had a thick dark smear on her mouth and cheeks. Goopy crumbs clung to her forehead and caulked the creases of her neck.

"Are you all done, sweetheart?" I asked.

She reached up for me with frosting-covered hands.

Day care's not hurting her, I thought as I pulled her out of her high chair. *I don't care what anyone says. She's doing just fine.*

I put the thought "I'm a bad mother" into a sticky little bubble in my mind. Then I blew it out the kitchen doors, across the deck, and over the back fence.

ONE WEDNESDAY EVENING, toward the end of the panic class, Glen instructed us to line up against the wall, then walk across the room as slowly as we could. This was hard for me. Even before I became a mom, I had a tendency to zip through one thing and then another. I had two speeds, "Fast" and "Cartoon Roadrunner."

But by now I'd learned that I could trust Glen. What I'd originally read as disinterest was just an innate calm. I knew he was helping me, and I went along with whatever weird ideas he had.

"Focus on your breath," Glen said. "Feel your feet on the floor, the swing of your arms, the set of your back. Anchor yourself with your breath."

After a few awkward scuffles, I kicked off my shoes, then felt myself settle into slowness.

Lift foot. Step slowly. Pause. Shift weight. Lift foot . . .

I tried to think about the individual muscles in my feet as they lifted and released. All those frail little bones, shifting in concert, like the strings inside a piano in a never-ending search for balance.

Halfway across the room, I glanced up and saw my fellow pan-ickers moving back and forth from one cheap stucco wall to the other, like zombies, or participants in a strange cult ritual. It was a reverse race. Whoever's slowest wins! So far the leader was Roy, who looked as if he'd taken only about two steps. Ivy was already on her way back, poor dear. She couldn't help herself. I was about in the middle of the pack, not first and not last.

"Don't worry about what other people are doing," Glen said. "Anchor yourself with your breath."

I looked down at my black socks.

"Feel how you balance your weight on your feet," said Glen. "Do you walk on the outside of your feet? On the inside?"

Lift. Step. Pause. Shift.

I'd spent a lifetime trying to ignore my feet and hoping other people would, too. I wear a women's size 10 shoe, but I'm only five feet six inches tall. I have always been embarrassed by my big feet. So there were many things I'd never noticed. Like how I placed more weight on the outer edges of my feet than the inner edges. Also, the bottoms of my feet were not flat as I thought. They were soft, rounded surfaces that caught the floor at different angles and then readjusted. The soles of my feet were making constant tiny adjustments, all in the service of keeping me upright. I was suddenly filled with gratitude for these feet.

Lift. Step. Pause. Shift.

And my weight. It didn't just go forward. It went side to side each time I lifted my foot. From one foot to the other, one hip to the other. Even my back had to turn slightly to accommodate the radical change that occurred with each step.

Lift. Step. Pause. Shift.

This went on for several minutes, until Glen finally broke the trance. "Okay, everyone, slowly make your way back to your seat."

I didn't want to stop. So this was walking! I wondered what other mysteries were in my body, in my breath, in all the things I'd taken for granted.

IT'S TIME TO CALL A TRUCE TO THE MOMMY WARS

Every mother I know has felt judged, at one time or another, about her choice to work or not work, most often by other women. Stay-at-home moms are overcoddling and wasting their education. Full-time "career" moms are coldhearted, reptilian women who care more about money and status than about their own children.

Oh, but the judgment doesn't stop there. Mothers who stop at one kid are depriving their child of siblings. The ones who have more than two kids are accelerating global warming. Mothers who don't breast-feed long enough are going to give their children asthma. Mothers who breast-feed too long are weird. Helicopter moms are over-scheduling their children, turning them into type A, anorexic basket cases, while the rest of us are depriving our children of important enrichment activities. Health-nut mothers judge others for putting Fritos and unnaturally flavored juice in the lunch box. Meanwhile, everyone pities the children of health-nut mothers, who have to eat that gritty whole-grain bread and the brown spotted bananas.

These are the kinds of judgments that get passed around casually in our personal lives. Then there's the public arena. There was the furor over tiger moms with the publication in 2011 of Amy Chua's *Battle Hymn of the Tiger Mother.* Should women push their children harder to be "successful" in school, music, and other pursuits? Next we were outraged over the May 2012 *Time* magazine cover, which showed a mom looking defiantly into the camera while breast-feeding her toddler next to the headline "Are You Mom Enough?" Are women breast-feeding too long or not long enough? This happened around the same time everyone had to weigh in on the pregnancy of the new Yahoo! CEO, Marissa Mayer, and her decision to take only a couple of weeks of maternity leave. What's wrong with her, anyway? We had barely settled back in our seats when we had to rise again to join the kerfuffle over Anne-Marie Slaughter's essay in *The Atlantic*, "Why Women Still Can't Have It All," which quickly became one of the most widely read articles in the history of the magazine. But instead of a dialogue

➤

about the structural issues that Slaughter said are holding us back, much of the reaction to her piece came back to personal choices. Should women change their definition of "having it all"? Should we learn to be content with what we have?

Why are we so obsessed with women's personal choices? Why are we so quick to judge mothers?

Maybe we judge because we feel conflicted about the choices we've made. We're afraid of screwing up what we're constantly reminded is the most important job we'll ever have—raising our children. We point the finger at others as a way of feeling better about ourselves. We wrestle with our feelings about how our own mothers raised us.

Whatever its cause, all this judgment is, of course, a distraction. The real conflict, which we all feel either directly or indirectly, is between *all parents* and the economic policies and social institutions that don't value the act of caregiving, that make it so damnably difficult to raise our children, stay economically viable, and keep ourselves and our relationships intact. Politicians of all stripes (mostly men) extol family values, but do we really value families when we don't offer parents paid time off after the birth of a baby? When affordable, quality child care is out of reach for so many families? When so few women have the support they need from employers to breast-feed, and half of us lack paid sick time?

As one author pointed out in a May 2012 *New York Times* opinion piece, "If 'the conflict' continues to be framed as one between women . . . it will continue to distract us from what we should really be doing: working together—women *and* men together—to change the cultural, social and economic conditions within which these crucial choices are made."

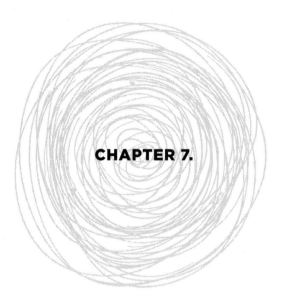

CHAPTER 7.

IN MARCH, THE ANXIETY GROUP ended, and all us panickers tearfully hugged good-bye. The circumstances of our lives had not changed—Roy and Ivy still battled their dragons at the office, Jesús and Camille were still exhausted parents—but we all felt a little less crazy, a little less alone in the world.

Over the next few months, anxiety released its grip on me, like a fist opening. I could concentrate better at work. At home, I could relax as I read Ruby a bedtime story without worrying about what I had to do the next day. I stopped snapping at Brian over little things. I no longer worried about having another panic attack.

Dogstar grew, and my department grew with it. In my first six months on the job, I hired my first five employees. I knew nothing about how to be a manager, and I was still learning how to handle clients. I decided to follow my instincts and hope that things would fall into place.

Thomas was one of my early hires. He was about average height and gelled his short, sandy brown hair to make it stand up from his forehead in a modern-day Travolta pompadour. He owned at least a dozen pairs of glasses, which constituted the centerpiece of each day's carefully selected outfit. Even if he was just wearing a T-shirt and jeans, the color of his glasses frames matched the drawing on the shirt. Quite often, his shoes matched, too. He brought in his own furniture to outfit his desk area: chair, lamp, shelves—modern pieces by obscure designers I'd never heard of that he'd scored on eBay. You've probably guessed by now that Thomas was gay. He was the kind of guy who exaggerated his gayness, often summoning his inner drama queen for laughs, which I found refreshing.

"I like things *just so*," he said, with a majestic wave of his hand when a coworker teased him about the fancy furniture.

Thomas had freelanced for Dogstar in the heyday of the dot-com boom. Stella remembered him as a brainiac who was great with clients, and who could also be arrogant, obstinate, and demanding. But when I interviewed him for a full-time position some four years later, there was no trace of arrogance. Thomas was in his early forties and just reentering the world of the Internet after waiting out the dot-com bust for a couple of years. He seemed humble and uncertain about his abilities. It's not easy to find people who are equally suited for both design work and managing clients. I decided to take a chance on him.

I soon discovered, however, that Thomas was a terrible procrastinator. He would get so worked up about big assignments that he would put them off until the night before they were due. This made his project managers spitting mad and forced the other designers on his project to put in late nights, too. Even his last-minute work could be brilliant, but it was often sloppy.

"I know. I'm sorry. I have to plan better," he said when I asked him why his project manager was angry and his document had glaring typos. "Big presentations paralyze me. My therapist and I are working on it."

Oh boy. Not knowing what else to do, I decided to throw myself into being his career coach. Thomas was game. We made work plans with mini-deadlines to help him pace himself. I started some of his presentations for him, to break his writer's block. We did timed writing exercises and had weekly check-ins. In my own way, I was introducing cognitive behavioral therapy to Thomas, helping him to bring awareness to his work, teaching him to replace his negative thoughts about himself with more positive ones.

And you know what? These efforts paid off. Thomas shook off the rust, became fluent again in the work, and got better at managing his time.

"You're the best boss I've ever had!" he gushed during one of our weekly check-ins.

No one had ever said that to me before. I was still a new manager and deeply insecure about my own abilities. I glowed from that compliment for days. From then on, I decided I would go above and beyond for Thomas. It felt great to be able to help him. Making him feel competent made *me* feel competent.

But as the months went by and his confidence blossomed, Thomas started angling for more responsibility. He would call my cell phone in the evening to complain about someone else's promotion while I sped through the grocery store with Ruby kicking her legs against the metal cart.

"Don't take this the wrong way, Roger's good at his job, but he's not a strategic thinker, and he's tone-deaf with clients. I'm the one who built that account!" he huffed.

"Can this wait until tomorrow, Thomas? I've got my hands full."

During one of my check-ins with Stella, I told her about our conversations.

"Watch out," she warned. "He's starting to act like Dot-Com Tom again."

I knew what she meant. Regular Thomas was funny and helpful and self-deprecating. Dot-Com Tom wanted more recognition, more pay, more authority. Regular Thomas was willing to work hard and share the credit with his project team. Dot-Com Tom was annoyingly entitled.

I tried to put it into perspective. Everyone had qualities that made them difficult to work with from time to time, including me. I could be impatient. I had to work hard to keep my temper in check. Thomas could be a drama queen, but he was also passionate about the work. I maintained that he needed a manager to steer him through his little storms of entitlement. Just as toddlers needed clear boundaries, maybe Thomas needed them, too.

ONE AFTERNOON, I INVITED Thomas to take a walk around the block while we had our weekly check-in meeting. As soon as we hit the sidewalk, he launched into his latest rant: other people getting credit that should have been his.

". . . If this were a different agency, I'd get a $50,000 bonus for what I've done to build up that account!"

"Thomas, no one gets $50,000 bonuses at Dogstar. Not even Stella."

"Well, I think you need to talk to her about me. I deserve a promotion."

"This is a small agency, Thomas. Are you saying you want *my* job?"

"Of course not. But I think you and Stella should talk about making room for me on the leadership team. Maybe I could help run the department with you. I'm ten years older than you, and I've been doing this work longer than you . . . I don't want you to take this as a threat, Katrina, but if I decided to leave tomorrow, Dogstar would be high and dry."

I was stunned. I had created a monster.

"This is how people start their own agencies, you know," he continued as we strode through the alley behind the Dogstar office. "They build up a relationship with a big client, and then they leave and take the account with them . . ."

"Okay. Hold it." I stopped in the middle of the sidewalk. "You need to take a deep breath," I said, trying to keep the anger out of my voice.

Thomas stopped short. To my surprise, he did exactly as I said. He took a deep breath.

"First of all, I want to acknowledge the great work you've done with your account," I said. "You've done *fantastic* work. Maybe the best of your career. You've come a long way in the months I've known you. You show enormous potential. If you feel you haven't been compensated appropriately, we can discuss that at your next review."

Thomas frowned slightly but continued to meet my gaze with clear blue eyes.

"Now I need to make something very clear," I said. "Are you ready?"

Thomas nodded. I had his full attention. This was a standoff. I was a mother. I knew what to do in a standoff. Take the high ground and stand firm. I continued in a low, even voice.

"Everyone in the company has something to offer. Something important. Every single person. This is *teamwork*. There are no superstars at Dogstar. We need team players."

I paused for a moment. Thomas continued to meet my gaze, so I continued.

"You have got to put your own contribution into perspective, Thomas. I hope you stay. I really do. But if you think you'll get better treatment at another agency, then you are welcome to go."

Thomas blinked. Something changed in the way he held his sandy brown, perfectly groomed eyebrows. The shift was barely perceptible, but I could see he was nervous. I'd called his bluff.

Thomas and I had both freelanced for other agencies; we both knew what they could be like. Cutthroat. No I'll-hold-your-hand-to-get-you-through-your-deadline, touchy-feely stuff. Thomas knew how good he had it. He had no intention of leaving.

The following week, at our next walk around the block, Thomas apologized.

"I've been thinking about what you said, Katrina. You're right. This is a team. I lost sight of that." Then he put his hand on my arm. "Thank you. It's not what I wanted to hear, but it's what I *needed* to hear. I still think you're a great boss. The best I ever had."

"You're not so bad yourself," I said, relieved that the crisis was averted.

AS IT TURNS OUT, managing temperamental toddlers had been excellent training for managing creative professionals like Thomas. The skills I picked up at home worked equally well, if not better, at work. I listened. I offered options. I set limits. I eschewed ambiguity. I did not engage in emotional turbulence. I kept my cool and waited it out. I was always available to problem-solve, and I did not hold grudges. I refereed disagreements between Thomas and his project manager the way I refereed arguments between Martha and Ruby over a shared toy at home. I gave both parties a chance to air their complaints, then enlisted their help in coming to a mutually agreeable solution. When they succeeded, I heaped on the praise.

I was also learning how to work with difficult clients. Our projects often involved large groups of people who were expected to collaborate intensely together, and the pressure inevitably brought out conflict. To borrow from *Anna Karenina*, each difficult client was difficult in its own way. You had your manic start-up founder who called the project manager's cell phone at all hours of the day and night. The vice president of a media conglomerate who demanded we make his site "the best thing on the Internet. Ever." In ten weeks. The two lovely women from a philanthropic foundation who politely shat on every single design presented to them. "It's not that we don't like them," they demurred. "We just know our executive director has something else in mind." They never explained what that might be.

Still, most of the people we worked for, when you got to know them a bit, were quite likable. They were just afraid. Fear was the proximate cause of every turf war. The marketing people were afraid that they would lose control of the publishing process. The technology people were afraid that no one understood what they did (which was usually true) and that we'd design something they couldn't build.

The salespeople were afraid they'd be left out of the loop and their commissions would drop. Everyone was afraid of something.

To be effective at our work, we had to look past what people said or did and address what they feared. Reassuring the IT director that we would design a site that was easy to build, or calling an extra meeting to ask the salespeople how to make a demo more useful, could save weeks of frustration. Addressing people's fears, even more than producing brilliant design ideas, was the best way to keep clients happy and projects on the rails.

But sometimes, we overlooked something. Then, all hell broke loose.

SEVERAL MONTHS INTO THE JOB, we won a contract with a large educational toy company. In her desperation to secure this important new client, Stella slashed our bid, which meant we had less time than usual to get the work done.

One afternoon I sat at a long rectangular table in our client's conference room with a dozen other people. Toys lined the walls—happy puppy and kitten characters eager to entertain children while teaching them the ABCs. We were redesigning their online store and had ninety minutes to gather all the information needed to finish our wireframes. I had come armed with a list of questions to make sure we got our answers before the time was up. Things were zipping right along, until Yolisha rushed in, thirty minutes late, and plunked herself heavily into a chair at the other end of the table. All eyes turned to her. She looked across the long table at me and frowned.

Yolisha was the vice president of marketing. She was a tall, big-boned woman who wore the biggest diamond ring on her left hand that I'd ever seen. I often found myself staring at her ring in meetings, wondering if it was hard to lift her hand.

"Hi, Yolisha," I said cheerfully. There was no point in showing my annoyance that she was late. The vice president of marketing could come and go as she pleased. I handed the person next to me a piece of paper to pass down the table. "Here's an agenda for you. We're on item number five—"

"We can talk about that later," she interrupted. "I just got out of a branding meeting. I need you guys to start thinking creatively about our new positioning."

This was not the first time an executive had shown up late to a meeting and tried to derail the agenda, nor would it be the last. Usually, we just went along with it, rather than argue. It was better to humor the client and then try to make up the time later. The problem was that we were on an abnormally tight schedule. Although I could never say it so bluntly to her, Yolisha wasn't paying us to think creatively about her positioning. She was paying us to finish the design for her online store.

"You're right, we should definitely discuss this," I said, a fake smile plastered to my face. "But according to the schedule, we must get the rest of the requirements today in order to finish wireframes next week."

Yolisha glowered at me and twisted her ring with her right hand. The boulder of a diamond sent sparks around the room, like a disco ball.

"What do you mean next week? Ellen's dashboard says they're due tomorrow. My tech guys are waiting to build."

"Uh . . . well . . ." I searched for a delicate way to answer. Yolisha was our client, and if she didn't like the cut of our jib, she could fire us. "We're delivering the final *sketches* tomorrow, but the technical team is supposed to get the full *annotations* next week . . . It's in the schedule."

Annotations were all the detailed notes that accompanied each sketch and would give the technical team the information they needed to build the new site. Annotations were tedious, time-consuming work, where we spelled out every last link, explained how it worked and where it went. This wasn't the only project I was working on, but even if it had been, the annotations would take two solid days of heads-down time to finish.

"No, you're not. You're delivering them tomorrow." She glared at me and twisted the ring.

All eyes turned back to me. The whole room seemed to be holding its breath, like spectators in an ancient Roman coliseum.

Here's something to know about me. Our house is on the border of two cities, Berkeley and Oakland. Brian often teases me that my emotions, too, live on this border. Although I am not proud of this fact, I can cross over from peace-and-love Berkeley to ghetto, slash-your-tires Oakland in nothing flat. In the split second that Yolisha and I stared into each other's eyes, I could feel this transformation take place inside me.

How dare she talk to me that way? I thought. *That bitch!* I had been busting my ass all week, and for what? She was a bully. A corporate bully. And because she was a VP, she could get away with it. I clenched my jaw and gripped the bottom of my chair. I wanted to march across the room and thwack her over her head with my pile of half-finished wireframes. It took an act of pure will to stay in my seat and say nothing.

After an awkward silence, Ellen, our project manager, jumped in with some soothing mouth noises. ". . . Let's take this offline . . . revisit the schedule . . . for now, to make the best use of everyone's time, perhaps we could get back to these questions. We want to make sure we address all your concerns . . ." It was a magical incantation of capitulation, something I had yet to learn.

It seemed to do the trick. A few heads nodded, and we returned to our agenda. A few minutes later, without a word, Yolisha stood up and stalked out of the room.

When we got back to the office that afternoon, Stella was waiting for us at the top of the stairs.

"Yolisha called," she said. My heart dropped in my stomach, which had plenty of room since there'd been no time for lunch when our meeting ran long.

"She's crazy," I said. "Ellen's dashboard was very clear. Annotations aren't due until next Friday—" I sounded like a child, even to my own ears.

"Katrina, we need to do it tonight." Stella was firm. I didn't like the way she said it. She wasn't upset, or angry, but she looked tense. She looked as if I'd disappointed her. "It was a misunderstanding, but if we don't deliver, the tech team is going to be sitting around twiddling their thumbs. It makes everyone look bad."

"That's not our fault!" I said. Then more weakly, "I can't get these done tonight, Stella." I felt like a little girl arguing with Mommy. I was disgusted by my sense of helplessness, by the whiny note I heard in my own voice. But mostly I was angry with Stella for caving in to Yolisha's demands. It *wasn't* fair. We were in the *right!* Why wasn't Stella standing up for us?

"It's okay. These things happen," Stella said, looking past me. She'd already made her decision and had moved into planning mode. "We'll circle the wagons. I'll order dinner in. Thomas isn't on anything right now. He can help. Ellen, you can stay, right?"

Ellen sighed, then nodded, then rolled her eyes, as if to say, in this order: *(1) This sucks. (2) Of course I can stay. (3) This is so unfair.*

I stalked off to my desk and braced myself to call Brian. My husband had a dizzying array of wonderful qualities, but an ability to be flexible when plans changed was not one of them.

"I have to work late tonight," I said, hoping to keep the conversation short. "Can you get the kids?"

"You have to work late?" he said. I could hear him trying not to get mad, trying to think through what this meant for his day. It was a Wednesday and we had Martha. He was working from home in the East Bay, which meant he would have to leave by three thirty in order to pick her up from preschool in San Francisco and make it back to the East Bay before six to pick up Ruby.

"Shit," he said after a long pause. "I have a four thirty phone conference."

"I'm sorry. I really need you to do this. Can you cancel it? Or maybe do it from the car?"

"Yeah, I guess . . ." He sighed. "So you're not going to see Martha at all tonight? You know we don't have her this weekend, right?"

"There's nothing I can do. It's a client emergency," I said. Then I tried to shift to planning mode. "There's some Annie's Mac and Cheese in the cupboard—"

"Don't worry about it. I can handle dinner." He hung up without saying good-bye.

I was grateful to Brian for getting the kids. But did he have to be so pissy about it? He'd had his share of client emergencies, and there were plenty of times when he had to work late and I had to get the kids. Why couldn't he be more understanding?

I popped open my work calendar on my computer screen. I was late to a meeting with one of my designers to review a draft of a presentation. I was supposed to have another meeting at three thirty with a project manager. Those could be rescheduled. Even so, how were we going to get the work done?

We set up an assembly line. Stella and Thomas each took a section of the wireframes, and after I gave them a quick tour of the basic design concepts, they started writing detailed annotations. I got to work on the wireframes that hadn't been sketched yet. Ellen became the official proofreader and used the company card to order a fancy pizza with goat cheese and basil from the restaurant next door. We ate at our desks.

Brian called at eight thirty as I was editing Thomas's first batch of annotations.

"I know you're busy," he said. "I just wanted to say I'm sorry for being such a crank. Everything is fine. Girls are in bed. Don't worry about a thing."

"I love you," I whispered into the phone. We had an open seating plan, which made it easy for anyone in the room to hear my phone conversations. "You're wonderful," I added.

"I'm a dork about the plan changing."

"I know," I said. "But I always buy the bread you hate. And I steal the covers. I guess we're even."

"We're even," he laughed. "Just finish up so you can come home."

I DIDN'T THINK IT WAS POSSIBLE, but by 1:00 AM, our wireframe factory was giddy as we made the finishing touches. Ellen set up the twenty-page document to print. Stella pulled out some orange juice from the fridge and a bottle of vodka from one of the cabinets—a leftover from the last holiday party.

"Just OJ for me," Thomas said. "I'm a teetotaler."

"We rock!" Stella took a big sip from her paper cup and swallowed. "You guys are superstars. This is real teamwork."

I beamed, took a sip of my drink, and leaned back in my chair. Now that I knew we were going to meet the deadline, I felt ten pounds of stress slide off my shoulders. It was a marvelous relief.

I looked over at Thomas, who sniffed his orange juice for freshness. I looked at Stella, with her Converse-sneakered feet perched on the table like a teenager. At Ellen, lips pursed in concentration as she carefully lined up each set of printouts to run through the binder machine. I was overcome with gratitude. There was no way I could have finished the work in one night by myself.

I took a sip of my drink, which was so strong it made my nose wrinkle. Stella had been right. If she had said no, Yolisha would have fired us. It didn't matter that she was wrong. This was how the game of business was played. The customer was *always* right. Especially when they were paying tens of thousands of dollars and had another half million dollars' worth of work waiting in the wings. If Stella hadn't given in, we could have lost the whole account. Yes, it sucked that I'd missed a night with my kids. So had Stella. Instead of whining, she had rolled up her sleeves and pitched in. She had been both a manager and a mother longer than I, and it showed. I had a lot to learn from her.

MOTHERS MAKE GREAT MANAGERS

There's no question that mothers face discrimination in the workplace. In one 2007 study, researchers at Cornell found that mothers are 79 percent less likely to be hired for a job when their resume is equally strong as those of women who do not have children. When mothers are offered the job, their salary is $11,000 lower than what nonmothers are offered, and they are held to harsher performance standards.

Despite this negative perception of our abilities, we are quite a catch for employers.

In her book *If You've Raised Kids, You Can Manage Anything,* Ann Crittenden says that mothers excel at work, not in spite of our parenting experience, but *because* of it. Raising children teaches us to sharpen our focus in the midst of distractions, enhances our interpersonal skills, and develops our ability to motivate others—all transferable skills.

➤

When I asked readers on my blog whether they'd gotten better or worse at their jobs since they'd had kids, this is what some of them said:

Nancy

Better, no question (especially now that they're older). I'm motivated to work as efficiently as possible so I can spend time with them—and I'm motivated to work as effectively as possible so I can keep up with their cash outflow!

Julia

Being a working mom has fine-tuned my focus at work . . . I am in "head-down, get it done" mode when tackling projects; the quicker I get it done and the better my client likes what I do, the fewer revisions I must make (cutting into my free time with family). In that way, being a working mom has increased the quality and efficiency of my work.

Liz

Definitely more effective. The more tactical reason is that I've gotten better at juggling the details (my mom, who started and ran her own company, always said, "If you know how to manage a carpool, you can manage a company") . . . As a mom I have become more confident as a person—more comfortable in my own skin. And, my priorities are clearer. As a result, I'm more comfortable with clients, more forthright with "c-level" execs, more willing to put my neck on the line in situations where stating an opinion may be risky, and better at identifying what's important . . . and what to let go of.

Deborah

I think parenting gives me more perspective about work, which makes me better at my job. I don't get as stressed about work deadlines, etc. I can be more efficient. I have developed better skills at working with others. My ego is not as caught up in workplace dynamics, and generally I feel more confident. Maybe that's just getting older, but parenting does require a new level of perseverance, which is helpful at work, too. Work can also feel like a "break" from family life—which is a good thing.

CHAPTER 8.

AT MY FIRST ANNUAL REVIEW in 2004, Stella gave me a raise. Brian and I decided to put our money to work for us—we hired someone to clean the house once a week.

This was not a simple decision for me. My mom had worked when I was little, and *she* didn't have a housekeeper. She was very careful with what little money we had. Growing up, my mother was more likely to shop at garage sales than at department stores. We rode the bus for years before she finally bought a car. Meals often featured either beans or peanut butter, and her idea of "eating out" was Two-for-One Night at Burger King. After we moved to Chicago, when I was ten, phone calls to family were strictly timed, to keep the long-distance bill down, and when we returned to New York to visit our father twice a year, she drove the twenty-eight-hour round-trip journey, to save the cost of airfare.

I inherited my mother's sense of thrift. I worked my way through college by waitressing and cleaning houses. Throughout my twenties I lived with housemates, rode my bike to work, and bought clothes, furniture, and other household items at garage sales and flea markets. I got my hair done at Supercuts.

Brian also grew up in modest circumstances, and yet the lesson he took away from his upbringing was very different from mine: *Don't take money very seriously.* He had no problem living slightly beyond his means and running up credit card debt. When we got together, I had to teach him how to balance a checkbook. For his birthday one year, I bought him a session with a financial advisor. Brian is a stubborn and proud man, but my genuine distress at his "laugh-now-cry-later" approach moved him. He changed.

And now it was my turn.

"I learned how to save," Brian scolded me. "Now you need to learn how to spend."

"I just feel weird having someone else clean my house. We're two able-bodied adults. We should be able to do it ourselves."

"We're two busy working parents with no family around to help," Brian corrected. "There's nothing wrong with paying someone to help. Plenty of people need the work."

"I know, but I feel weird about it. And the money—"

"Is only money! What's more important, saving a little money, or having more time with the girls?"

He had me there.

We hired a friendly woman from El Salvador named Dinora to clean the house every Tuesday. I was apprehensive, but the first time I came home exhausted from work and found a sparkling clean house awaiting me, I was hooked. Brian came in from his office and we took a tour of our house, with its gleaming floors, sparkling toilets, and dust-free shelves.

"I'll give up eating before I give up this," he said.

So it began. Soon, we hired a neighbor to mow the lawn and weed the garden. We hired a handyman to recaulk the bathtub. We sent out Brian's work shirts to be laundered. We ordered a box of fresh produce from a local farm collective to be delivered directly to the house once a week. We hired a parade of IT people to climb up into our dusty attic and tinker with our buggy wireless network. We embraced the convenience of online shopping, getting everything we could—clothes, birthday gifts, books, computer supplies—from the web, after the kids were asleep. Yes, we paid extra for shipping, but at least we didn't have to spend a precious Saturday afternoon dragging the girls around the mall.

Sometimes it felt as if we were paying other people to live our lives for us so we could work, but I could see that all this help made an enormous difference. I could read Ruby an extra bedtime story instead of scrubbing the toilet. Brian could join us for dinner once in a while, instead of getting stuck troubleshooting our network. We could take the girls to the zoo on the weekend instead of pulling weeds and mowing the lawn.

The girls were growing so quickly—I didn't want to miss any more time with them than I had to. Soon after Ruby learned to walk, she learned to run. Her vocabulary was exploding with words like *violet* and *usually* and *mountain lion*. We celebrated her two-year birthday with a party at the YMCA Kindergym (where we paid an additional fee for setup and cleanup).

As I watched a half dozen little girls jump around the bouncy castle, I flashed back on the parties my mother had organized for my sister and me when we were little, with relay races, and pin-the-tail-on-the-donkey, and bobbing for apples on the front porch. She always made the most elaborate cakes—from scratch, not a mix—and decorated them with fruit and candy and flowers. I had assumed I would be like my mom and pour my creative energy into my children. Instead, I made cupcakes from a mix and paid the Y staff to assemble little paper goodie bags with lollipops and temporary tattoos that parents used to lure their children back into the car when the party was over.

IN THE FALL OF 2005, MARTHA STARTED kindergarten at a public school in San Francisco. She learned to pull herself across the monkey bars on the playground until she wore calluses in her little palms. She started spelling words and counting to twenty, then thirty. Suddenly, she could read books, and I lost track of how high she could count. The following January, Ruby turned three, and I began the child care search over again, finally settling on a sweet little preschool run out of a converted house near the BART station. The school practiced a Reggio Emilia curriculum; as far as I could tell, that meant they let the kids play a lot, which was fine by me.

Life was getting more manageable, partly because the girls were getting older, and we were all sleeping better, but also because we had learned to buy back our time.

Up and up our expenses rose. When I sat down each month to pay bills, I chanted Brian's mantra in my head:

It's only money.

It's only money.

It's only money.

"How do families do it when both parents have to work full-time and they're still living paycheck to paycheck?" I asked Brian.

"Tell me about it," he said. "How do single parents do it?"

ONE SUNDAY MORNING, I PACKED up some snacks for Ruby and Martha and headed to a local café to meet up with my friend Lee, a single mom with two kids. Lee and I hadn't seen much of each other since I started my job and she'd adopted her second child. She suggested we meet at Tumble & Tea, a kind of mothers' paradise where the grown-ups sipped lattes and children climbed an indoor jungle gym, played dress-up, or occupied themselves with the toy trains.

We settled our kids in the play area, then found a comfortable couch where we could keep them in our sights.

"So how've you been? I haven't seen you in months."

"Great! Everything's been great," she said in her character-istic breezy way. Her auburn hair was cut in a flattering pixie, and she wore big silver hoops in her ears. "Just busy. You know how it is."

Ruby plopped herself on the floor at our feet and began to lick a small cut on her ankle.

"Ruby! What are you doing?" I said.

"I'm drinking my blood," she answered.

"That's disgusting, honey. Stop that!"

"Mama! I told you already. I'm a vampire!"

"Come on, Roo!" Martha called from the jungle gym. "We're playing fairies!"

Ruby sprang to her feet and ran off to join the girls.

I watched her for a moment, delighted by her weirdness, then turned back to Lee. "So what's your secret? How do you do it all, anyway?" Lee had a full-time job as a manager for a civil service agency. "I mean, I'm barely making it work, and we don't even have Martha full-time. And I have Brian's help. Are you, like, Wonder Woman or something?"

"You really want to know?" she asked, squinting at me through her cat-eye glasses.

I nodded.

"Medication," she said, lowering her voice. "Oh, and I call in a sick day about every other week."

"Seriously? But you're always so poised and . . . cheerful about everything." I felt like a terrible friend. Lee and I had known each other for a decade—long before we had kids. I'd been so caught up in my own life I had no idea she was having such a hard time.

"Girl, you don't know the half of it." She shook her head and wiped a crumb from her scone off her leg. "Sometimes I hear a punk rock song on the radio and I think, *That's what it sounds like in my head.*"

Lee said things weren't so bad when it was just her and Kanya, but then she adopted Sann and had to return to work. Suddenly her anxiety went through the roof. Some nights, she couldn't sleep, not because the baby was awake, but because she stayed up worrying. She broke out in hives. She had heart palpitations and became convinced that she was going to have a heart attack—just like Jesús in my anxiety management class— but when she went to the doctor, they ran some tests and told her she was fine. She didn't feel fine. She felt as if she was losing her grip.

"I started wondering if I was going to be one of those people who have to stop working and take disability," she said. "I started wondering if I was cut out to be a parent at all."

Lee said she started getting irritable with the kids. One evening, Kanya, who was six, was playing too loudly and woke up her baby brother. Before Lee could catch herself, she slapped her daughter.

"That night I called a parental stress hotline. I said, 'I slapped my kid.' The woman on the phone said, 'It certainly is a red flag.' That's when I started therapy and I started taking antidepressants. I had this old-school psychiatrist, and I was crying in his office about how bad my life was. He said, 'Sweetie, it's not cancer.'"

Across the room, Sann and Kanya pushed around a giant ball while Ruby and Martha hung upside down from the jungle gym, their matching purple cotton sundresses hanging in their faces.

"How are you now?" I asked.

"Better. But the line between 'Everything's okay' and 'I'm on the verge of total collapse' is so thin," she said. "A few weeks ago my car got stolen, and right after, Sann fell and had to get stitches. Suddenly, we were on the edge again."

I knew exactly what she meant. A few months earlier, Ruby had gotten strep throat, and between the sick time and work deadlines, our lives were chaos for about two weeks. When I thought about it, there were so many factors that could make parenting a vigorous exercise in love or a daily nightmare: how many kids you have, their ages, their individual temperaments; how much support you have from family and friends; how much money you make; the number of days you work, and the hours you work; how much vacation and sick time you get. Then add in whether your partner is carrying some of the load or making it heavier. And whether you or your kids have health problems. And how good their day care or school is, and how long your commute is. There are so many things that go into the equation, and they're not static. All it takes is one thing too many: a kid who doesn't sleep, a sick babysitter, a stolen car, a bad day at work—anything that is one thing too many, and suddenly, you learn that your well-being is about as solid as one of the forts Ruby and Martha made in our living room out of blankets and pillows. One nudge in the wrong direction, and everything comes tumbling down.

MEANWHILE, BACK AT WORK, Dogstar's reputation was growing. We won new projects with an art museum, a natural history museum, and an international nonprofit that designed beautiful, modern houses for the poor.

I gave my first talk at a design conference. Afterward, the organizer handed me a packet of yellow carbon-copied evaluation forms. I raced back to my hotel room so I could read them. Most of the comments were positive, three or four stars out of five.

"Good speaker," one said. "Very personable," said another. The next one wasn't so complimentary. "You say 'um' too much! Join a local Toastmasters!"

I felt my face flush. What was Toastmasters? I looked it up. It was a club for people who wanted to get better at public speaking. I decided to buy a book about public speaking instead—I didn't have time for clubs.

The next time I was to speak at a conference, I practiced my talk twenty times, eradicating every single *um* from my speech. My evaluations came back all fours and fives.

At my second annual review, in 2005, Stella promoted me from "director" to "principal" and gave me another bump up in salary.

My responsibilities were the same, but the title on my business cards looked more impressive. The promotion came with a packet of legal documents that said I was entitled to what seemed like an enormous amount of stock options, options that would be worth real money if the company ever went public. Brian and I decided that if the company was sold, we would move to a neighborhood with less crime where the schools were more reliable.

By 2006, I had nine full-time staff reporting to me, plus another three or four freelancers working at any given time. There were so many projects to oversee, so many fires to put out. Sometimes it was stressful, but it was also satisfying to feel myself grow more adept in my role. I promoted Thomas and another designer named Beth to my old title, director. They helped oversee projects, which gave me time to continue to do public speaking.

THAT SUMMER, BRIAN AND I TOOK the girls camping at Feather River. By this time, Martha was almost six, and Ruby was three and a half, old enough that we could look at the sky once in a while, instead of constantly scanning the ground in front of her to see what she might trip over or stick in her mouth. It was an idyllic week swimming in the river, catching small fish with our hands, taking long walks in the woods.

One afternoon, Brian and I snuggled side by side on a cot in our dark, one-room wood cabin, waiting out the wicked midday sun while the girls napped on top of their sleeping bags, still in their bathing suits. Their cheeks were flushed and damp hair clung to their foreheads. They looked like sweaty, mosquito-bitten little angels. I felt perfectly content, the most relaxed I'd been since Ruby was born.

"Let's have another one," Brian whispered in my ear. He ran his big warm palm lazily down my back, over my hip.

"You're crazy," I whispered back. "We're just starting to get the hang of this."

"Someone's missing," he said. "You know it's true."

I knew what he meant. Maybe if Martha lived with us all the time, it would be different. On weekends, when it was the four of us, we were a happy, chatty, bustling family. But when Martha went back to San Francisco on Monday morning, we were two adults and a child. It was different. I had nothing against having an only child, in theory, but I *wanted* another one. To make us complete.

"Do you know how much I love you?" Brian ran his palm lightly across my arm. "Do you have any idea?"

"I'm not ready yet," I said softly. "What about my job?"

"You can quit your job. Come freelance with me."

I didn't want to quit my job. Things were going so well.

There was a slight breeze and I could hear the faint rustling of leaves overhead. The air was dry and smelled of ponderosa pines baking in the sun. Brian continued to run his hand over my hip, my butt, kneading the flesh. It was making me sleepy, and it was a turn-on at the same time.

"Are you going to stay with me forever?" he said, and I could hear his smile behind my ear.

"You know I am. There's nowhere else to go," I giggled.

"Then let's make us another one," he said.

"Now?" I let out another small giggle. "The girls are sleeping *right there.*"

"Right now."

His hand moved to my stomach, then farther down.

"Can we talk about this later?"

"Talking isn't going to get it done," he teased. "I know how to get it done."

I laughed and pushed his hand away. "We're not getting pregnant today," I said firmly.

But for the next several weeks, it was all I could think about. I knew I had to be crazy to even *consider* having another baby. We had two beautiful girls: happy, smart, creative, interesting little people with all their fingers and toes and normal, healthy brains. What if we had another child and something was wrong with it? My cousin's son had been born with cerebral palsy. Her days revolved around her child, taking him to endless appointments with specialists, closely monitoring every aspect of his development, and doing hours of physical therapy at home, every single day. I knew several women who had children with severe learning disabilities and it was the same for them. Their lives were given over to their children. Was I willing to take on the risk, no matter how small, of something going wrong?

Even if we had a healthy baby, what if caring for another child was just too much for us to handle? The logistics were daunting. Two kids to bathe and feed every morning and evening, and three on the weekends. Two drop-offs every morning, three on Mondays when we had Martha. As the kids got older, it would become more complicated. Three sets of homework to supervise. Three social worlds of playdates and sleepovers and sporting events to coordinate. Three kids who might get the flu or lice or pinworms or break a bone. Three was a lot more than two. It was 50 percent more. It was another bedroom. It was three more years of diapers.

And then there was the emotional part. Having another child meant giving up control. Again.

Before Ruby, I could fool myself into believing that I was a free agent in the world, that I answered to no one. Sure, Brian and I were partners, but if things went sideways with us—and I hoped they never would—we could always split up. Although I loved Martha, I was her stepmom. She already had a mom. I could at least fool myself into thinking that if I disappeared, it would be a big bummer for her, but it wouldn't ruin her life.

After I had Ruby, the illusion vanished. I was tethered to her *forever*. She was my daughter *forever*. There was no escape clause. I would always be her mother, she would always be my child, and to some extent my happiness would be out of my control.

Soon after Ruby was born, my aunt Linda sent me a picture of a baby elephant holding its mother's tail in its trunk. Beneath it read a quote by the writer Elizabeth Stone:

> *Making the decision to have a child is momentous. It is to decide forever to have your heart go walking around outside your body.*

That was the beauty and the horror of becoming a parent. If something bad happened to Ruby, it would be as if it happened to me. Did I really want more of that? Did I really want *another* heart walking around outside my body?

I was like a gambler who couldn't stand to leave money on the table. Why couldn't I just take my winnings and go home?

Less than two months after our camping trip, I took a pregnancy test and it came back positive. This should not have been a surprise. We had stopped using birth control soon after our trip to Feather River. The only surprise was that it happened so fast. I'd barely had time to get used to the idea. Was this really what I wanted?

BUYING TIME

By international standards, Americans are hopeless workaholics; we work some of the longest hours in the developed world.

Married couples in the United States spend, on average, 130 hours per week on paid and unpaid work combined (about 65 hours per person). This estimate does not include mental tasks like coordinating schedules and planning events—you know, the stuff we do when we're daydreaming in a meeting or sitting on the toilet. But our hard work is not enough. Research shows working parents "increasingly feel that they do not have enough time to get things done at their jobs."

How do we cope? We look for ways to buy back our time.

Sociologist Arlie Hochschild painstakingly details this phenomenon in her book *The Time Bind:* "The time-starved mother is being forced more and more to choose between being a parent and buying a commodified version of parenthood from someone else." Of course, fathers are faced with the same conflict, but as Hochschild explains, mothers still do more of the household work, and the burden tends to fall more heavily on us.

"Increasingly," she explains, "new products and concepts are being developed to extract smaller and smaller bits of time and effort from family life and return them to the family—for a price—as ready-made goods and services."

What are these goods and services? Prepared meals. Errand-running services with names like "Beck and Call" and "TaskRabbit," and day cares that arrange for transportation to swim lessons and gymnastics classes. Party organizers. Matchmakers who will coordinate your child's playdates (like a dating service for children!). In-person and phone-based tutors. "Sick day" centers that will watch a feverish child so you don't have to miss work. Personal concierge services that can shop for your next health care policy or find you a new accountant.

Here's how one such Boston-based company markets its service:

How much is it worth to stop being frazzled and feel rested and ready to go at work? . . . If a personal concierge can keep you from realizing at three in the morning that you forgot to send out a Mother's Day card, the odds increase that you'll get a good night's sleep and be fresh and ready to go the following day when your boss hands you another emergency project.

If you have enough money, you will never again have to sign for your own deliveries, check on your elderly parents, return your overdue library books, file your receipts, wrap and ship Christmas and wedding gifts, RSVP for parties, send thank-you cards, or book your next vacation.

Then you can put all your free time back into work!

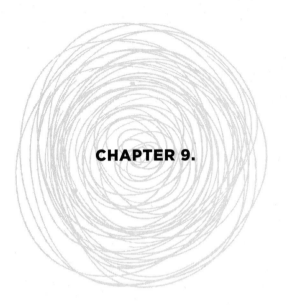

CHAPTER 9.

I WAS AT THE GROCERY STORE one Saturday morning, pulling a can of black beans off the shelf, when I felt an unsettling warmth in the crotch of my pants. I stopped, hand in midair, as if trying to determine which direction the wind was coming from. Nothing. I placed the can of beans in the cart and shuffled toward the checkout. Then it happened again. Another little gush, this time unmistakable.

I was two months pregnant and bleeding. That couldn't be good. I abandoned my cart halfway down the aisle, stacked high with apples and crackers and cornmeal for the polenta I'd planned to make for dinner, and walked cautiously toward the parking lot, as if I were holding a bowl of soup in my belly and didn't want it to spill.

By the time I pulled into our driveway, my hands were shaking. I felt light-headed and dizzy, and an unpleasant pain tugged at my abdomen when I stood. I shut the car door, hunched forward, and made my way up the front steps.

Ruby and Brian were sprawled out on the floor of the family room playing a memory game, surrounded by cards with drawings of pink elephants.

"Mama!" Ruby always made me feel like a celebrity when I came home. It was one of my favorite things about being a mom.

I smiled at her instead of grabbing her for a hug as I usually would, then carefully lowered myself to my knees. "I'm bleeding," I said to Brian. "It hurts." I kept my voice calm so Ruby wouldn't be alarmed, but I was starting to get scared.

"How bad is it?"

"Bad. I think I might pass out."

Brian jumped to his feet and grabbed the remote off the coffee table. "Ruby, good news. You get to watch a cartoon!"

"Toons!" Ruby said. "I want Maisy!" We rationed Ruby's television time, which meant it was always a welcome treat when she did get to watch.

Brian turned to me. "I'll pack up. We're going to the hospital."

"I'm sorry," I said. I wasn't sure what I was apologizing for, but it seemed like the right thing to say.

"Don't be sorry. Just rest. Stay calm."

I lay down on the rug, aware that I was probably bleeding on it. My mouth felt like cotton. *So this is what it's like to have a miscarriage,* I thought. I'd always thought a miscarriage was like a bad period, but this was much worse. I was freezing cold, even though it was a warm fall morning.

A few hours later, I lay on a hospital gurney in a dark room while an ultrasound technician with a smooth black ponytail prepared her equipment. Brian and Ruby held hands behind the gurney, waiting.

I thought about the baby inside me, probably the size of a peanut. He didn't seem real to me yet—although I had an intuition he was a he, not a she. But in my mind he was still just growth, a barnacle that gave me wicked morning sickness and made garlic, fish, and coffee smell like poison.

The truth is I had scheduled this baby into my life as I might schedule a long vacation. I had been extremely lucky to get pregnant the first month we tried, which meant my pregnancy leave would coincide with summer—a nice time to be at home with a baby. I was already thinking ahead. If we had to try again, maybe we could still have a baby in the fall. That wouldn't be too bad. Then I thought selfishly of the four weeks of "morning" sickness (more like "all day" sickness) I'd suffered, and how, if I was having a miscarriage, I would have to start with that all over again.

Our technician introduced herself as Jenna. In a kind, gentle voice, she told me everything she was going to do before she did it, just as she'd probably been taught in technician school.

"Now I'm going to squirt gel on your belly," she said. It was warm. "Now I'm going to put this magic wand on your skin. It should be nice and smooth." It was. She kept her wand on my belly, which had just started to pooch out, much earlier, I noticed, than it had when I was pregnant the first time. She turned her gaze to the screen.

"Maybe you should take Ruby outside?" I whispered to Brian. We hadn't even told her I was pregnant yet. It was too soon. I didn't want her to be confused.

"Of course," he said. "Come on, kiddo. Let's look at the pictures in the hallway . . ."

I'm having a miscarriage, I thought, as Jenna stared at the screen. *It will be over soon.* I didn't feel dizzy or light-headed anymore. I wasn't even particularly upset. If this had to happen, I was grateful that it was happening *now,* so early, before I started to feel the baby move.

Somewhere between the grocery store and the hospital, I had moved past fear and sadness and back to familiar territory—logistics. I hadn't bought the groceries—what were we going to make for dinner? Martha's mom was supposed to drop her off at noon—would Brian remember to call her to say we would be late? I was supposed to pitch an important client in New York Monday. Would I be in any shape to fly?

"Do you see that?" Jenna's voice broke through my thoughts. "Oh, honey, this is good."

She turned the monitor toward me, but it took a moment to understand what I was seeing. I saw a black circle—my womb—surrounded by white chalky background. On the bottom of the circle, a white blob curled in on itself, like a bent barbell. At its center a faint light pulsed.

I let out a sob. I hadn't expected this. That blinking light. My baby's heartbeat. The whole world narrowed down to that silent pulse of light, as if it were trying to send me a message in Morse code. *I'm here. I'm here. I'm here.*

"What's wrong with Mama?" Ruby said. Brian lingered in the doorway with Ruby perched in the crook of his arm, like a marionette.

"It's okay, darlin'." Brian wiped a tear from his cheek. "We're just looking at Mama's tummy to see why it's hurting. I think we found the puzzle piece."

"Like Curious George?" Ruby said. She had a book about Curious George, who goes to the hospital after he swallows a puzzle piece.

"Yes, just like Curious George."

"Oh," she said. "My tummy hurts, too."

We were all very quiet for a while. Jenna moved the wand around, trying to get the best picture.

"I'm sorry. I'm going to have to switch to the vaginal ultrasound. Can you hang in there for another minute?"

"Of course," I said. She pulled out a long gray wand, like a giant medicalized dildo. I squeezed my eyes shut, grateful for the sheet Jenna draped over my lower half that obscured Brian's and Ruby's view.

"If you could open your knees a bit . . . there."

I felt a soft tap on my shoulder. It was Ruby, standing next to the gurney. She reached up to hold my hand. Brian stood behind me and held my other hand. We stayed that way, until Jenna pressed a button to print a picture.

"There you go. Your . . . uh . . . little puzzle piece." She smiled and handed the photo to Brian, who took it with his other hand. The photo showed a dusty gray, alien-shaped blob. Our baby.

LATER THEY WHEELED US to another room. Ruby colored with crayons and the coloring book Brian had remembered to pack, while Brian called Martha's mom and she graciously offered to drop off Martha later, when we were back home. Then the doctor, a petite woman who looked as if she couldn't possibly be a day over twenty-five, entered the room. She explained that I had a bad case of subchorionic bleeding—there was a problem with the way the placenta had attached to the womb. There was a fifty-fifty chance that it would end in a miscarriage. She said I should try to focus on the positive.

"Lots of people get this in early pregnancy," she said. "And they go on to have healthy babies."

I glanced over at Ruby, who was absorbed in her artwork, oblivious to adult conversation.

"What do we need to do?"

"You just have to wait and see. If it doesn't resolve, you'll have a miscarriage. If it resolves, the baby will be fine. There's no halfway. The best thing you can do is rest. Avoid walking around. Lie down as much as you can. No lifting things. You work?"

"Yeah. I have an office job."

"You'll probably want to take some time off."

I remembered about my business trip. "I'm supposed to fly to New York tomorrow."

"Absolutely no flying," she said.

In the car on the way home, I pulled my cell phone out of my purse to call Stella.

"What should I say?" I asked Brian. I hadn't told Stella I was pregnant yet. For some reason, I dreaded breaking the news. When I was pregnant with Ruby, Stella had been pregnant, too, and we had bonded over our growing bellies. But I had a vague sense that it would be different this time. Even though I knew she'd be happy for me, I couldn't help but feel I was cheating on my job by having another baby. I half expected Stella to feel the same way.

"Whatever you do, don't apologize," Brian said. He sounded angry, but I knew he was just being protective. "This isn't your fault. Women are always apologizing for things that aren't their fault. Men don't do that."

"Men don't cancel business trips because they're pregnant."

Brian kept his eyes on the road. "Katrina, just tell her what happened."

Stella picked up on the third ring.

"Hey! What's up?" She always sounded happy to hear from me. I loved that about her. Even on a weekend, when she was with her kids and the last thing she needed to think about was work. I could hear screeches and yells of children in the background.

"Do you have a minute? I have some bad news."

"Uh oh . . . Let me go outside. It's really noisy in here," Stella's voice dropped several notes. Despite her cheerfulness, she was one of those people who was always primed for bad news. "We're at Pump It Up . . ."

Pump It Up was a popular place to host kid birthday parties, especially for busy parents who didn't have the energy to host a party at home. It was basically a giant, windowless building next to the 980 freeway, full of bouncy castles and balls and inflatable things that could be thrown and jumped on, without anyone getting hurt. Like the YMCA Kindergym on steroids. I waited until the background sounds on the phone faded away.

". . . Okay, that's better."

"I'm pregnant," I blurted out.

"Oh!" she said. "This is bad news?"

"No, no! That's the good news. Sorry . . ." Brian's eyes darted at me, then snapped back to the road. "The bad news is we had to go to the hospital. There's been a problem. They said I can't fly." I put it on the mysterious They. Not my fault. It's Them.

"Oh . . ." Her voice was concerned. I could almost see her, standing in the parking lot, in her alert stance: legs hips-width apart, leaning slightly forward on the balls of her feet as if she was waiting for a softball pitch. "How bad is it?"

"We don't really know. I'm having a lot of bleeding. They said I might need to go on bed rest." The doctor hadn't actually said the words *bed rest*. But I wanted to keep it simple, and I wanted Stella to know it was serious and out of my control.

"Oh," she said again. I could hear a lot of things in that one utterance. Concern for my well-being. Disappointment that I couldn't fly to New York. And something else. Judgment? Disdain? Stella almost never got sick; when she did, she sniffled into the office anyway. She seemed to believe other people's illnesses were a result of bad habits and a weak moral fiber. More than once she had rolled her eyes when I told her someone in my group had called in sick. It bothered me that she might see me that way, too.

There was a long pause, during which I thought of a hundred ways to apologize. I looked over at Brian, who gripped the steering wheel, his thick eyebrows furrowed, and said nothing.

Finally Stella spoke. "I'll see if Kimberly can go. She's really impressive in pitches . . . We'll be fine. Don't worry about a thing. Just get your rest."

We hung up. I felt disappointed in a way I couldn't articulate at the time. I felt dismissed. I didn't want to let Stella down, but I had. On the other hand, she seemed to recover with record speed. Maybe she didn't need me that much after all.

I thought about Kimberly, a project manager who was a year or two younger than I, with long, light brown hair and pretty blue eyes. I'd never thought of her as competition before. Kimberly didn't have kids; she had nothing holding her back, and that bothered me, too. I had the first twinge of a new feeling. A Mommy Track feeling. It was the beginning of being left behind.

"What's wrong, hon?" Brian settled a warm, heavy hand on my knee.

"Nothing." I slouched back in my seat and perched one foot on the dashboard. I closed my eyes and imagined the flickering light in my belly, like a candle in a dark room.

I HADN'T PLANNED TO TELL ANYONE at work I was pregnant until I hit the magical twelve-week mark, when you're supposed to have the all-clear. But I found it impossible not to tell people. How else to explain why I couldn't come into the office?

"I'm pregnant," I told Roger, one of the project managers, on Monday over the phone. "There have been complications. I have to work from home this week."

"Congratulations!" he said. "I hope you're okay. Just let us know what you need."

I spent the next week lying on the couch in my living room glued to my laptop and the cordless phone. Every time I stood or walked to the bathroom, the bleeding increased and I got a dark tugging sensation in my belly, as if the baby were yanking on the cord to get my attention. *Mama! Don't forget about me, Mama!*

Brian readjusted his schedule so he could pick up Ruby every day from preschool. It was hard not to get up and move around. The house got very messy, and we ate pizza for dinner almost every night, but I willed myself to stay put.

Stella called the first day back from her trip.

"How was New York?" I asked.

"Totally great. We were a great team. Kimberly has so much charisma. I think we're going to get the project."

"That's great!" I tried to sound cheerful through gritted teeth. "I'm sure you guys rocked it."

"So how long is this going to go on?" Stella asked.

There was no right answer. As long as the bleeding continued? Even the doctor couldn't say how long that would be. Some women spent their entire pregnancies on bed rest. I had seven months to go. Stella sounded impatient, and I didn't blame her. She had a business to run. She was relying on me. Although there was a lot I could do from my couch—edit proposals, review my designers' work, participate in meetings by phone—it wasn't the same as being in the office, and I was useless in pitching new business.

"Let's give it a week," I said. "Hopefully I'll be better by then."

The bleeding didn't stop, but it slowed after the first week, and I tentatively started coming into the office. Luckily there was an Italian leather couch in the reception area. It had hard stiff arms but the cushions were soft. I made that couch my new, temporary office. I folded up my coat to make a pillow and lay down while I reviewed proposals and presentations. I asked people to sit in the reception area so I could conduct weekly team meetings and my one-on-ones with staff while lying on my side. Some of my coworkers gave me strange looks at first, but once they found out there had been complications with my pregnancy, they seemed happy to pull up a chair and get to work.

This went on for weeks, then months. Sometimes the bleeding would disappear for a few days, only to return without warning. Finally, one day when I was six months pregnant, I realized the bleeding had stopped. An ultrasound showed my baby was indeed a boy, and he was growing just fine.

After the thumbs-up from my doctor, I went full speed ahead again, flying around the country to pitch new work and speak at conferences. I put together a new talk called "How to Manage a User Experience Team without Losing Your Mind." The more I worked on it, the more I realized I had a lot to say on the subject. I'd come a long way in the last three years, from not knowing the first thing about being a manager to telling other people how the Big Girls do it.

When I was seven months pregnant, I gave the talk at a design conference in Las Vegas. It was the last session of the conference and everyone was pretty punchy, including me. I relaxed into the talk, made some unplanned jokes, and had brief dialogues with people in the audience. I wasn't exactly Jon Stewart up there, but I knew what I was talking about, and I wasn't afraid to have a personality. I did not say *um* even once.

My evaluations were excellent—five stars almost across the board. Some people said it was the best talk of the whole conference. When I got back to the office I was positively thrumming from my success.

"Why don't you present your talk to the Doggies?" Stella suggested.

I set up a projector in the conference room a few days later, and people crowded around the table with their lunches. Stella sat quietly through the whole thing, looking intently at the screen where my slides were projected. It was unnerving to have her sit there for so long, not interrupting me.

"That was fantastic," she said finally when I snapped my laptop shut.

"Really?" I said. Sometimes I could be such a slut for praise. It was embarrassing.

"Yeah, really. That was excellent. You should turn it into a book."

"You think I could turn it into a book?"

She leaned back in her chair and folded her hands across her abdomen. People muttered their thanks and wandered back to their desks, but the two of us stayed behind.

"Oh yeah," she said when we were alone. "*Definitely.* Plus, you can write, so it would actually be a *good* book. Write a proposal and I'll take it to my friend Agnes. She's a publisher in the East Bay."

Stella had coauthored a couple of books of her own about web design in the mid-'90s. She leaned forward, warming up to her idea.

"It will be easy for you, Katrina. You already know what the book is about. Each one of these slides could be a chapter. Start with a table of contents. You know, just brainstorm a list and send it to me. I'll add my notes. It doesn't have to be perfect. It's just to start the conversation. Then write a page or two describing what the book is about, who it's for, you know, that stuff."

"I guess I could do that," I said.

"If we find a publisher, you can write it and I'll design it," she said, flashing me her one-hundred-watt smile.

I never would have thought of turning this talk into a book, but with Stella in my corner, it seemed easy. Not only that, it seemed *inevitable.* It was the logical next step in my career.

I dashed off a proposal in three days. Stella made her phone call, and before I knew it, we had a meeting with the publisher. A few weeks later, they made us an offer. Just like that, we had a book deal. I would write it, and Stella would design it, just as she had suggested. The plan was to start when I returned from maternity leave.

"KATRINA, YOU'VE GOT to be kidding me. How do you think you're going to work full-time and write a book when the baby comes?" Brian asked. It was evening, the girls were tucked in bed, and I lay on the couch while Brian rubbed my swollen feet.

I took a deep breath. "I know, it probably does sound crazy, but think about what a great opportunity this is—"

"I can't believe I'm hearing this," Brian said. He let my foot drop gently in his lap. Then he ran a hand around the thickest part of his hair, making a half circle around his bald spot. "I can't believe you would even consider this. You told me you were going to quit your job when the baby comes."

"I said *what?*" Deep in the recesses of my tired Mommy brain, I remembered something about a conversation we had several months ago, something about cutting back at work. But quitting? Did I really say I would *quit?*

"You said you would quit."

"No, what I said was I would talk to Stella about going part-time," I said. I think that's what I'd said. Wasn't that what I'd said? "Anyway, I don't want to quit. Quitting is a last resort, if Stella won't let me go part-time."

"You. Told. Me. You'd. Quit." Brian said. He pushed my feet off his lap and turned to face me. He looked focused and furious, as if he were prepared to draw a sword in a duel.

"No. I. Did. Not."

We stared at each other for a good thirty seconds in silence.

"Okay, listen," I said finally. We didn't have to fight about this. We could be reasonable. "It doesn't make sense for me to quit. I have so much flexibility at this job. If I have to go back to freelancing, I'm at my clients' beck and call again, like you are now. Plus, I have all those stock options now. Do you really want to give that up? And the book . . . I *really* want to write this book. Brian, they are going to pay me to write a book, a book that is going to catapult my career. I can't turn that down . . ." My voice trailed off at the end. It was intimidating to argue with Brian when he was angry. Brian listened, stone-faced, to my entire argument without blinking. *How does he do that?* I thought.

"We are barely getting by as it is, Katrina. We're making this work, but *barely.* Don't you realize what another child is going to do to this delicate balance we have? There's a big difference between having two kids and having three kids."

"But we have Martha only on the weekends. So when the baby's born, it will be more like 2.3 kids—" As soon as I said it, I could hear how offensive that statement was, but it was too late to take it back.

Brian stood up abruptly. "I can't even believe you just said that. Martha is not a third of a kid. She's a whole kid, and with this baby, that makes three. If I thought you were going to keep working full-time—plus a *book?*—jeez, Katrina. I *never* would have suggested we have another baby. You're going to lose your mind if you try to work full-time after this baby is born, and so will I."

He stormed out of the room, thus ending the conversation.

But Brian was only the second most stubborn person I knew.

He'll get over it, I thought. I sank back into the couch and looked down at my belly, which rolled like ocean waves as the baby inside me changed position. There was no way I was going to let the baby derail my career, just as it was starting to feel like a *real* career. I didn't know how, but I was determined to make it work.

LET'S ALL WORK A THIRTY-HOUR WEEK

I've noticed that in morning work meetings, my colleagues tend to be more attentive and get a lot done. As the day wears on, our meetings become less and less productive. Then I read a story on *Salon* by Sara Robinson that described this phenomenon, showcasing research proving that long hours "kill profits, productivity, and employees."

Since your boss probably hasn't read the story, and chances are you're still stuck, like so many Americans, working *fifty or more hours* a week, and since that leaves you very little time to read anything except this book, I will share the highlights here:

- Most people assume that if you increase your hours by, say, 50 percent, you will get 50 percent more work done. Not true.
- Study after study shows that for *industrial workers,* productivity dramatically decreases after eight hours a day.

➤

- *Knowledge workers* (people like me and most of my friends) have only six good hours of productivity a day. After that, we are cooked noodles.
- Studies also show that when companies reduce workers' hours back down to forty per week, their businesses become "significantly more productive and profitable."

Sometimes there are short-term gains when people work sixty or seventy hours a week. However, as the article points out, the risk of burnout begins after one week:

Without adequate rest, recreation, nutrition and time off to just be, people get dull and stupid. They can't focus. They spend more time answering e-mail and goofing off than they do working. They make mistakes that they'd never make if they were rested; and fixing those mistakes takes longer because they're fried . . . [Some software teams] descend into a negative-progress mode, where they are actually losing ground week over week because they're so mentally exhausted that they're making more errors than they can fix. De-

spite 150 years of research proving that working long hours is bad for everyone, Americans now work some of the longest hours of any country in the industrialized world. Shouldn't we know better?

Robinson blames this on a culture problem created by a bunch of geeky, antisocial, workaholic software programmers from Silicon Valley who were upheld for their "passion" and made not working on the weekend seem terribly old-fashioned.

But most of us, whether we have children or not, can't work this way.

CHAPTER 10.

MY MATERNITY LEAVE BEGAN three weeks before my due date. On the first day home, I let Ruby linger over her cereal and then snuggled with her in the rocking chair. We read all of her "Olivia the Pig" books, basking in this rare, unhurried time together. Finally it was time to gather up her lunch and go to preschool.

"I want to talk to the baby first, Mama," she said.

"Go ahead," I said. "He's listening."

Ruby, who stood at about hip height, put her hand on my watermelon belly.

"Hiiiiii, Baby," she cooed in the sugary, indulgent, Big Sister voice she had practiced for months. "Are you coming *soon*, Baby? Are you coming *tomorrow*, Baby?" She turned to me and asked, as she often did, in her regular voice, "What the Baby sayin' now, Mama?"

"The baby says, 'No, definitely not. I am *not* ready to come out yet.'"

I said this with more force than I intended. The truth was, *I* wasn't ready.

When I was pregnant with Ruby, I couldn't wait to go into labor, but this time was different. I had a long list of things to do. After I took Ruby to preschool, I went straight home and got to work. I organized the baby clothes, paid bills, cleaned out the downstairs closet, and took the girls' outgrown coats to Goodwill. The next day, I took Ruby to the doctor to catch up on her shots, which made us both cry, but it felt good to be done with it. Then I took her to the dentist for an overdue cleaning. I upgraded our cell phone plan because we kept surpassing our minutes, and took both cars in to get the oil changed.

As the week wore on, I progressed to more exotic errands. I had our kitchen knives sharpened. I dropped off the broken lamp at a repair place on San Pablo so they could fix the socket. I bought a watch for Brian to replace the one that broke three months before and replaced the girls' various hair clips, which had all mysteriously disappeared from the downstairs bathroom. (One day, months later, I would find a sculpture they'd made from those hair clips at the bottom of their toy closet.)

For someone young and single, this might sound like a dreadfully dull way to spend a week, but as any busy mom can imagine, I was in Getting Things Done heaven. This was better than a gourmet meal or luxurious sex or a Caribbean cruise. After years of letting entropy have its way, I finally had a chance to beat it back.

I could have gone on like this for at least another month, if it weren't for the fact that my body was ripening like a peach in the sun. The skin under my belly button tingled and burned from the stretching. I couldn't eat more than a few bites at each meal because, although I was hungry, the food had no place to go; the baby had taken up every square inch of available space. I had a host of strange pregnancy symptoms no one tells you about—leg cramps, nosebleeds, an overactive gag reflex, and the dreaded "mask of pregnancy," a strange ruddy-brown coloring on my cheeks and upper lip. Of course, I'd had these same symptoms when I was pregnant the first time around, but hormones had conveniently washed the memory clean away, so it was a surprise to find myself here, again, dabbing at my bloody nose and gagging on my toothbrush.

Everywhere I went, strangers wanted to know, "When's that baby coming?" They said this with wary looks on their faces, as if they half expected me to squat down and give birth right before their eyes.

"In a few weeks," I'd say. But I knew better. Babies almost never obey their due dates. They can safely arrive anytime within the six-week window I had just entered.

"Tomorrow's the day," a homeless man yelled across the parking lot as I pushed my grocery cart toward the car. "That baby's gonna come tomorrow!"

I laughed. "Two more weeks," I yelled back.

That night, at about 11:00 PM, my water broke and I woke up in wet sheets.

Damn it, I thought groggily. *The baby's coming.*

And then I bolted upright. *Oh my God! The baby's coming!*

Brian snored loudly beside me. There was no point waking him yet. He would need his sleep. I crept downstairs, and quietly surfed the early labor contractions alone, in the dark living room.

At daybreak, I called my friend Dawn, whose daughter went to Ruby's preschool. She had slept with the phone by her bed for the last ten days and was poised for action. She picked up on the first ring.

"Showtime?" she asked, not even bothering to say hello.

"It's showtime."

"I'm on my way!" she said. Five minutes later she appeared on our porch with her daughter, Sophie, both still in pajamas, to take Ruby home with them.

FAST-FORWARD THROUGH TWO DAYS of mind-bending pain that reminded me, again, what an absurdity it is that everyone comes into the world this way. Brian held my hand as I labored at home, and then at the hospital, huffing and puffing through what I half hoped would be a natural childbirth. I had hired a doula—a young, attractive single mother I'd found on Craigslist. She showed up at the hospital full of perky energy but grew surly and cold when I started vomiting, as if I wasn't doing it right. When I cried for the epidural, she gave up on me; she abandoned the soothing words and acupressure points and started taking pictures. And I'm glad she did, because they remind me of the particulars of that morning: how Brian cut the cord with a shaking hand, how my red-faced newborn son rooted around like an angry baby seal on my chest, how I wanted to cry with love and relief but stopped myself because I've always felt uncomfortable letting other people see my tears.

A nurse took my son from me so she could wash him, weigh him, dry him, and bundle him up like a seven-pound super burrito, thick ointment glistening on his eyelids. Then she settled him into Brian's arms. The doctor finished her work, and one by one, the medical staff left the room.

A feeling came to me then, a feeling I had never experienced before or since. It transcended happiness. I felt that for the first time in my life, I could take in the world as it truly was—dark and light, pain and joy—and it was all made holy. Perfect.

I had been exultant after Ruby's birth, too, but this was different. Maybe it had to do with the fact that this would be my last baby, or maybe it was the cathartic ending to months of worry and uncertainty, not knowing if he would make it. And now here he was, safe and sound. Baby Jake had arrived. No one was missing anymore. Everyone I loved was right here on earth.

The room had turned very cold, refrigerator cold, as if they were afraid the baby would spoil. A lone nurse puttered about, washing things, putting things away, clanging things, and all the while, giving advice in a loud, friendly voice.

"May 10, May 10," she singsonged. "A wonderful day to have a baby . . ."

I gazed at my husband in silence as he traced his index finger around the swirl of our newborn son's dark hair. I wanted to bask in this feeling and then swoon into sleep. I hadn't slept for two nights, and in my delirious, postpartum euphoria, I believed that sleep was the magic elixir. If I could sleep, I could infuse this new understanding, this new sense of wholeness, right into my body. No one would ever be able to take it away.

". . . May 10 is Mother's Day in Mexico, you know," said the nurse.

Brian looked up at me and whispered, "He's beautiful, Katrina. Thank you."

I closed my eyes and imagined the feeling baking into my skin, hardening like shellac.

CHAPTER 11.

I LAY ON MY BACK ON A PLUSH, king-size bed at the Washington Court Hotel. The lights of the Capitol building glowed through the gauzy curtains, throwing ghostly shadows across the bedspread. The cool blue numbers on the alarm clock read 1:49 AM. Out in the hallway, the ice machine hummed, and with ever-diminishing frequency, I heard the clatter of the elevator passing my floor.

Tomorrow—*today*, rather—I was scheduled to give a presentation about managing design teams at a highly regarded industry conference. But first, I needed to sleep.

And that meant Jake needed to sleep.

Jake, all seventeen chubby, cuddly pounds of him, lay beside me, practicing a new gurgle he'd just invented. He punched me playfully with a pudgy baby fist. "Isn't this fun, Mom?" he seemed to be saying. "We're having an adventure!"

Barely three months old, Jake was not sleeping through the night. At home, he usually went down for a few three-hour blocks, waking just long enough to nurse and pass out again. But not tonight. Tonight, he was in full-on conventioneer party mode. All he was missing was a lampshade.

I rocked him back and forth on the bed. I carried him around the room. I sang all the lullabies I knew. When I ran out of lullabies, I sang "America the Beautiful" because, after all, we were in our nation's capital. He stared at me with his big brown eyes that turned down in the outer corners, just like his father's, until each song ended. Then he gave me another spazzy, playful punch.

Time for DEFCON 2: I swaddled Jake in his Miracle Blanket, which looked like a miniature straightjacket and was supposed to give infants a soothing, womblike feeling of safety. The "miracle" thus performed was, presumably, sleep. Cocooned neatly inside this complex piece of cotton origami, Jake furrowed his brow and groused his disapproval.

I had no choice. I went to DEFCON 1. I unbuttoned my pajama top and nursed him, still lying on my side. When he was done, instead of rolling his eyes and passing out, he gurgled and grunted and wiggled and worked himself up even more.

Whatever happened to "sleeping like a baby"? Maybe he was teething. Ruby got her first tooth early, at four months. Maybe the time change had thrown him off, or the unfamiliar surroundings. The blue numbers on the alarm clock coolly announced it was 2:26 AM.

It wasn't Jake's fault. We shouldn't have come here. Back in March when the conference organizer asked me to give this talk, I should have looked down at my pregnant belly, did the math, and seen a bright red neon sign flashing NO in capital letters in my head.

What I said instead was: "I'll be on maternity leave . . . I'd have to bring the baby with me."

"No problem," she enthused. "We can find someone to hold the baby while you give your talk."

How could I possibly say no? I had to bust down the doors to get my first speaking engagement, and now this woman I barely knew wanted me to speak at a prestigious national event. Her company was going to pay my travel expenses, get someone to mind the baby for me, and kick in a small stipend. A stipend! That was practically a speaker's fee! Heck, it was practically an honorarium! How could I refuse?

So here I was. Playing hostess to a one-boy rave, wondering why I let myself get talked into this by someone who *didn't even have children.*

It was 3:13 AM. The longer we didn't sleep, the more frantic I became, which meant I would be that much less likely to sleep when Jake finally did. I had prescriptions for both sleeping pills and Xanax for emergencies like this, but because I was breast-feeding, I couldn't take them.

If I didn't sleep, how was I going to give a forty-five-minute talk to one-hundred-plus strangers? I had averaged four hours of sleep a night for the last three months. On a good day, I was spacey and slow, like the dim-witted neighbor on a '70s sitcom. What was I going to be like on a bad day?

At some point, I dozed off. All too soon, Jake was crying and I was wide awake. The heartless clock glowed 6:11 AM.

It was too early for breakfast. I pushed away the thought that it was barely 3:00 AM California time. I nursed my boy and then unfurled him from his Miracle Blanket bondage and rolled him onto his stomach for a little "tummy time." He hated "tummy time," but the pediatrician said it was important for building his neck muscles.

I sat at the desk opposite the bed, pulled out my handwritten notes, and flipped open my laptop to rehearse my talk. I was scheduled to perform Katrina's greatest hit, "How to Manage a User Experience Group without Losing Your Mind." It seemed like ages since I gave this talk in Vegas for the first time.

"Hello," I said groggily, to no one in particular. "My name is Katrina Alcorn, and I'm here to talk to you about managing user experience teams . . ." I clicked to the first slide on my laptop and began reciting my introduction.

"Today I'm going to focus on the people part of management . . ."

"Eh!" Jake bobbed his head up and down like a lizard picking at insects.

I clicked to the next slide. It was a *New Yorker* cartoon of two men sitting in a bar. One was telling the other, "Then I made the leap from skilled labor to unskilled management."

"Ehhh!" Jake said again. *You're ignoring me!*

I flipped him over on his back and propped him up against the billion or so pillows they give you in a fancy hotel room. Then I continued rehearsing, while looking into his eyes and talking in my singsong baby voice.

"When I FIRST made the LEAP from skilled LABOR to unskilled MANAGEMENT, I didn't really KNOW what I was DOING . . . (No I didn't, Jakey! I acted like I did, but I didn't!) . . . I didn't have a MENTOR. I'd never taken a MANAGEMENT CLASS . . . (No I didn't, silly boy. Not one class!) . . ."

This went on for another couple of slides, but my boy was not fooled. He knew I was doing a boring grown-up thing, and his protests grew louder and more urgent. I gave up, slapped the laptop closed, pulled Jake onto my lap, and bounced him on my knee. I was so tired I wanted to die. We both smelled like sour milk.

Time to shower. I set Jake on the bath mat, and he lay there kicking and punching good-naturedly at the ceiling.

When I was clean and toweled off, I placed Jake in the exact center of the bed and propped him up again while I got dressed. He sucked on his fist and grunted fashion advice. I decided to wear my tan maternity pants because, although I could squeeze into my normal clothes now, I wasn't ready to give up the wide elastic maternity waistband. I pulled on my nice nursing shirt, the black one that looked like a regular shirt except for the discreet flap of fabric that could be pulled aside when needed. When I wore the shirt and Jake nursed, you couldn't see any skin. A regular Miracle Shirt.

The rising clatter of the elevator and the other sounds of morning had finally drowned out the ice machine. The world was waking up, whether I was ready to or not.

I pulled out the baby carrier and strapped Jake to my chest, facing toward me, both of us groaning with the effort. He was big for three months. At his last checkup, our pediatrician called him "monumental," which seemed an especially apt description today. He weighed as much as the Lincoln Memorial. I hung my conference badge over his back, and we rode the elevator down to the conference hall.

The keynote session had just begun. The woman who designed the pill bottles for Target was speaking. I'd heard about her. It sounds mundane—designing medicine bottles—but the new labels had saved people's lives because they were so easy to understand. I walked in, hoping to stand inconspicuously at the back of the room, but Jake was feeling rowdy. He had a whole panoply of sound effects for occasions like this. Every so often, he cut loose with a little babbling or an indiscreet gurgle. One of the many young hipster designers shot me a look, as if I'd just let out a fart in church. I exited out to the hall and jiggled up and down on the balls of my feet a bit to settle Jake. We tried it again a few minutes later, with the same result. I decided to walk around with him for a while.

It's always a good idea to attend a couple of sessions before you speak at a conference, just to get a feel for the audience. Each conference is its own temporary world. It has its own culture and its own running jokes that usually start at the keynote presentation and float from one session to the next like dandelion seeds. If you can grab ahold of one of those seeds, it makes your presentation stronger, more confident. It tells people, *I'm one of you.*

I tried entering another session again an hour later, when Jake was calm. Two minutes in, he made one of his random baby rhinoceros sounds, and it echoed off every wall. Back to the lobby.

I sleepwalked through the mostly empty halls, with a bowling ball strapped to my chest until it was time for my presentation. We made our way back to the lobby where a woman wearing a flouncy H&M skirt and glasses with thick, black hip-hop frames waited for us.

"Do you want to go in early and get set up?" she asked.

Her name was Meghan. I think. Or was it Erin? She was here with her husband and son, who was a month or two older than Jake. I met her only the day before, but we immediately bonded over our kids, and she volunteered to hold Jake during my talk.

"Let me nurse him one last time," I said, "just to make sure the tank is full."

"Good idea," Meghan said.

When we were done, Jake went to her without a fuss. Thank God. I kissed him good-bye on his head, which still had that new baby smell, like warm bread dough.

The session room was bigger and fancier than any of the rooms I'd spoken in before. Stately. The carpet was a rich burgundy and impressive-looking chandeliers hung high overhead. I set my notes on the podium and a technician clipped a wireless mike to my maternity waistband. The first slide of my presentation was up on the giant screen behind me. My name in lights.

I fetched a bottle of water from the table in the back as people shuffled in. Was it me, or did they look particularly grim? If I'd been able to sit in on even one session that morning, I would have a better idea of who these people were and how my talk fit in with other things they'd seen and talked about. Instead, I stood before a room full of total strangers.

Someone I'd never met before walked to the podium to introduce me, reading from handwritten notes on a large white index card.

"Now we're going to hear from Katrina Alcorn of Dogstar Studio in San Francisco. Katrina manages a team of a dozen user experience designers . . ."

I wondered how Jake was doing. If he started to cry, would I be able to hear him? I was already sweating. I wasn't normally a sweaty person, except when I was lactating. *Oh, God,* I thought, *I hope I don't have armpit stains.* I snuck a glance at my chest—didn't think so. Not yet anyway. I wore breast pads to keep from leaking through my bra. If I'd thought of it, I would have stuck an extra one under each armpit. Thank God the Miracle Shirt came in black.

It was my turn.

"Welcome! My name is Katrina Alcorn. I'm here to talk with you about managing user experience groups. Before I begin, I'd like to get a sense of how many of you are managing teams now . . ."

Only a sprinkling of hands went up. That was okay. The conference organizer told me my talk was supposed to be "aspirational." They were here because they thought they might want to be me someday. That was good.

I quickly walked through the agenda and my *New Yorker* joke. No one laughed. That was okay, too. We were just getting warmed up.

After briefly touching on the different types of user experience teams and the kinds of things I looked for in a new hire, I clicked to a slide with the title "Katrina's Cardinal Rule: Don't Hire Closed-Minded People." Below the title was a close-up photo of George Bush scowling and wagging his finger. This killed in Vegas.

"Don't hire blamers," I said. I paused a beat. "People who are closed-minded or unwilling to learn from their mistakes." There was an uncomfortable silence. A few people shifted in their chairs. Someone coughed.

And then, too late, it hit me: I wasn't in Northern California anymore. This was Washington, D.C. Some of these people voted for Bush. *For the love of God, why did I leave this slide in?*

I looked down at my notes, trying to remember what I was supposed to say next, with George Bush pointing his accusing finger at my sweaty back.

It took me a few slides to get back on track, and by then all hope for glory was gone. I spent the next forty-two minutes standing stiffly behind the podium trying to keep from fainting.

When it was over, I practically ran from the room. Meghan held Jake in her lap. He was sleeping. Like a baby.

"He did great," she said as I scooped him up.

I couldn't get out of D.C. fast enough.

WE ESCAPED ON AN AFTERNOON FLIGHT, took a cab from the airport, and arrived home an hour past Ruby's bedtime. Brian had let Ruby wait up for us, and she met us at the door, jumping around in her pink nightie and grinning like an elf. But when I sat down to nurse Jake, she started to cry.

"I just want my mommy to myself!" she sobbed, exhausted.

I felt so bad for her. She was only four years old. It was so hard to share.

When Jake was done, I passed him to Brian, pulled Ruby onto my lap, and buried my nose in her hair, which smelled like bubblegum shampoo. That was Jake's cue to scream for his mommy.

All I wanted was to take a bath and wash the sticky D.C. summer off my body. My back ached from lugging Jake around conference halls and airports, and I reeked of stale airplane food and milk.

A few weeks later, I received evaluations from the people who saw me speak. I rated two and a half stars out of five. Exactly average. Frantic, I went online to check the other speakers' scores. Maybe this was just a tough crowd. Most of the other speakers had at least three stars, if not four or five. So, I wasn't exactly average. I bombed. I totally bombed.

Brian tried to console me.

"How many of the other speakers could have done what you did?" he said. "Flying across the country alone with a baby, no sleep . . ."

"No one is grading on a curve for me because I'm a mom," I wailed.

It stung. I didn't have time to go to many industry parties or blog about design. I did a fraction of the schmoozing and writing that I should do to be seen as a leader in my field. This was what I did to stay ahead—I spoke at a few out-of-town conferences a year. And it was always a sacrifice. It was hard on Brian when I was away. It was hard on Ruby. It was exhausting to fly across country, ten times more exhausting to do it with a sleepless baby. So what was it all for?

I tried to explain all this to Brian, who listened patiently, without saying a word. The longer I spoke, the more his eyes glazed over.

I knew that look. He still gave the *appearance* of listening, but somewhere behind his eyes, a thought had formed, a conclusion had been reached. He thought I was being *neurotic.* I felt my anger rise. I gave up with a sigh, slumped against the sofa, and crossed my arms over my chest, feeling utterly misunderstood. Without so much as a word, we had slipped onto very thin ice. Brian tried to put a hand on my shoulder, and I shrugged him away.

"I need a time-out," I said.

I won't think you unkind if you, like Brian, wonder at this point, *What did you* think *was going to happen?* It's only now, years later, that I can fully articulate why I agreed to speak at that stupid conference while I was still on maternity leave.

Experts say the "make it or break it" decade for our careers is that ten-year stretch between ages thirty and forty. That's when urban professionals clock long hours and pile up airline miles. When we're supposed to write white papers on weekends and stay out on weeknights to schmooze at industry events. Inconveniently, they're also the years when women are likely to be pregnant, nursing, and raising young children. Weekends are for playdates, volunteering at the preschool fundraiser, and folding laundry. Weeknights are for trying to catch up on sleep and folding more laundry.

We can't compete with our book-writing, jet-setting colleagues, and we begin to get passed over for raises and promotions. Before we know it, we've drifted off the Fast Track and onto the Mommy Track. Or we simply park our car in the driveway and stay home for good. Either way, most of us never see the Fast Track again. Because once you get off it, it's very, very hard to get back on.

Of women in the United States who take a couple of years off to be with their babies and then try to go back to work, about a quarter can't. Those who do manage to get work in their field lose an average of 18 percent in earning power (and that number goes up and up the longer they take time off).

Consider that women who don't have children make 10 cents less on the dollar than their male counterparts. That's a real problem for women—a maddening, bafflingly intractable problem.

Now consider that mothers make *27 cents* less on the dollar than their male counterparts (whether those men have children or not). Single mothers make *34 to 44 cents* less. That's not just a problem for women. That's a crisis for American families.

I didn't know any of this when I agreed to fly across the country with my three-month-old, lug him around the conference for two days like the world's cutest albatross, and then embarrass myself in front of a bunch of indifferent strangers. All I knew was that a powerful feeling in my gut told me to say yes, and keep saying yes, no matter what.

A GI BILL FOR MOMS

Both anecdotal and empirical evidence show that women's opportunities in the workplace have a way of mysteriously evaporating after they have children. The news media began to refer to this phenomenon as the "Mommy Track" in 1989, after a career consultant named Felice Schwartz set off a furor with an article in the *Harvard Business Review*. In the article, she claimed that women managers cost corporations more than men do, because they require things like flexible schedules to accommodate their pesky family responsibilities.

Schwartz suggested that companies divide their female employees into two groups, based on their level of career commitment. Group 1: "Career-primary" women who'd be willing to work long hours, travel extensively, and, when needed, relocate without letting any personal obligations get in the way. Group 2: "Career-and-family" women who'd happily accept lower pay and a dead-end job if it meant they could take a sick day when little Johnny had a fever.

In other words, Schwartz's proposed solution was to take the implicit Mommy Track, in which mothers are informally and unfairly passed over for raises, choice assignments, and promotions, and make it explicit *corporate policy*.

There are more problems with this strategy than I care to list, but here are a few:

1. It's exploitative—taking advantage of women when they most need their income to support a family.
2. It's unrealistic. Our needs (both men's and women's) change over time. How many of us—with children or without—can truly put career front and center at all times?
3. It's discriminatory. (No one suggested dividing fathers and nonfathers into separate groups.)
4. It shows an amazing lack of creativity, requiring women to fit into the existing work culture, rather than finding ways to make that culture work for everyone.

Companies need women at all levels, and they *especially* need women in leadership roles. Numerous studies have shown that companies with more women in leadership roles outperform their competitors. They do better on the stock exchange, and they make higher profits.

Many possible reasons have been put forth for this correlation between more women and healthier companies. It could be that we're better listeners, that we have a more "open and inclusive style of management," or that diverse groups (such as those that mix genders) tend to make better decisions. One recent study published in the *Harvard Business Review* suggests that women may simply be better leaders. Or maybe, as Congresswoman Nancy Pelosi pointed out in a 2012 interview, the years some of us spend raising children actually give us important diplomacy and interpersonal skills. (Important biographical note: Pelosi spent more than a *decade* as a stay-at-home mom with five children before running for political office.)

All too often, employers look at the years we stay home with young children as a black mark, wasted time. Even a request to work a reduced schedule is seen as a lack of commitment to our jobs.

This is what needs to change—this attitude about the time people spend caring for family. Instead of pushing us onto the Mommy Track, employers should be looking at creative strategies like job shares so women can stay in leadership roles, or better "on-ramps" to help us transition back to the Fast Track when we're ready.

Government, too, can help by providing incentives and programs to help working parents. This isn't an ideological argument—throughout our history, politicians of all stripes have stepped in to help correct economic deficiencies. Just one example: In 1944, faced with millions of veterans coming home from World War II with valuable skills that did not easily translate to the workforce, Congress passed the GI Bill. The bill provided loans to start new businesses, and tuition and living expenses to attend college. One needed only ninety days of active duty to be eligible—no combat experience required.

This investment in the future of our country unleashed a massive amount of untapped human capital. By the time the program ended, in 1956, more than two million veterans had attended college and more than six million had received some type of training with help from the program. Today historians and economists conclude that the GI Bill was one of the *most successful, profitable government programs in U.S. history,* speeding our long-term economic growth and helping bring about the emergence of the middle class. For every $1 invested, the government and the economy received almost $7 in return.

➤

➤ Why wouldn't we make a much smaller but similar investment for mothers and fathers who take years off (unpaid) to raise children? It wouldn't just improve the economic stability of families; it would be an investment in the economic well-being of our country.

CHAPTER 12.

BEFORE JAKE WAS BORN, both Stella and I had carefully avoided any specifics about my maternity leave. I think we were both afraid of what the other would say. But I knew what I wanted.

I wanted six months off. Six months, I believed, would give me time to recover from the birth and get through the worst of the sleep deprivation. It would give me unhurried time to establish breast-feeding and bond with my new baby. A six-month leave would also give me time to help Ruby adjust to having a new brother. Soon after Jake was born, she had begun to regress, crying more often when she didn't get her way and even wetting the bed—something she hadn't done since she had outgrown diapers two years before. I was pretty certain that like many older siblings, Ruby felt anxious and displaced by the new baby. Six months off would give me unhurried time with Ruby, to reassure her that all was well.

Most of that time off would be unpaid, of course, but Brian and I had planned for this, and he had steady freelance work. We could afford it. I just needed to know I'd have a job when I was ready to come back.

I'd almost broached the subject with Stella many times when I was pregnant, but I never knew how to begin. In some circles, people consider a six-month maternity leave suspiciously un-American, a European-style luxury that reveals a lack of professional commitment. We have the dubious distinction of being one of only a handful of countries in the world (along with Papua New Guinea and Swaziland) without paid maternity leave. Between our *cultural disdain* for time off and the lack of *paid* time off, fewer than half of working mothers in the United States manage to stay home for even *three* months. It did not help matters that my boss was one of them.

Stella had gone back to work very early. If I remember correctly, she'd taken only a few weeks off with her first child and a month or two with her second. Both times, she'd brought a nanny to the office, who'd hand the baby over at three- or four-hour intervals to nurse. Although Stella boasted about her early return to work as an achievement, I suspected she felt a bit cheated. She had the added pressure of being the primary breadwinner in her house—running a design firm paid a lot more than her husband's job. Even if she felt the business could run without her for a few months, she couldn't afford it financially. Asking this woman for six months "off" would be asking for something she couldn't even give herself.

Stella never brought it up, either. Perhaps she was afraid that if she told me how soon she wanted me back at work, I would quit.

Instead, she suggested I hire a nanny and graciously offered to make room at the office for my nanny to watch the baby, just as hers had done. But I couldn't afford a private nanny, and besides, I wanted those early months to be about the baby, not work.

I tried to think about it from Stella's perspective. She was a busy working mom, too, and she had a business to run, after all. She *depended* on me. If my maternity leave made *her* life harder, then of course she would want me back sooner. And who could blame her?

I didn't see any point in trying to negotiate. Instead, I did everything in my power to make sure things would go smoothly in my absence, reasoning that if Stella felt my department was in good hands, she would be willing to let me take more time off.

THOMAS WAS MY TICKET TO six months' leave. Lately, he'd been jockeying for more responsibility. I was optimistic that with a little grooming he would excel in my job. *Maybe the new job demands would give him a place to channel his energy and help tame his inner drama queen,* I thought.

Back when I was still pregnant and I brought it up, Thomas jumped at the opportunity. As soon as I came off of bed rest, he began to shadow me in pitches and management meetings. I spent hours coaching him how to staff and scope new projects, basically teaching him all I knew about "How to Manage a User Experience Team without Losing Your Mind." I typed detailed notes about my various responsibilities, until I'd assembled a little manual of operating instructions for my job. I told Thomas who could help him with different tasks so he wouldn't have to do it all himself.

It occurred to me that I might train Thomas so well that they might never need me to come back—but that was a risk I would just have to take. Who knows? Maybe we could arrange some type of a job share when I came back—a promotion for him, and more time for me to work on the book.

And sure enough, soon after my maternity leave started, Thomas began calling me every week or two to tell me things were going great. Actually, they sounded *more* than great. During one of these conversations, he told me he thought he'd found his calling. "Are you sure you want to come back?" he'd asked. "I want to be *you.*"

Maybe this job share could work out after all, I thought. But soon after my thwarted conference presentation in D.C., Stella called and the fantasy evaporated.

"Your team is going to mutiny," Stella said. "We need you back."

This came as a complete surprise. I'd set things up so perfectly I thought people would hardly notice I was gone. Technically, I wasn't really *gone* at all. I still checked my work email almost daily, and was available by phone, if important issues arose. I had come in to the office with Jake at Stella's request, while on unpaid leave, to interview a potential new hire. And I'd represented my company (for better or worse) at that conference in D.C. It didn't occur to me to get paid for that time, beyond the piddling conference stipend. This was all part of the unspoken pact I thought I was making with Stella—*I'll pitch in when you really need me. Just please let me stay home with my baby.*

"What do you mean?" I said to Stella. "Thomas just called me last week. He said things are going great."

"They aren't," Stella said. "He's turned into Dot-Com Tom again. He's making everyone crazy. Soraya will barely speak to him, and I think Owen might be looking for another job. Seriously, Katrina, people are going to quit soon if you don't come back and do something."

After much discussion, we came to an agreement of sorts. I would come in the following week to talk Owen and Soraya off the ledge. ("Bring the baby," Stella said. "Everyone loves to see babies.") After that, I'd start coming in on a part-time basis and work my way up to four days a week by the time Jake was six months old. It was generous of Stella to let me ease back in this way. Still mindful of the deal I'd made with Brian, I told her I couldn't come back a full five days a week.

"I don't know, Katrina," she said, hesitating. "No one else on the leadership team works four days a week."

"No one else has a new baby," I observed, trying to keep the anger out of my voice. In fact, of the six people on the leadership team, the only other person who had a child besides Stella and me was Vicente, and I knew from our discussions that his wife did the lion's share of the child care.

"*I* worked full-time when my kids were babies," Stella fired back. "*I* never had the luxury of working four days a week."

Ouch. The resentment I'd suspected was there finally broke the surface. She didn't get this much time; why did I think I was entitled to it?

Because you need this time, I could hear Brian say. *We need you to take this time.*

"I'm sorry, Stella, I guess I'm not as strong as you," I said. "I just know I can't do five days a week. Not yet."

When Stella saw that I was going to hold firm, she relented. What choice did she have? Let Dot-Com Tom run the department into the ground?

"One year," she said. "We can try it until Jake is a year old. I can't commit beyond that."

At last, we had an explicit agreement. I would take a prorated cut in salary and benefits, of course, but I could keep my stock options and, most important, my job.

In the meantime, I formed a new secret plan. I would take my management skills to a new level. I would show Stella and everyone at Dogstar that I could get more done in four days a week than most people could in five. When Stella saw that this was working, she would agree to continue our arrangement beyond Jake's birthday.

And so, when Jake was four months old, I went back to work.

ON MY FIRST DAY BACK, I interviewed my staff. It was just as bad as Stella had said. Owen was threatening to quit. Soraya told me she was demoralized by the way Thomas treated her in front of her project team. Chang was annoyed with the way Thomas would march into meetings, dominate the conversation, make random abstract suggestions, then disappear when the real work had to be done. Norman, who would rather impale himself on a rusty spike than say an unkind word about anybody, told me Thomas went all Robin Williams *Dead Poets Society* while facilitating a client workshop, strutting around the room dramatically as he talked, hopping up on a side table so he was perched above the rest of the group, dangling his legs in the air. Beth just rolled her eyes.

"No one understands Thomas but you," she said.

The project managers were in a tizzy because Thomas was two

months behind on his time sheets—they couldn't bill our clients until they had that information.

Stella was fed up with the way Thomas used their weekly check-ins to have the kind of sessions he was used to having with me.

"I never agreed to be Thomas's therapist," she complained.

It was my fault. I'd spoiled him. Thomas thought that's what his manager was supposed to do, listen to his problems.

My second day back at the office, I invited Thomas to lunch.

"I don't know how to bring this up with you, so I'm just going to start," I said after we ordered.

"Okay . . ." He looked as scared as I felt. This was going to be a tricky conversation.

"Thomas, it's all good. You're not in trouble."

"Okay . . . ?" His blue eyes peered at me through sky-blue glasses frames.

"I just think there are some things that have gotten out of sync while I've been gone. And that's normal. I mean, you've been doing a lot of great stuff. But I think some of the things that you think are going well aren't shared by everyone."

"Like what?"

I did my best to describe some of the feedback from his co-workers, without getting into embarrassing specifics. As I talked, I watched the look on his face transform from deer-in-headlights to downright defensive.

"No one ever trained me to be a manager," he sputtered, leaning away in his chair.

"Thomas, listen to me. You're not in trouble. This isn't about what you did wrong. This is just about squaring your perceptions with some of the other feedback I've gotten."

Squaring your perceptions . . . Jesus, where did I pick that one up?

Thomas looked as if I had punched him in the head; he had no idea how hard I was working to soften the blow.

"You have a wonderful, brilliant mind, Thomas," I said after swallowing a bite of pasta. This was easy to say, because I believed it. "But sometimes people can't keep up with you. If you're going to continue to supervise people, we need to work on translating your ideas in ways that they can understand."

I continued in this manner, trying to make the bitter pill taste like crème brûlée, all the while hoping I didn't sound like a phony, or let my tiredness show, stealing glances at my watch—I'd forgotten to pump before we left the office. I made a joke about the time sheets, but there was nothing funny about it. It was ridiculous that I had to tell this "brilliant" designer to keep up with the basic requirements of his job.

When I was done, it was Thomas's turn. He had made the pivot from defensive to angry. He told me at length how much pressure he was under while I was away. *You know, while I was pushing a person out of my body.* I felt my temper rise but held my tongue.

"I never wanted your job," he said finally. "I never wanted to be *you*."

I stared at him, trying to think of an appropriate response. And then I felt my milk come down.

"I think we should head back to the office," I said.

A MONTH LATER, DOGSTAR MOVED to a roomier office space in a more upscale part of town. At Thomas's insistence, our desks were right next to each other at one end of a long mezzanine.

As the weeks went by, and I ramped up to my four-day-a-week schedule, the tension between us was palpable. Everyone could feel it. It was not just Thomas who had changed. I had less energy than I had before Jake, and less time. I cut back my one-on-ones with my team members to a curt fifteen minutes—there was no time for listening to Thomas's, or anyone else's, problems. Thomas probably felt a lot like Ruby did. *Where did Mommy go?* Often I felt the urge to say something reassuring to him, but something always stopped me. I didn't want to be Thomas's therapist, either.

For many of us, before we have kids, the drama of the office can occupy center stage in our lives. Everything is so important! The turf wars: *Who's making a power play? Who's feeling threatened? So-and-so is in the boss's doghouse . . .* The childish behavior: One coworker lashing out at another because he's had a bad day. So-and-so is whining that she never gets the cool projects. The gossip: *Guess who kissed whom at the office holiday party?*

After we have kids, our priorities shift. We begin to see these dramas in a new, often unflattering, light. Petty turf wars become repugnant, and childish behavior is intolerable. One survey of three hundred women found that "toxic culture," not the "glass ceiling," was the main reason senior women leave corporate roles. We don't have time for this crap. Literally. Time has become a limited resource, as precious as clean water or fertile soil. We resent squandering it calming a client's tantrum because he doesn't like a logo, or fielding idle gossip. More than ever before, we need the grown-ups to act like grown-ups.

I felt this shift occur in me after Jake was born, and I've observed this same phenomenon in many of my friends. When I went back to work, I became keenly aware that any extra effort I gave at the office was effort that I was not making for my new baby, his jealous older siblings, or their exhausted, overworked dad. This meant I had less tolerance for anyone who wasn't holding up his end.

This new urgency around time was not only changing my relationships at the office, it was affecting our social life, too.

Before Jake, Brian and I had kept up with a few friends who didn't have children, but now the gap between us yawned wider. Stretched to the max, we unconsciously started dividing the world into two types of people: the ones who made life easier and the ones who made life harder. Ironically, the ones who made life easier were often the ones who were stretched as thin as we were—other working parents. When everyone in the house came down with the flu, it was other overworked parents who dropped off soup or picked up infant Tylenol at the pharmacy. Our friends who didn't have children, even the ones who doted on our kids, couldn't understand why we went to bed so early, or why we didn't reciprocate their invitations to dinner, or why it took three weeks to plan one evening out, or why we might not *want* to plan time away from our kids.

I confided in one of these friends how stressed out we felt.

"Maybe you should stop wearing a watch," he said.

Stop wearing a watch? Wow, that's all it was? The problem wasn't that I had too much to do, but that I just needed to chill out and stop worrying about what time it was!

We didn't want it to happen, but soon it became easier to just lose touch.

Maybe this is just one of those things that happen with any kind of big life change. Who understands what someone going through a divorce needs better than someone who's been through their own divorce? Who understands what someone with breast cancer needs better than someone who's been through their own health crisis?

But here's the point: Raising children isn't supposed to be a crisis. It's supposedly the natural order of things, something that a vast majority of adults choose to do. So why do so many of us wind up so isolated? Why does our social circle shrink instead of expanding just because we're raising children? If it really takes a village, where are the other villagers?

AN ESSAY I ONCE READ BY the historian and *New Yorker* writer Jill Lepore helped me to make sense of the alienation I felt. She explains that we didn't used to be parents and nonparents. For most of human history, to be an adult was to help care for children. In fact, the word *parenting* is relatively new, dating back to the mid-1800s. This is how ordinary life looked then:

> *Born into a growing family, you help rear your siblings, have the first of your own half dozen or even dozen children soon after you're grown, and die before your youngest has left home. In the early 1800s, the fertility rate among American women was seven to eight children; adults couldn't expect to live past sixty. To be an adult was to be a parent—nearly everyone lived in households with children . . .*

We lived and worked in the constant presence of children, sharing the work of raising them. Then, as the birthrate began to go down, our familiarity with children, and our collective sense of responsibility for them, began to change. The article goes on to explain that by 1922, parenting had begun to look "mystifying" to people who did not grow up caring for siblings and neighbors and cousins:

> *Looking after babies and little kids is skilled labor, but, as the number of children dwindled, so did the number of adults who had any real skill. The growing uprootedness of American life meant that many first-time parents couldn't count on grandparents, or, really, on anyone.*

Today we're in a new phase of this ongoing social experiment; we are raised in smaller families and may wait until our thirties or forties to have children of our own, if we choose to have them at all. Many of us have so little exposure to children that we may never even hold a baby until we give birth to one. We're bewildered by the "skilled labor" of parenting and often left to sort it out for ourselves. When we do have a baby, many of us cross a great divide, from being a carefree single adult with no one to look after but ourselves to suddenly feeling the weight of extraordinary, grave responsibilities.

I'd felt some of this with Ruby, but after Jake was born, there was no denying how profoundly different my life was from those of nonparents. When I looked back across that divide at people like Thomas—a single gay man in his forties—I felt profoundly misunderstood. And I wouldn't be surprised if he looked back at me, equally bewildered, and thought, *What happened to her?*

FAILING THE FAMILIES WHO NEED PAID LEAVE

It's not just wealthier countries like France (sixteen weeks), Denmark (fifty-two weeks), and Sweden (sixteen *months!*) that offer paid parental leave. It's also poorer countries like Bolivia (twelve weeks), Cambodia (ninety days), and even the Democratic Republic of Congo (fourteen weeks). Here's what our lack of paid leave has gotten us:

- Having a baby is a leading cause of "poverty spells" in the United States—when household income dips below what's needed to cover basic needs.
- The United States ranks thirty-seventh of all countries in infant mortality—paid family leave has been shown to reduce infant mortality by as much as 20 percent.
- In a 2011 report called *Failing Its Families*, Human Rights Watch found that our lack of

➤

paid leave in the United States contributed to "delaying babies' immunizations, postpartum depression and other health problems, and caused mothers to give up breastfeeding early." (The report also found that for many women "merely revealing they were pregnant and requesting leave triggered tensions with employers, and sometimes demotions or pay cuts.")

I was lucky that when Jake was born, I was eligible for several weeks of California disability leave, which paid a percentage of my salary. (Don't ask why nursing an infant child is considered a "disability.") I was also lucky that my employer supplemented that leave for the first few weeks. And luckier still that when my paid leave ran out, I could afford to take a couple of months of unpaid time off to bond with my baby.

But most women in the United States don't have any of these options. In fact, the women most in need of paid leave—low-income workers—are least likely to get it. They are also less likely to have sick pay or vacation pay to help cover time off after a baby is born.

CHAPTER 13.

AFTER JAKE WAS BORN, my body went into overdrive to keep him fed. My breasts seemed to be under the mistaken impression that I'd had twins. My breasts were like two Jewish mothers that followed the baby around saying, *Did you eat yet? You look thin. You need to eat!*

I was a milk fountain. Sometimes my milk went shooting across the room before Jake could get his mouth on my nipple, and sometimes it came out so fast he choked and it came out his nose. This probably sounds weird to someone who has never nursed a child, but I was inexpressibly proud. I could feed my child from my body! And I was feeding him the healthiest food he could possibly eat. It would nurture him his whole life, shielding him from respiratory infections, digestive problems, ear infections, even asthma, cancer, and diabetes.

I fully intended to continue breast-feeding until Jake was one year old. Back when Stella's daughter, Claire, and Ruby were babies, we pumped in one of the four private bathrooms our old office had. Although I've heard many women complain about pumping in bathrooms, I didn't mind terribly. All I cared about was that it was private and the door had a secure lock. Pumping, after all, is nothing like nursing. The idea that someone other than my husband might witness the bovine experience of being hooked up to a machine explicitly designed to pull milk from my breast was mortifying.

But the day we moved in to our new office, about a month after I returned to work, I immediately discovered there were no private bathrooms. The women's room had three stalls, and the only outlet was next to the door, which meant pumping in full sight of any woman (including clients) coming in or out. The conference rooms were encased in glass, like aquariums.

Everyone was in a flurry to unpack, put away their files, and set up their workstations. I didn't want to bother anyone with my dilemma, so when it was time to pump, I simply taped a sign to the bathroom door saying PLEASE COME BACK IN 10 MINUTES, then pressed the lock on the door handle and got to work. I plugged in my Medela Pump In Style, a breast pump cleverly disguised to look like a stylish backpack, and set it on the sink. I assembled the bottles and suction cups and tiny plastic hoses with the precision and economy of motion of a high-class burglar. Finally, I unbuttoned my shirt, unsnapped my nursing bra, removed the pads, and set them faceup on the sink.

Someone jiggled the door handle, the lock popped open, and one of the designers opened the door.

"Can you come back in five minutes?" I said, hunching over my exposed chest.

"Sorry!" she said, quickly shutting the door.

Apparently the lock wasn't very secure. I pressed it down again, then positioned the suction cups so my nipples pointed straight out, and turned on the pump. It began to wheeze and groan rhythmically. Within a few seconds, milk began to drip, then trickle into the bottles. That was the cool part, watching all that milk filling up Jake's bottles. When he nursed, I didn't get to see it. I marveled at the sheer quantity. No wonder he was "monumental." No wonder I was hungry all the time.

Two minutes later, the door flew open, and I heard a woman gasp.

"I put a sign up!" I protested, my back to the door. "Can you come back?"

Before I could finish talking, she'd slammed the door shut.

Apparently the sign wasn't big enough, either. A moment later, Soraya burst in.

"Oh, hi!" she said, surprised, and then beelined for an open stall.

I gave up, dropped the suction cups in the sink, and quickly reattached my bra and buttoned up my shirt.

After cleaning up, I marched over to the office of our HR director, Pauline, and begged her to help me find a private space to pump. Luckily, we had five conference rooms—four more than our old office. Pauline arranged for Conference Room B to be set aside as a "mothers' room." One of our project managers, Kimberly, would be coming back from maternity leave in a month or so, and she'd need a place to pump, too. Pauline dug up some old red paisley tablecloths and helped me attach them to the glass wall with lots of thick translucent packing tape. Then Orlando, the office manager, sent an email to everyone saying, "Don't book meetings in Conference Room B. Remember, 'B' is for 'Baby'!"

Every three hours, I ducked into Conference Room B and shut the door. The walls between the conference rooms were paper-thin and I wondered if people could hear the mechanical groaning sounds of the pump in the adjacent rooms. But at least no one walked in on me anymore.

Soon, I got into a routine. I learned to position the suction cups so that I could hold the left one with my right hand, pinning the right one in place with my arm. (The "hands-free nursing bra" had not been invented yet.) I used my left hand (I'm left-handed) to write notes on a proposal or make fundraising calls for Ruby's preschool. (I had agreed to solicit all the food donations for Ruby's preschool auction—I'm almost certain people could hear the pump over the phone, but no one ever commented on it.)

After about ten minutes, both bottles were usually pretty full. Every time I snapped the pump off, I was surprised by the sudden quiet while I patted my breasts dry with a paper towel and made myself presentable again.

Then to the kitchen to wash everything up. Occasionally when I walked in, a coworker was fixing his or her coffee at the kitchen counter. I didn't want to make anyone uncomfortable, so I tried to act nonchalant, but they usually left quickly, to my relief. I thought about using the sink in the women's bathroom, but that was shared, too. It was also smaller, and of course, there was no sponge or dish soap.

After washing and drying the pump parts, I put away the milk. We had one shared refrigerator. Stella had always put Claire's bottles on the top shelf in full view and joked at staff meetings not to mistake her milk for the half-and-half. That seemed a bit outré for me. I stored Jake's bottles on the bottom shelf, in an attempt to be discreet.

One day, during a short lull between meetings, I stopped at my desk to check email. As usual, I was about thirty behind. I scanned my inbox until one subject line jumped out at me: "Bodily fluids."

From: Eugene Romero
Subject: bodily fluids
Date: October 10, 2007 2:18:52 PM PDT
To: everyone@dogstar.com

_____

I'm against them being stored in the company refrigerator.
Just my 2 cents.
+++
eugene romero
senior design engineer
dogstar, inc.

....

I stared at the computer, stunned. I barely knew Eugene. He was a tech guy who'd been hired while I was on maternity leave. He was a bit on the quiet side, like a lot of tech guys, but he seemed nice enough. He had sent the email to everyone in the New York and San Francisco offices, more than forty people.

My whole body flushed with shame. If I had been alone, I would have burst into tears. What kind of Neanderthal was this guy? Did he have any clue how fucking hard this was? Was everyone else thinking the same thing? Even worse—had I done something wrong?

I had been trying to make the best of my return to work, but I didn't want to be here. I wanted to be at home with my baby, not pumping milk and sharing the kitchen with clueless, childless men.

I couldn't bear for anyone to see me cry, so I swallowed back the humiliation and turned to Thomas, whose desk was about ten feet to the right of mine.

"Have you seen this?"

He hadn't. He walked over to my desk and peered over my shoulder. A moment later, his hand flew to his heart.

"Oh my God! I can't *believe* he sent that! He should be *ashamed* of himself!" In that moment, I loved him. He was Regular Ol' Thomas. Sensitive Thomas. My friend Thomas. "Besides, what's the big deal? It's not like it's urine or *poo* or something," he said, wrinkling his nose.

Out of nowhere, Stella appeared at my desk, looking worried.

"Don't get mad," she said quickly. "It's okay. We're handling it."

"Stella. This is so inappropriate."

"I know. Just don't get mad. Let me handle it."

She walked away. And that was that. There was nothing more to discuss. I wanted to show I was a good sport, so I gathered up my notebook and went to my next meeting, trying not to dwell on whether or not my coworkers were thinking about my bodily fluids.

Over the next few days, a few of my colleagues (one dad and two moms) whispered to me how appalled they were by Eugene's email. Otherwise, there was an odd silence about the matter, and Eugene's complaint was left hanging, unaddressed.

THAT WEEKEND, I CALLED SOME of my mom friends to commiserate. As it turned out, most of them had endured pumping humiliations of their own. Some were told to pump in bathroom stalls (technically this is illegal) or rooms that didn't lock. The worst story I heard was from my old friend Jackie, who lived with her husband and toddler in Denver.

Jackie had a complicated delivery, and her newborn needed major surgery after birth. She'd worked extra-hard to establish breast-feeding during her baby's lengthy hospital stay. Like me, she fully intended to continue breast-feeding for the recommended first year.

"I had a child with health issues, and there are so many health benefits of breast-feeding," she told me. "I wanted to give him every extra advantage."

When her baby was five months old, Jackie packed up a rented hospital-grade breast pump with the same complicated mix of emotions that I felt—sadness, relief, guilt—and returned to her job at a large, highly regarded nonprofit that touted itself as "family-friendly."

On her first day back, Jackie's male boss said, "You know, people are going to look at you differently now that you're a parent. Most people here don't have kids."

"I didn't know what he meant," Jackie told me, "but it totally freaked me out. The message I took from that was *Don't rock the boat.*"

Around that same time, a coworker asked her if she'd "read any good books" while she was on maternity leave. The question was so profoundly out of sync with the five exhausting months she'd spent running back and forth between home and the Children's Hospital that she didn't know what to say.

"They think you're lying on a beach when you're on maternity leave," Jackie said. "They have no idea."

The HR department didn't offer any information for moms returning to work. A lactation consultant told Jackie that her employer was legally obligated to provide a private place to pump (not a bathroom). So on her first day back, she asked the human resources administrator where she should go. The woman directed her to a tiny, windowless "telephone" room with a chair, a phone, an electrical outlet, and a sliding door that didn't shut completely.

"It was basically a converted closet," Jackie said.

Jackie talked to all the working moms at her office. Most of them said they'd stopped pumping earlier than they wanted to because it was too hard. A few were walked in on repeatedly while pumping in conference rooms, and one coworker was told she had to pump in a room full of foul-smelling solvents. Another said her male supervisor was so uncomfortable with the physical aspect of her pregnancy that he told her not to discuss it at work.

"He basically wanted her to be a floating head with no body," said Jackie.

Eventually, Jackie explained her dilemma to her boss and suggested the only reasonable solution she could think of—using her own cubicle. Her boss's response was surprising for a man in his forties with a wife and young children at home.

"He said, 'Whoa! You can't be doing that,'" Jackie recalled. "'Those people who sit around you don't have kids. You're going to freak them out!' . . . He didn't offer to help or talk to HR with me or anything."

Jackie went ahead with her plan anyway, and her boss never said anything. An awkward stalemate, to say the least.

I thought about Jackie, exhausted from nighttime feedings, hunched over her desk, arms wrapped around her chest to hold a nursing wrap in place, hoping no one would walk by, and I wanted to cross my own arms over my chest. Not surprisingly, she gave up after four weeks.

"It was just too hard. I nursed at home in the evenings, but gave up pumping during the day. And then, of course, my milk supply went down and I had to stop. I felt so guilty about it."

This all happened more than a year ago, but she still was clearly upset. Even over the phone I could hear the anger in her voice.

MONDAY MORNING, EUGENE sent another company-wide email. He'd had some sort of epiphany over the weekend, and he realized he'd been wrong. Then he sent me a separate email, begging me to let him apologize in person. He called himself an "asshole," which was a promising start. We arranged to meet in Conference Room B. *(B is for "Bodily Fluids"!)* Eugene was waiting for me when I got there, arms and ankles crossed, looking as if he wanted to crawl into a hole in the ground. He told me how his mother berated him on the phone for an hour, and he realized what a big mistake he'd made. He wasn't a Neanderthal. He wasn't even an asshole. He just didn't know any better.

"Listen, I want you to know how hard this is," I started to say. "Coming back to work. I mean, with a baby at home . . ." Then I trailed off. What was my point? I actually felt sorry for Eugene, squirming red-faced in his chair. How could he possibly understand what this was like? I was a working mom and he was a single dude in a black turtleneck sweater.

"It's okay," I told him. "We're good. All is forgiven."

BREAST-FEEDING IS
GOOD FOR BUSINESS

Breast-feeding is one of those issues, like licorice or *Star Trek,* that drive people to extreme views. So I think it's important to mention that some women simply can't breast-feed, for a variety of reasons, and they shouldn't be made to feel guilty about it. Period.

That said, the benefits of breast-feeding are indisputable and they affect us all. Not only does breast-feeding improve the health of the mother and child, but it can also save employers money in absenteeism and turnover, and save billions in health care costs.

Studies show the United States could save $13 billion a year if women were able to breast-feed exclusively (not supplementing with formula or solid food) for the doctor-recommended six months. And yet, only 14 percent of mothers are able to breast-feed that long. A lot of these women can and want to, but they lack support from their employers to do so.

If you are one of those women, it may be helpful to know that your boss is *required by law* to accommodate your need to nurse. The law used to be fuzzy on this, and it used to vary from state to state. But since the health care reform bill was passed in 2010, it's crystal clear.

By law, employers in the United States must provide breast-feeding employees with reasonable break time and a private, nonbathroom place to express breast milk during the workday, up until the child's first birthday. The law has some nuances, like an exemption for small businesses, so it's worth reading it for yourself. Here it is:

SEC. 4207. REASONABLE BREAK TIME FOR NURSING MOTHERS.

Section 7 of the Fair Labor Standards Act of 1938 (29 U.S.C. 207) is amended by adding at the end the following:

"(r)(1) An employer shall provide—

"(A) a reasonable break time for an employee to express breast milk for her nursing child for 1 year after the child's birth each time such employee has need to express the milk; and

"(B) a place, other than a bathroom, that

➤

is shielded from view and free from intrusion from coworkers and the public, which may be used by an employee to express breast milk.

"(2) An employer shall not be required to compensate an employee receiving reasonable break time under paragraph (1) for any work time spent for such purpose.

"(3) An employer that employs less than 50 employees shall not be subject to the requirements of this subsection, if such requirements would impose an undue hardship by causing the employer significant difficulty or expense when considered in relation to the size, financial resources, nature, or structure of the employer's business.

"(4) Nothing in this subsection shall preempt a State law that provides greater protections to employees than the protections provided for under this subsection."

CHAPTER 14.

NOBODY REALLY KNOWS HOW HARD it is for a war veteran to adjust to civilian life except other veterans. Nobody really knows how hard it is to care for an elderly parent except others who have done that backbreaking work. Likewise, nobody really knows how hard it is to be a working parent except other working parents.

I am sure Eugene, young, single, with no children, thought he was busy. All Americans are busy. When I was young, single, with no children, I thought I was busy, too. What I couldn't see then, because I hadn't experienced it yet, was that all around me, people quietly carried burdens much greater than mine.

The American work culture doesn't make many accommodations for these burdens. This creates all kinds of logistical problems for us, but it also creates emotional ones. We feel alienated and alone, which only makes our burden feel heavier.

From five thirty each morning, when I startled awake to the sound of Jake crying in the next room, to ten each night, when I closed my laptop, my day was a blur of perpetual motion. If everything went perfectly, my days could be exhilarating. *Katrina wins the race against entropy!*

But when everything did not go perfectly, I got smacked with the double whammy that every working parent has felt—scrambling extra-hard just to catch up and being in a constant state of apology to people who had no way of understanding the difference between busy and Busy.

I'm sorry I'm late. I had to pump.

I'm sorry I can't stay longer. It's time to get my kids.

I'm sorry I have to skip the conference. I can't afford more nights away.

I'm sorry I have to miss the pitch. Jake has a fever.

I'm sorry. I'm sorry. I'm so so sorry.

Although I was working "only" a four-day-a-week schedule, we had one more child than when I worked five days. Brian and I both were moving as fast as we could, and yet, certain tasks were still not getting done. Jake was behind on his immunizations. I needed new glasses. All of us were overdue for a trip to the dentist. Martha had a school play coming up, the same day as Ruby's parent-teacher conference.

When were we supposed to make time for all this stuff—the stuff that was part of living a normal life but didn't seem to fit into *our* normal life? Someone had to collect the paperwork to refinance the mortgage when the interest rates dropped. Someone had to pick up the dry cleaning, get the oil changed, buy stamps, organize family photos, get our taxes ready, plan birthday parties, RSVP for other kids' birthday parties, buy and wrap the party gifts, shop around for life, car, and home insurance, stock the earthquake kit, bake brownies for Martha's basketball team potluck, take Ruby to her swim lessons, poison the ants, buy Jake a raincoat, return the overdue library books and princess movies, invest our retirement savings, chaperone Ruby's field trip, and pay the bills.

Add to that the work obligations that fell outside of work hours. Dinner to schmooze an out-of-town client. Industry conferences and gossipy networking events and launch parties, some of which we hosted at the Dogstar office. It was bad form to miss them. For Brian, there was invoicing and accounting, negotiating contracts, learning new software programs and countless other business-related tasks for which he didn't get paid.

Luckily, we were consultants. It was our job to plan and execute difficult, complex projects.

"What we need is a good project plan!" Brian declared, confident that this would fix our problem.

So each Sunday night, after the kids went to bed, Brian and I hunkered down at the kitchen table to create our plan for the week. We listed everything we needed to get done, decided which ones were top priority, and then made an elaborate spreadsheet that divided each day of the upcoming week into his-and-her thirty-minute increments. It specified, in fastidious detail, every child drop-off and pickup, every grocery-shopping trip, and every weekly chore. It included work meetings that were expected to start early or run late, business trips, and professional networking events. It included important school events, like Martha's science fair and Ruby's preschool art show. In an effort to stay healthy, we scheduled time to work out, and time to see friends.

This Wonder Schedule even included time to create the next week's schedule (two people @ one half-hour time slot). It was color-coded by category (work, kids, personal) and took up half the refrigerator. Looking at it filled me with an odd mixture of hope (I can do it all!) and dread (not a moment to spare!). On paper, there was time for *everything,* as long as nothing went wrong . . .

But, of course, things *did* go wrong. The car got a flat. A friend called for a favor. The water heater broke and flooded the floor. When any of these things happened, it was like the proverbial butterfly effect that caused the hurricane; one wrong move could set off a chain of events causing the whole schedule to collapse.

The worst was when one of us got sick, because chances were, all of us would get sick, which meant being stuck in the house for a week or more, missing work, missing school, missing sleep, getting bored off our nut on *Scooby-Doo* cartoons.

We did everything humanly possible to avoid this. We took daily multivitamins. Brian began getting allergy shots once a week. At the slightest hint of a cold, I doled out herbal treatments to the kids like echinacea or homeopathic remedies that promised to boost their immune systems. Brian and I took the grown-up versions of these magical elixirs. One entire shelf in the kitchen was devoted to tinctures, packets of Emergen-C, plastic tubes of Airborne, and things I could barely pronounce like Oscillococcinum and thuja leaf.

We avoided sugar because I read that sugar compromises the immune system. We bought brown rice, never white, and ate whole-grain breads and Kamut pasta. I sprinkled brewer's yeast on the kids' yogurt and, for a special treat, let them lick white powdery acidophilus right off the spoon.

We canceled playdates if anyone's forehead felt even slightly warm, and our friends did the same. Every working parent we knew was terrified of germs. We washed our hands as though we had obsessive-compulsive disorder, and when we went out, I carried lavender-scented antibacterial wipes in my purse. I eyed every doorknob and banister with suspicion. I flushed public toilets with my foot. I was worse than Howard Hughes.

And yet, after Jake started day care and I returned to work, we got sick and sick and sick again. Chest colds. Unexplained fevers that lasted five days. Rashes that bloomed on the kids' bellies and under their arms, then faded away. Head lice, which might infest only one of the kids but required us to treat everyone in the family and wash every towel, sheet, and blanket in the house. Once, Martha got a stomach flu in the middle of the night. She tried to get to the bathroom, but didn't get any farther than the top rung of the ladder on her bunk bed, where she vomited like a sprinkler head, somehow managing to hit all four walls of her bedroom. Really. All four of them. It couldn't have been easy. The last thing she had eaten before bed was an entire pint of strawberries. It looked as if a dying animal had run around the room, bleeding on every surface.

Bronchitis. Sinus infections. Pinkeye. Walking pneumonia. Asthma attacks. Strep throat. Whooping cough.

Whooping cough? The disease that was supposedly eradicated in the 1940s? Yes, that whooping cough. Both Jake and Brian got it. That one earned us a free house call from two very concerned nurses from the Centers for Disease Control. They shut down Jake's day care for a week, so that even after he was well enough to go back, he couldn't.

In three months, Brian and I missed ten days of work between us to stay home with sick kids. If the rest of the year turned out to be anything like those three months, we would miss more than forty days of work. How could this be?

I had six paid sick days a year—generous, considering half of American workers don't have any. But it wasn't close to covering all the days one of our kids was sick. Of course, I could always use my vacation time, but I needed that to cover the random "professional development days" at school and holidays that only children and postal workers get (César Chávez Day, anyone?).

I asked our pediatrician for advice. She was in her fifties or early sixties and had seen it all. I trusted her implicitly.

"Why do we keep getting sick?" I asked during one of our many visits to check on a child's lingering cough. "What are we doing wrong?"

"Oh, this is normal," she said, as she tucked her stethoscope away in a pocket. "Children get on average eight to ten colds and fevers a year."

Eight to ten illnesses a year? Per child? It was absurd and, yet, consistent with everything we had experienced. When we got home, I did the math.

Let's say, on average, your kid has to be home from school one day per illness (some illnesses don't require any missed days of school, while others can knock your kid out for a week, easy). That's nine days per year, per kid.

Let's say you have two kids, and their nine sick days a year over-lap by half. That means you need to take an *average* of thirteen to fourteen days off a year to be home with a sick kid. Some years will be better, others will be worse. Of course, that number does not include the days when you, the parent, are sick. And no matter how many green smoothies you drink for breakfast, if you're up all night with a sick kid, you're bound to get whatever is keeping him awake.

My rule was to never, ever, take a sick day for myself unless I was throwing up. My frequent sniffles and coughs garnered sympathy from some of my coworkers and the stink eye from others.

Why are you exposing me to your germs? they wanted to say.

And I wanted to reply, *I can't afford to take a fucking sick day. I have three kids!*

This was the silent conversation we carried out, time and time again, in my head.

Often, when one of the kids was sick and Brian was unavailable, I worked from home. It was generous of Stella to let me do this, but let's face it. It sucks to field conference calls on mute while your feverish child is moaning on the couch. It just does. You feel as if you're neglecting your kid when she needs you most, and you feel as if you're letting your coworkers down, too.

WE WERE NOT ALONE in our battle against illness. All our friends seemed to be in the same bind. My friend Jenny's family, in particular, was deluged with illness that winter. Jenny had two children a little younger than Jake and Ruby. Her husband and the kids seemed to trade illness back and forth like Pokémon cards. At its worst, Jenny came down with whatever latest bug they had, which quickly morphed into an infection, and her eardrum burst. She started crying in her doctor's office as green gunk oozed out of her ear.

"How do I stop getting sick?" she sobbed.

Her (elderly male) doctor looked down his glasses and delivered the most unhelpful piece of parenting advice I have ever heard: "Don't pick up your baby when she's sick."

Then, because she was still crying, he suggested she make an appointment with a psychotherapist.

We working parents rallied for each other, dropping off hot soup, picking up each other's kids from day care, and running to the pharmacy for each other over the weekend. We shared herbal remedies and information about allergy shots and amino acids. Rebecca swore by homeopathy. My friend Alma insisted I schedule an appointment with her acupuncturist.

Brian tried to look on the bright side. "One day we're going to look back at this time, when the kids were so little, and say, 'Those were the salad days.'"

It didn't feel like the salad days. It felt as if we were climbing a mountain that disappeared into the sky. I wanted desperately to get to the top, to relax and enjoy the view. But with every step the oxygen grew thinner.

AMERICANS AND SICK TIME

Globally, 145 countries guarantee paid sick leave to workers because it's not just good for our health, it's good for the economy. The benefits in many of these countries will make you sick with envy. Most cover *up to a month or more* of sick days. In many countries, single people have even more days of paid sick leave than workers who are married, because they may need the time to care for sick children, elderly parents, or other loved ones.

Unfortunately, here in the United States, about half of us don't get any paid sick time, including 80 percent of low-wage workers. In other words, the more you need it, the less likely you are to get it.

Studies show that if we had just a measly seven paid sick days a year, the U.S. economy would save *$160 billion* through increased productivity and reduced turnover. This would save employers an average of $255 per employee per year in lost pro-ductivity—more than the cost of absenteeism and medical and disability benefits. Best of all, we'd all be less sick.

This would be a great first step, but it still wouldn't come close to covering the time many of us with families need. That's one reason some companies are beginning to experiment with Results-Only Work Environment (ROWE), where employees are evaluated by results rather than by arbitrary measures like face time or hours worked. One of the core principles of a ROWE is that employees can have *unlimited paid time off,* as long as they get their work done. This requires companies to treat employees like adults, trust them to be responsible, and hold them accountable instead of wasting time and resources tracking things like attendance and vacation time. Companies like Gap Inc. say ROWE has revolutionized their business, boosting quality, accountability, and productivity and reducing turnover in the production team by 50 percent.

CHAPTER 15.

WHAT MADE IT ALL OKAY was Magic Fridays.

Friday was my day off from work. I could slow down and give my brain a much-needed break as I caught up on chores, volunteered at Ruby's preschool, and fit in some exercise. Fridays were the buffer that kept me, and our family, on the right side of the razor-thin line between "everything's fine" and total collapse that winter after Jake was born.

By spring 2008, we were enjoying long stretches when no one got sick, and things began to look up. Jake started sleeping through the night. Ruby was finishing up her last year of preschool and getting used to having a little brother. Martha was sailing along in second grade with glowing reviews from her teacher. Brian negotiated a new contract that had him working only four days a week. It meant less income, but we agreed we needed the time more than we needed the money.

Suddenly, we *both* had Fridays free. That's when Magic Fridays really began.

If the weather was nice, Brian and I might ride our bikes up into the Oakland hills, then roll down and soak in a hot tub at Piedmont Springs. Or we'd do chores together in the morning and have sex in the afternoon, something that was almost impossible at night when we were both so tired. Sex? During the day? It was like a mini-honeymoon. Even buying groceries and washing the car were fun because we were together, with no one to interrupt us, and no reason to hurry. We had time alone to talk. I fell in love with Brian all over again. Magic Fridays made me feel like a person, not just someone's mother or manager or maid. They were a peaceful oasis, a sanctuary. Slowly but surely, we began to heal from the stress of the last few years.

To keep Fridays free, I became even more efficient the rest of the week, often working weekends to get my work done. If someone accidentally scheduled me for a Friday meeting, I begged them to move it or at least to let me call in.

With great reluctance and a twinge of regret, I told the publisher I wasn't going to be able to write the business book. Stella couldn't afford to pay me to write it and have someone else help run my department. And I couldn't afford to do it on my own time without giving up Fridays.

"Maybe we can talk about it again next year," Stella said. "Your kids won't be young forever. It will get easier."

I was officially on the Mommy Track now. My job was to baby-sit my staff, our clients, and their projects. Most of the time I was too tired to care, although sometimes, it hurt more than I wanted to admit. But it seemed petty to complain. I knew lots of women would kill for my job and a four-day schedule.

PART OF OUR MAGIC FRIDAY ROUTINE was to count our blessings. I could do this for hours, up and down the hills, in and out of the hot tub, before and after sex. It made me feel rich.

Even with the colds and viruses, our kids were healthy in the big sense—no chronic diseases or disabilities.

We didn't have financial problems. Brian and I both made good money. It was sometimes unsettling that he was self-employed, but he always seemed to wrangle work when we needed it. We'd finally paid off my school loans and the credit card balance. It felt good to know we had no debt beyond the mortgage, and we were actually saving a little for the future. There were no fancy cars or exotic vacations, but we didn't need them. What we needed was financial stability, something neither of us had growing up. We had that now. Unlike my parents, I never had to worry about whether we had enough money to pay for a car repair, and I was still getting used to the idea that I could simply buy clothes for my kids that fit, instead of getting them two sizes too big, so they could wear them longer.

We were happily married. When we weren't overwrought, we were kind and loving to each other. Our kids picked up the atmosphere of kindness, and they, too, were thoughtful and generous with each other. Martha was fully integrated into our family and her mom's San Francisco family as well. She had a new stepdad, a kind and considerate man who adored and doted on her.

We owned a lovely house on a quiet street with a big yard, fruit trees, and a swing set. After bouncing all over the country before we met, we both felt settled and at home in the Bay Area. We marveled at the bizarre stereotypes people often had about Berkeley and Oakland—to us it was paradise. We couldn't imagine living anywhere else.

I had a lot to be thankful for, a ridiculous Chinese wedding banquet of blessings, where the dishes just keep coming and coming without any apparent end.

Of course, it couldn't last.

Stella had been clear from the beginning that my four-day workweek was temporary. Unfortunately, my plan to win her over did not seem to be working.

It wasn't that I couldn't do my job. I crammed five days of work into four and got paid for four. I made myself available for important meetings and calls on Fridays if there was no other day the client could do it. I did not miss deadlines or leave important tasks undone, and the feedback on my work from clients and staff alike was relentlessly positive.

No, my ability to do my job wasn't the problem. The problem was jealousy.

Pauline told me that Norm and Roger had complained that I was setting a bad example. While there were two others in the office who worked a four-day week, I was the only person on the leadership team who did so. Stella worried that soon everyone would start asking to work a reduced schedule.

"Well, why can't they?" I asked Pauline. "If everyone can get the same amount of work done in four days and save the company one day a week in salary, wouldn't that be good for the business?"

"I doubt Stella would see it that way," Pauline said with a shake of her head.

Like most managers, Stella had a thing about people being in the office. Her assumption was, if they weren't at the office, they weren't working—I was one of the few exceptions to that rule. It bothered her to see the office emptying out before 6:00 PM. About every other month, we wasted half a leadership meeting speechifying about how we needed to crack down, and all of us, as leaders, needed to set a better example. Invariably, I found myself on the politically incorrect side of this silly argument, not because of my circumstances, but because it was, well, silly. After all, these were highly paid creative professionals. They were expected to make clients happy and produce smart designs, not punch a clock. I really believed that as a matter of principle. But I also had a hard time not taking this argument personally.

"Just because someone is sitting at their desk doesn't mean they're working," I pointed out in one of these discussions.

"Well, that's a problem, too," Stella said.

"If we're trying to be good managers, we should be looking for ways to motivate people to do their best work," I continued.

"But face time is important, too," Norm chimed in.

Eventually I would drop the subject and we'd move on to something else.

ONE DAY, VICENTE PULLED ME ASIDE to tell me that Thomas had been complaining to him about my schedule. I was surprised. Thomas had never said a word to me about this. I got defensive.

"That's ridiculous," I said. "I also work nights and weekends. But Thomas doesn't see me doing that, so it doesn't count?"

"Katrina, there's no problem with your schedule," Vicente said. "You and I both know this is just Thomas being Thomas." Vicente had a daughter about Ruby's age. His wife worked part-time. I didn't need to explain things to him.

Nonetheless, as the months passed, I could almost hear the slow hiss of my social capital leaking out of some unseen hole.

MY ANNUAL PERFORMANCE REVIEW was scheduled for an afternoon in mid-September. Our review process was formal and quite thorough. They call these "360 reviews" when everyone—peers, managers, and subordinates—give feedback. Pauline's job was to collect this feedback, remove people's names, and give it to me to look over in preparation for the actual review with Stella.

The first time I scanned through the feedback, I glowed with all the praise:

"Katrina is a role model for everyone at Dogstar: She writes, she speaks, she is an amazing mentor to her staff . . ."

"Katrina is one of the best bosses I've ever had . . ."

"Katrina is at the top of her game in all aspects of her job . . ."

But as I read through more carefully, I noticed another, more subtle, theme running throughout.

"Katrina's biggest obstacle is her limited availability . . . "

"The biggest challenge I see for her is how busy she always seems to be, especially considering her limited schedule . . ."

"Katrina works short days and is out of the office Fridays . . ."

"Time is the great limiter as far as growth right now, but it might not be in the future. It will be up to Katrina to decide."

A group narrative had formed about me, a silent consensus reached. "Katrina is great, but . . ." If I let things continue this way, I knew the feedback would only get harsher. Meanwhile, I already felt atrophy setting in on my design skills. The only thing I did anymore was manage; I hadn't tried to speak at a conference in almost a year, and had no plans to. I'd given up on the book. Maybe if I didn't care about doing a good job, or if I didn't have so much of my identity wrapped up in my work, I could have let it go. But I couldn't bear the thought of becoming mediocre. Even if Stella let me continue with this schedule, the status quo was not an option. I would rather quit than be mediocre.

"I DON'T WANT TO QUIT," I said.

The kids were asleep. Brian and I lay side by side in bed, reviewing our options.

"Well, you can't go back to working five days a week, that's for sure."

I sighed. "I know, but I love my job. I'm never going to find another job like this."

"Katrina, there are web agencies all up and down San Francisco. They would snap you up in a heartbeat."

"I don't want to work for those other agencies. They work people to death."

"Right. Your job is only working you *half* to death," Brian said, readjusting the pillow under his arm. "That's much better."

"What I really need is a wife," I said. This was a running joke between us. We both needed a "wife."

"Well, if you really want to go back full-time, I could stop working and stay home with the kids," Brian said.

"Seriously? You'd do that?"

I'd never even considered this option before. I always assumed if one of us stopped working to be with the kids, it would be me.

"If it meant that much to you," Brian said, rubbing my arm with his free hand.

"You'd go crazy with boredom."

"No, it would be fun," he said. Then after a pause, "As long as it was *temporary.*"

We lay there in silence as I let the fantasy play out in my head. Brian standing in the doorway, wiping his hands on his apron as I arrived home from work each day. The house clean, Ruby's homework done, a hot dinner waiting for us on the table. Did I want that life? Would I be jealous that he had so much more time with the kids than me?

"Could we live on your salary?" Brian's question broke through my reverie. Since I managed all the bills, he really didn't know the answer.

"It would be really tight," I said. "Even if we pulled Jake out of day care, we'd have to cut back. We definitely wouldn't be saving for the kids' college, or our retirement."

"That would be okay if it was just a few years, right?"

"Yeah . . ." I said. "But how do we know you'd be able to *get* work in a couple years?"

I knew at least three women who took a few years off to care for their kids and then couldn't get jobs. Would it be different for Brian? Our field was changing so fast; it was hard enough to keep our skills up now. I thought back to how precarious our finances had been when Ruby was a baby. Did I really want to go back to living that way? Counting the days until each paycheck would hit the bank?

"This is stupid," I said. "We both need to work. We both *want* to work. It just doesn't work for me to have a full-time job."

"So what do you want to do?"

I didn't want to do anything. But the choice was clear.

"I'll quit," I said, finally. "I'll go back to freelancing."

We went to sleep. It was Sunday, September 14, 2008.

THE VERY NEXT DAY, Lehman Brothers announced it was filing for bankruptcy. The Dow plunged five hundred points. The media warned we could be entering the worst financial crisis since the Great Depression. It was the beginning of the global financial crisis. I thought of the famous black-and-white Depression-era photo of the mother with seven children. I thought of long lines of barefoot children begging for bread and out-of-work businessmen sleeping on park benches.

Brian's freelance gig was about to end in two weeks, and he didn't have another project lined up. Under those circumstances, it would have been insane to quit my job.

Far be it from me to do something insane. The next day, I told Stella I would come back full-time.

THIS IS YOUR BRAIN ON PARENTING

Do you ever feel as if being a parent has turned you into an expert multitasker? It probably has. Studies show that in mammals, caring for their young is associated with improved learning ability and fearlessness.

For example, experiments show that mother rats outsmart their childless counterparts at navigating mazes and capturing prey. That's because in pregnant and nursing mice, dendrites, the special cell structures that are necessary for communication between neurons, are doubled. And glial cells, which are important communication conductors, are also doubled. This is what allows mother mice to learn mazes more quickly than others. (Sorry, dads, I have not read anything indicating that fathers experience a similar boost in brainpower.)

Of course, even with our extra dendrites and glial cells, we mothers still have our limits. Studies show that the amount of multitasking working parents do has doubled since the mid-'70s. Research also shows that *too much* multitasking has the same effect on our IQs as a bong hit. It makes us do stupid things. And yet, life with young children often requires an absurd, stuntman level of multitasking—something we do more than half our waking time.

Our heads are crammed with mundane chores and challenges—the donation for the teacher gift, the overdue DVDs, the work file we need to resend. One kid won't eat food that's not white. The other kid is starting to use the potty and doesn't own any underwear. So we miss our train stop. We return the DVDs to the library without a DVD in the case. We burn the rice. We write cryptic notes on the calendar that we can't read an hour later. We promptly lose our new pair of glasses, search for them frantically for twenty minutes, only to find them on top of our own head.

I first noticed the stoner effect of multitasking after Ruby was born, when I randomly started switching around dates and times. I arrived an hour early for a dentist appointment. I showed up for a meeting at her day care in the wrong week. It became a joke between Brian and me—how I should write everything on my body, like that guy in the movie *Memento*. Haha! Funny!

After Jake was born, it stopped being funny. I left my debit card in the ATM twice in two months. I would lose my train of thought in midconversation. Another time, in my rush to get in the house with a crying baby and his cranky older sister, make dinner, and simultaneously answer an urgent email, I left the keys in the front door lock and didn't discover them until the next morning.

I began to worry that I had some sort of incipient dementia. An informal poll of my mommy friends reassured me that I was not alone. Lee said she showed up with her kids for an Easter egg hunt a week early. My friend Lily said she started running a bath for the kids, then forgot about it until it overflowed the tub. Another mom I knew told me she had a full basket of groceries with her two kids in tow when she realized she'd left her wallet at work. And another said she managed to actually *buy* her groceries and even pack them into the car, but when she turned on the car to drive home, the frantic cries from the parking lot informed her she'd forgotten to pack her *daughter* in the car; luckily, no one was hurt. My favorite was from a mom from Ruby's school, who confessed that the night before, she'd found her son's pajamas in the freezer, next to the ice cream. *Right where she'd put them.*

CHAPTER 16.

THE SAME MONTH I AGREED to go back to work full-time, Ruby started kindergarten. I had lobbied the school district for months to accept Ruby into a small public elementary school about a mile from our house in Oakland. The school was not much farther than our designated neighborhood school, but it was miles away in terms of the quality of education. It had a diverse, involved community of parents, a strong principal, and experienced, dedicated teachers. While other schools were cutting arts programs and anything that didn't have a direct impact on test scores, the school I wanted Ruby to go to had managed to raise funds for Spanish classes, a dedicated art teacher, and an antibullying curriculum. In addition to learning to read and write and do math, kids learned gardening, quilting, and video animation. And unlike some of the other public schools in the area, there was an after-school program that was open until six, so I wouldn't have to worry about where Ruby would be between the time school let out (1:25 or 2:45 PM, depending on the day) and the time Brian or I picked her up after work.

That spring, to my enormous relief, we got the phone call telling us Ruby's transfer had been accepted. We felt as if we'd just won the lottery, and in a sense, we had. Getting Ruby into a good public school meant we didn't have to figure out how to pay for private school, which would have cost the equivalent of a medium-priced college tuition. I was still holding out the hope that we could save up enough money to move to a better neighborhood when it was time for Ruby to enter middle school. But this gave us more time.

I WAS EXCITED FOR RUBY to start this new adventure. In just the last few months, she'd transformed from a toddler into a little girl. She could write her name and even wrote short letters to Martha, if I spelled the words for her. She asked me to quiz her on addition, and she could spend hours drawing or painting with watercolors at the kitchen table. She invented thirty-two imaginary friends (we counted) and gave them names like "Stick" and "Apple Juice" and "Toilet Paper Girl." She often carried on good-natured conversations with Stick while drawing pictures of fairies and cowgirls and flowers. I could see her mind was ready to open up to a world of learning.

Ruby and I combed through her closet the night before her first day of school, looking for the perfect outfit. She settled on the skirt I'd found online with the wide elastic rainbow waistband and the giant photo print of a kitten. I braided her slippery fine hair into two "princess braids," making a little tiara of woven hair around the crown of her head.

I'd arranged to take off the entire week as vacation, keeping Jake home with me and picking up Ruby when school got out, rather than sending her straight into the after-school program. In this way, I hoped I would ease her transition into school. The first day, I planned to surprise her with a trip to the ice cream parlor to celebrate. Later we would have her favorite dinner—Annie's Mac & Cheese with steamed broccoli—when her dad got home from his client's office, and she would tell us about her new school.

Martha had started third grade the week before. If Martha had lived with us full-time, the girls would be at the same school, but instead, she and Brian left early to drive to San Francisco. I tried not to feel disappointed about the fact that we couldn't all be together on Ruby's first day.

Ruby didn't seem to mind—she was chatty and relaxed when we arrived on campus, a bunch of '70s-style portable buildings that the teachers and students had transformed with bright, happy murals, and surrounded with gardens of wildflowers and herbs and vegetables. It looked like a children's paradise.

But when we entered her new classroom, Ruby went silent. All around us, children were drawing and stacking Legos and filling child-size shopping carts with plastic food while their parents looked on protectively or chatted with the teacher. I held Jake in my arms while he chewed on his fist, enthralled by the activity. Ruby gripped my hand and tried to bury her head in my skirt.

"Hon, don't you want to draw?" I coaxed.

"I don't know," Ruby said in her smallest voice. "I think I want to go home with you."

I pretended not to hear her, thinking it would be better to focus on the positive.

"Let's look at all the fun toys in your new classroom, Ruby." Together we cautiously perused the puzzles and the doll station before making our way to the art table. Art was Ruby's number-one favorite thing—one of the many reasons we'd tried so hard to get her into this school. I knelt beside her while she got to work on a picture of a kitty with giant green ears.

After a few minutes, the teacher, a woman with long gray hair and Birkenstocks, rang a brass bell.

"Okay, boys and girls. It's time to say good-bye to your moms and dads and come sit down on the rug."

Most of the other kids began to tentatively make their way to the rug while the teacher, Ms. Morrill, took out a guitar. Ruby dropped her crayon and clung to my arm.

"Honey, go ahead and sit on the rug. It's okay," I said.

She gripped my arm tighter and began to cry.

"Sweetheart, you're going to be just fine. Mommy will pick you up when school is over. You can tell me all about your fun day."

"No!" she sobbed, and dropped to the floor. "Mama, don't leave me!"

I struggled to keep my balance with thirty pounds of one-year-old Jake in my arms, while Ruby wrapped herself around my leg.

"Ruby, honey, get up . . ." I whispered.

She just suctioned herself to me more tightly.

I glanced around the room—most of the children had settled themselves onto a square, and the moms and dads were making their exits. Ms. Morrill had started to sing a song about "rainbow children," and the children on the rug watched her in a trance, as if she were the Pied Piper. A few stragglers hugged their parents—they, too, were obviously having trouble saying good-bye, but they did so quietly. Meanwhile, the more I tried to calm her, the more Ruby increased the volume of her distress.

"No, Mama! I want to go home with *you!*"

"Sweetheart," I whispered, trying to sound loving and firm and confident, "you're going to be Just. Fine. Mommy's going to go now . . ."

But I couldn't go, not with her clinging to my leg like a blue-eyed barnacle. I tried to gently peel off her fingers with my one free hand while I held Jake with the other arm.

Another parent kindly offered to take over. With her help, I extricated myself from my daughter, who was now sobbing in great, stormy gusts.

"I love you, darling. I'll see you this afternoon," I said as I stooped to kiss her braids. Then I sped for the door.

IN THE COURTYARD, dozens of parents lingered with each other, chatting and occasionally dabbing at their wet eyes—both happy and sad their kids had just completed a new rite of passage.

I was too upset to talk with anyone. I could hear Ruby's wails follow me across the play yard, each one a stab through the heart. I felt as if I'd betrayed the person I loved most in the world. It wasn't a rational feeling; it was primitive and raw, like that day, five years before, when I'd dropped off Ruby at Thania's and she'd clung to me, and I'd left her anyway.

You're being ridiculous, I told myself. *Ruby's a big girl now. She's going to be fine. It's just kindergarten!*

But when I returned with Jake at 1:25, Ruby met us in the courtyard, looking just as miserable as when we'd said good-bye that morning. As soon as she saw us, she broke into fresh sobs.

"Evan told Albert to punch me!" she said, hurling herself at my legs. "And then Albert hit me!"

Evan and Albert were friends from her old preschool—we'd known them and their families for two years. They'd never done anything like that before. Later, I got the story from Albert's mom. There had been some sort of disagreement. Ruby kicked Albert, and then Albert hit Ruby. And then they were both sent to The Office.

Yes, you read that right. On the first day of kindergarten, my daughter, the one with the princess braids and the rainbow-kitty skirt, got sent to the principal's office for *fighting*.

Ruby was crying when I picked her up on Tuesday. And again on Wednesday.

I had expected this first week to be tough, but I had not expected this.

On Thursday I waited outside at 1:25, filled with dread. When she saw Jake and me, she ran to greet us, arms open.

"Mommy!"

"She had a better day today?" I asked Ms. Morrill hopefully as I hugged my girl.

"No, she did not have a good day," Ms. Morrill said, shielding her eyes from the sun so she could give me her full attention. "She had three meltdowns in class. It was very disruptive."

On Friday I picked up Ruby at two fifteen so she would get a short taste of the after-school care program. As soon as she saw me, she burst into tears.

What was I going to do? Starting Monday, I would have to be back at work, which meant she'd be in after-school care until five thirty.

I talked to Brian and to the other parents we knew. Everyone assured me that it would get easier. But as the weeks wore on, it became clear Ruby was not adjusting to her new school as we had hoped. She cried so hard, and clung so long on the days that I dropped her off, that her teacher asked me to take her to the office so the principal could escort her to class each morning, to minimize the disruption.

I'll just have to try harder to help her through this, I thought. I picked her up early on Fridays, when I worked from home, and once a month, I cut out of work for a couple of hours to volunteer in her class, but there wasn't enough time for everything, and often I found myself sneaking glances at my phone, checking my work email. I looked like one of those moms I used to hate, those Crackberry moms who cared more about their jobs than about their kids. The first person who pointed this out to me was going to get a smart phone in the ear.

BRIAN AND THE OTHER PARENTS were right, of course. It did get better . . . right around *spring break* the following year. For those several long months in between, I don't know who suffered more, Ruby or me.

I've often wondered if I had been home more when Ruby was younger whether she would have adjusted to school faster. Maybe it wouldn't have been so bad if I'd been able to pick her up early a few days a week. Or maybe, even if I'd been a stay-at-home mom who greeted her at two forty-five every afternoon with fresh-baked cookies, she *still* would have had a rough adjustment. It's impossible to know.

What I do know is that despite all the work I'd done to beat back the Mommy Guilt when Ruby was a baby, it had returned full force. Mommy Guilt is like herpes. You never really get rid of it.

I carried the guilt inside me, but of course it didn't stay there. Occasionally, it erupted in an explosion of anger. Brian bore the brunt of this. These eruptions were almost always over insignificant lapses—changing Martha's schedule without clearing it with me, forgetting to take out the garbage—things I would take in stride under more relaxed circumstances. It wasn't fair, but looking back I think he was the only person I could safely lash out at without fear that I would (a) cause some irreparable psychological damage, or (b) get fired.

All this hand-wringing that I did, that so many mothers do, is a form of self-torture. But knowing that doesn't mean we can stop it. Think about what we're trying to do. This modern life—where the majority of moms and dads both work; where extended family networks have broken down (either through physical or emotional distance); where kids go to school all day and then get shuffled to after-school activities by paid caregivers; where those caregivers, many of whom are truly wonderful people, may change from year to year—this is all a relatively *new* social experiment. How do we know it's not hurting our kids? How much time away from their parents is too much? How much of this harried, hurried lifestyle is rubbing off on them? We don't know. It's too new for anyone to really know. So we mothers scan the horizon, looking for trouble, and when we see it (like when we have a child who isn't adjusting to school well), isn't it natural to wonder if we're doing this wrong?

WHAT KIDS REALLY WANT

In 1999, a researcher named Ellen Galinsky published a breakthrough study about navigating work and family life, aptly named "Ask the Children." She talked with children around the country from the ages of eight to eighteen, as well as their parents, to find out what was on their minds. She found quite a mismatch between what adults think children need and what children say they need.

For example, children were asked, if they were granted one and only one wish to change the way their mother's or father's work affected their lives, what would it be?

More than half the adults guessed that the children would wish for more time with their parents. And it's true that children *did* want more time with their parents. But granted only one wish, most of them wished their parents could be "less stressed and less tired." Only *2 percent* of parents guessed their kids would say that.

➤

> If you're struggling with Mommy Guilt, here's another interesting finding from that same study: When it came to time with their parents, children yearned most for more time with their fathers, whom they saw less than their mothers.

CHAPTER 17.

WHEN YOU'RE WORKING and raising kids, life is held together with a very delicate string. One tug of the string—an illness, a sleepless night, a flat tire—and the whole apparatus, your whole carefully constructed life, starts to come undone.

At first, working five days a week wasn't much different from working four. There was always more to do than there was time to do it. But now, without Magic Fridays, I sensed that the string that held our life together was beginning to fray.

Meanwhile, reports about the economy grew more and more dire. In October 2008, the stock market plummeted in its worst week in seventy-five years. Governments were taking over banks in Europe and Iceland to keep them from failing altogether, and the U.S. government began bailing out banks here at home. New terms entered our lexicon: *credit-default swaps, subprime mortgages, toxic assets, too big to fail.* Unemployment skyrocketed from 5.6 to over 7 percent, and still, companies were laying people off in droves. I was glad I had decided to hunker down, do my job, and try to ride out the storm.

In November, Dogstar scored a major coup—a new project with a large media company. We had worked for months to win the work, rewriting our proposal more times than I could count to accommodate the client. In the end, we agreed to some punishing deadlines, but the client had us over a barrel. The economy was in free fall, and paying clients were evaporating like morning mist. We planned to compensate for the lack of time by staffing the project with one of the biggest teams we'd ever used. It would take four or five user experience designers—about half my full-time staff—the same number of visual designers, plus two project managers. The logistics were daunting: The client's business, editorial, and technology teams were spread across the country. We would have to coordinate with all these groups across three different time zones.

Brian's long-running contract had just ended. His journalism background and experience designing media sites made him a perfect fit to lead this project. I didn't have anyone on staff with his abilities who wasn't busy holding on to other clients. Stella and Vicente agreed I should ask Brian to come aboard.

I had mixed feelings about this plan. Brian had freelanced for us before and it had always worked out. But even when projects went well, it was a strain for both of us. As his manager, I had to be extra careful not to appear to take Brian's side in any disagreement. To avoid this, I needed him to be above reproach in everything he did, which, he pointed out, wasn't always fair to him. As his wife, I wasn't crazy about all the travel he'd have to do. But Brian wasn't deterred.

"Hon, it's going to be totally worth it. Just think what an amazing portfolio piece I'll have at the end of this," he said.

How bad could it be? I thought.

THE DAY THE PROJECT STARTED, our life kicked into hyperdrive. Because some of the client's team was on the East Coast, three hours ahead of us, each day started at 9:00 AM sharp with a nationwide conference call. Brian couldn't drop off the kids at school and get to the office in time for his meeting, so I started taking the kids to school. Once at Dogstar, Brian holed up in a conference room with the rest of the San Francisco team, where they reviewed and revised the previous day's work with each other and all the various members of the client's team. Most days those reviews went straight through without a break until late afternoon.

I continued to leave at four every afternoon to get the kids. Whenever Brian's meetings ended, he drove home, spent a few minutes with the kids, and then went to his backyard office to work on wireframes until midnight or 1:00 AM. In other words, after a full day talking about the work, he still had to *do* the work, so there would be new work to talk about tomorrow.

After a few weeks of this, I pleaded with Brian to delegate more responsibility.

"To who?" he snapped. "Everyone has too much on their plate already. *I'm* the one who can't let this project fail."

I couldn't think of a good answer. The entire team was already looking pale and worn. As a freelancer, Brian could fall back on the letter of his contract—after all, he didn't sign up for this brutality. If he did that, the project probably *would* fail. Dogstar would be completely *screwed*. The client would sue us or refuse to pay. And then *I'd* be completely screwed. That's what he couldn't let happen.

I asked the project managers to cut back on the reviews, but the client was unusually demanding, and they had a hard time holding their ground. I convinced Vicente to bring on another freelancer to help with Brian's workload. Two weeks later, I fired that freelancer myself when he completely botched a site map and Brian had to pull an all-nighter to fix it.

Despite our careful consideration, we had walked into a trap. Brian was killing himself working for me, which meant I had to do more of the parenting on top of my demanding full-time job. It was part of a perverse law of physics that says when one parent works harder, the other must work harder, too. Our relationship was symbiotic. Like the crocodile and that bird that eats the junk on his teeth, except more romantic. We relied on each other for everything— emotional support, financial support, physical well-being. We'd become one organism, the Alcorns. When he didn't do the dishes, I did them. When I couldn't get the kids, he got them. I paid the bills. He took out the garbage. Many times one of us would voice the thought the other was just about to speak. We completed each other's jokes. When he missed Martha, I ached for both of them. When I gave a good presentation at work, he was exultant. So of course, when he found himself ambushed by a particularly difficult project, we were both ensnared in its net.

WE HAD WALKED INTO THIS PROJECT with eyes wide open. What we didn't account for, what we had no way of knowing, was that the client, Vlad, was a complete and utter nightmare.

When we first pitched the project, Vlad was just one of several important-looking men sitting around the conference table, pecking away at his BlackBerry and excusing himself to take urgent phone calls in the hall. Our main client contact was a laconic, smart, and reasonable Midwesterner named Arnold. Vlad was Arnold's boss, and once the project started, he did a bait and switch. Next thing we knew, we weren't working for the level-headed Arnold, we were working for Vlad, the egomaniacal careerist from New York. Brian discovered we weren't in Minnesota anymore when, very early in the project, Vlad screamed at him to "shut the fuck up!" over the phone. Twice.

When Vlad came to town, it was worse. One day he was standing over Brian's shoulder when Brian opened his laptop and turned it on. Up popped the home page of *The New York Times* website. "That's your home page?" Vlad said, as disgusted as if it were a porn site. "They're our *competitor*."

The message was clear: *You are working for us. You'd better join our church.*

This kind of thing happened with clients from time to time. When we worked with software companies, we were supposed to use their software, no matter how buggy or unusable it was. When we worked for a sneaker company, they admonished Stella for wearing the competitor's brand. When we worked for a company that sold gum, every meeting room had a big bowl of chewing gum in the center of the table. You were encouraged to chew it. For all I know, everyone who works with Kool-Aid has to drink the Kool-Aid.

But Vlad was something we'd rarely encountered. When he wasn't sputtering with rage, he was witty, sophisticated, and charming. We were all taken in by his Manhattan style, his energy and aura of success. He showed a lot of teeth when he smiled, which was often, although the smile never extended all the way to his eyes. He carried himself like a man who spent a healthy amount of time at the gym, although where he found the time, no one knows, since he seemed to work at all hours. Unlike most clients, he didn't seem to be afraid of anything. While most clients just want to do a good job and harbor a fear that they'll lose something if they don't (status, credit, responsibility), Vlad's motivations were baldly self-interested. We were to make him look good, no matter the cost.

It was at Vlad's bullying insistence that we caved in to having daily "revs" of the work, as he called them, which was why Brian and the rest of the team were working around the clock. Vlad insisted we set up a videoconference link every morning so that he could see what our team was doing when he was in New York. He wanted the link to stay open all day. He called this "remote collaboration." Our team called it "the nanny cam."

WITHOUT MAGIC FRIDAYS, there was no release valve for this stress. Brian started drinking more in the evenings, as he toiled away on his schematics. When I brought it up, he accused me of henpecking him. I could feel a wall building up between us.

In early December, when Brian was flying to the client's office in Minneapolis, he had his first panic attack ever. It was horrible, as panic attacks always are, but thankfully it came toward the end of his flight. As soon as he got back, he visited his doctor and came home with a bottle of Ativan.

I hadn't had a panic attack since Ruby was a baby, but I remembered well what they felt like. I felt terrible for Brian, and strangely responsible, as if I'd infected him with a panic virus.

THE WEEK BEFORE CHRISTMAS, we flew to Upstate New York with the kids to visit my family. Vlad had tried to convince Brian and the whole design team to work through the holiday, but this time, one of the project managers put her foot down, and Vicente backed her up. Vlad groused about the lost week, but he backed down. Brian got a week off.

Unfortunately, it wasn't much of a vacation. For six days we shuttled back and forth among my mom's house, my mom's parents' house, and my dad's parents' house. It was too cold to go outside, so we sat, ate, drank, and talked while the children and their cousins raised mayhem around us.

My grandmother on my mom's side, "Gran," broke the news that Grandad Eric had just been diagnosed with a melanoma. The doctors were running tests. They didn't know yet if the cancer had spread. Gran was distracted and upset.

When we went to my mother's house, she plopped down on the couch with a glass of wine in her hand and started crying.

"I think Rick and I might be splitting up," she said, tears dripping down her cheeks. Rick was her current husband—her fourth. They'd been together for only a couple of years, so I didn't know him well. My mother, so competent in her work life, seemed to have no skills when it came to picking a husband and staying married. Rick walked into the room, saw her crying, did an about-face, and walked out. Later we all ate dinner together in silence.

My dad and his wife, Fran, drove up from Connecticut. We met at his parents' house. They were very affectionate with each other, Dad and Fran, and they showered presents on the kids.

"At least you guys are doing okay," I said to them.

Then Fran reminded me about her fibromyalgia, diabetes, heart problems, and insomnia. Dad, who is epileptic, chimed in good-naturedly that he just switched medications and had to wait a year before he could drive again, which made getting to work at his computer programming job very difficult, especially in winter.

While we were listening to all this, Brian stood up to go to the bathroom, tripped, and then caught himself by grabbing the edge of the couch.

"Are you okay?" I said, standing up with Baby Jake in my arms.

"Fiiine. Jus' fine," he slurred. Then he lurched toward the bathroom, beer in one hand, feeling for the doorknob with the other.

I'd never seen him like this before. *Was he drunk?*

When he returned, I got up to use the bathroom.

"Give me the baby," he said, and reached his free hand toward me, the other one still holding the beer bottle. I could barely understand what he was saying. I had seen Brian after a few too many drinks, but never like this. He was like a *Saturday Night Live* parody of a drunk person.

I met his bleary-eyed gaze, and instead of feeling concern for Brian, I was overcome with rage. This visit was hard enough. Now I was going to be on my own taking care of the kids until he pulled himself together. In the meantime, he was going to embarrass both of us in front of family we saw only once every couple of years.

"No," I said firmly, aware that my dad and stepmom were witnessing this spectacle. "You'll drop him."

"I'm fine," he said. "Give him to me."

"No," I said firmly. "Stop. Drinking."

Brian stared at me for a moment, then took a long, slow swig of his beer, taunting me. Dad and Fran sat quietly on the couch, heads bowed politely, as if in prayer.

I left the room, still holding the baby. Brian followed us into the bathroom.

"You're acting crazy," I hissed, turning to face him. "Get out!" I hoped my dad wouldn't hear, but I was glad he was nearby, in case I needed help. I was getting scared.

"I'm not the crazy one," Brian sputtered. "Gimme the baby."

"No! Get out!"

He blinked at me, then slowly backed away. I shut the door.

What the hell was wrong with my husband?

I found out later.

Brian had brought his prescription for Ativan, which was supposed to help him manage his new fear of flying, but he'd been so stressed out by the miserable visit that he'd taken two pills that afternoon. Never one to follow directions, he'd tacked on three or four beers for good measure. There were side effects.

SOMEHOW WE GOT HIM TO BED and he slept it off. In the morning, he didn't remember any of it. I told him everything, sparing no loathsome detail, and he just looked at me blankly as if I were describing something I'd seen on TV. He apologized, though it sounded insincere since he had no memory of doing the thing for which he was apologizing. At least he took responsibility and didn't just blame the drugs or shrug it off.

I knew I should forgive him. We should never have gone to New York. It was obvious he was breaking down from stress.

But I wasn't ready yet. The string had just snapped.

WORKING PARENTS, A MARRIAGE OF INCONVENIENCE

How does the stress of being working parents affect our marriages?

It's hard to say. Research shows that people who have children become less satisfied in their marriages, whether both partners work or not. And there's no question that "dual-earner parents" feel the time bind. According to a national survey commissioned by Care.com, 62 percent of working parents said they are too stressed from juggling work and family obligations to have sex with their spouses. In this context, you would think that the divorce rates have skyrocketed, but that's not the case. Divorces peaked in the '70s, back when my parents split up, then started coming down. Today, the more education and economic independence a woman has, the more likely she is to stay married. Sociologists say this is because the balance of power has shifted and women are better equipped to negotiate for what they need.

➤

> Still, it's hard to deny that the stresses of working and parenting affect our relationships.

In a recent ethnographic study, researchers from UCLA videotaped thirty-two families continuously for one week each. What these families had in common was they had two or more children and both parents worked outside of the home. While logging 1,540 hours of video, the researchers found—surprise, surprise—"a fire shower of stress, multitasking and mutual nitpicking."

According to one of the (young, childless graduate student) researchers, watching the families in their daily battle with exhaustion was the "very purest form of birth control ever devised. Ever."

CHAPTER 18.

AS THE WEEKS WORE ON, a ruthless monotony took hold. It started raining, a steady Northern California rain that seemed as if it would never stop. We marched grimly forward without pause, forgetting about life outside our to-do lists.

I snuck out of a meeting to take a call from Ruby's school. She wasn't feeling well, the office manager said. Could I come pick her up? I got these calls every couple of weeks. Sometimes Ruby was sick; sometimes she just didn't want to be at school. It was impossible to tell over the phone.

I could see Brian in one of the glass-walled conference rooms, huddled around a speakerphone with his project team. Everyone looked tense, which meant they were talking with Vlad and his merry crew in New York. I looked at the clock—if I left right now, I could get Ruby home, plunk her down in front of a *Wonder Pets!* cartoon, and then dial in to my 3:00 PM staffing meeting . . . I sighed, then grabbed my keys and coat.

Each day was made up of stolen moments. I was rarely doing what it looked like I was doing. At work, I was thinking about my kids. At home, when I should have been *focused* on my kids, I was working.

I tried to surrender to the idea that this was temporary. Brian and I told each other this constantly, to keep from fighting over our lack of time, the way underfed rats might fight over a scrap of food.

"This is just the way it is right now," we'd say, "there just isn't enough to go around."

When I sat at my desk to catch up on email, I was stealing time from a presentation I was supposed to be putting together about new business strategies. I warmed my cold hands under my thighs while I tried to make sense of a proposal for a Twitter application. A new boom was under way. We were reinventing the Internet, reinventing the way people related to one another. We called this new phenomenon social media, although I didn't see anything particularly social about it.

At 10:00 AM, I walked around the corner to have breakfast with a colleague from another web agency. We met every six months or so to talk shop. This kind of networking was a key part of my job, but it also meant stealing time from the proposal I should have been editing.

Mid-conversation, my colleague abruptly looked down and started tapping his phone with great intensity.

"Everything okay?" I asked, alarmed.

"Yeah, yeah, I'm just tweeting about my waffle."

A FEW WEEKS AFTER CHRISTMAS, Brian flew to New York for yet another business trip. His fear of flying had not improved, and if it hadn't been for the Ativan, I don't know how he could have done it. He arrived home a few nights later at 11:00 PM. I'm normally a light sleeper, but this time I didn't hear him come in. Our wacky neighbor had been conducting late-night weight-lifting sessions in his backyard. The clanging of the metal kept me awake, so I was wearing earplugs.

Sometime around midnight, Brian nudged me out of a deep fog of sleep. I looked up to see him standing over my side of the bed, shirtless, holding Jake to his chest. He looked alarmed. Barely awake, I pulled the spongy purple foam out of one ear.

"What's going on with him?" Brian said.

I bolted upright. "What do you mean?"

"Listen," he said. "Something's wrong with his breathing."

Jake's breathing was shallow and labored. Each time he breathed in or out, he emitted a strange, high-pitched whine. I had never heard anything like it. Was something blocking his airway? Immediately, my mind went to the worst scenario I could imagine—somehow he'd swallowed one of my earplugs.

I snatched him from Brian and pounded his back. Jake coughed, a gagging-choking-barking sound. Nothing came out.

We whisked him into the bathroom. I shut the door while Brian ran hot water through the showerhead to make steam. Then I sat on the toilet lid with Jake on my lap and really looked at him. He wasn't upset and he was definitely conscious, but it was as if he was breathing softly through a whistle.

"Call 9-1-1," I said.

I took Jake downstairs to the rocking chair to wait. I didn't want to wake Ruby, and I didn't want to upset Jake, because that could make his breathing worse.

"The ambulance is on the way," Brian said.

It felt as if we were in a movie, the kind of movie neither of us could stand to watch. Within minutes, we heard sirens, then there were firemen at our door in their strange overalls, looking brave and capable and concerned. They didn't have time to do more than ask a couple of questions before the ambulance arrived, and I was ushered onto a gurney with my pajamas still on and Jake still in my lap. Brian handed me the diaper bag on our way out the door.

"Your cell phone's in there," he said.

The closest hospital was only a mile away. When we arrived, there was a flurry of questions, mostly the same ones I had already answered in the ambulance about Jake's age (one and a half) and health history (no allergies, no problems). The ER doctor examined him, ordered a nebulizer with epinephrine, and rushed off. A machine on the wall started whirring. I held a mask under Jake's nose, as the nurse instructed. Every once in a while he tried to bat it away but he was too tired to put up much of a fight.

"Do you know what's wrong with him?" I asked one of the doctors.

"Well, for starters, he has croup," she said. "It's probably from a virus, and that's what's causing that barking sound when he coughs. But he's also having a reaction to the croup. The sound you hear when he breathes is called *stridor*. It's from the inflammation in his airways. Very dangerous if not treated properly. Do you hear how he makes the sound when he breathes in and also when he breathes out?"

"Yeah. It's horrible."

"That means he has inflammation in his upper and lower airways."

"Is he going to be okay?"

"Oh, sure! We see this all the time. We just need to bring the inflammation down and he'll be fine."

I exhaled. That's when I realized I'd been holding my breath for an hour.

As soon as she left, I called Brian.

"It's okay," I said immediately. "We have a name for it. Croup."

"Croup?"

"Yeah. It's another one of those things that kids get all the time." I said this breezily. I didn't want to scare him any more than necessary by going into the details. "They said we'll probably be here all night, but he's going to be okay. You should go to sleep."

"Thank God," he said.

We hung up. I still hadn't asked him about his trip.

For the next two and a half hours I sat with Jake on a thin, plastic-coated mattress, holding the mask near his face. Nurses came in every half hour or so, nodded at us, and exited again. Mostly we were left alone. At first Jake was passively annoyed, but the stimulating effects of the medicine woke him up. The mask was far enough from his face that I was breathing it, too, and we both got the jitters. It became a wrestling match as I tried to keep the mask close enough for him to breathe the medicine, and simultaneously keep him from pitching himself off the bed, which had no side arms to hold him in. Twice he knocked the mask out of my hand so hard that the line pulled out of the wall and a nurse had to reattach it.

I felt so lonely. I wanted my mom. I wanted her to sit with me and take turns holding this jazzed-up, wheezy, cranky baby. But of course, my mom was far away, in Upstate New York. My dad was in Connecticut. My sister was in Seattle. Brian's whole family was in Detroit. Everyone was far, far away.

There were no friends I could call, not at this time of night. Asking another stressed-out, sleep-deprived mom to spend the night with you at the hospital was like asking to borrow a month's salary. I couldn't bring myself to do it.

Now that I knew Jake was going to be okay, the horror of what could have happened began to sink in. I never should have worn the earplugs to bed. What if Brian's flight had been delayed? Oh God, I couldn't stand to think of what would have happened if Brian hadn't been there and I hadn't woken up. Or what if I *had* woken up, but Brian still wasn't home? I would have had to take Ruby in the ambulance, too, and now I'd be trying to soothe an exhausted, terrified six-year-old as well as wrestle a sick toddler.

THE MEDICINE WAS MAKING us both thirsty. Jake began crying for his bottle.

"Can we have some water?" I asked a nurse when she popped her head in.

"Sure," she said, and then never returned.

Another nurse came in twenty minutes later.

"Could we please have some water? We're both very thirsty."

"Uh-huh."

She came back, ten minutes later, empty-handed.

"We called your insurance company," she said. "They said you have to go to your HMO's hospital. We can't admit you here."

Apparently, we were in some kind of triage room. We'd been here for three hours, but we hadn't been officially "admitted."

"Oh. So what happens now?"

"Well, there's an ambulance on the way to transport you. They'll be here soon."

"Okay. Do you think we could get that water?"

"Yes."

She came back five minutes later with three medics from the new ambulance. No water. It was after 3:00 AM.

That's when I lost my temper.

"I'm not going anywhere until we get some water!"

She looked at me, startled, and disappeared. I never saw her again. A moment later, one of the medics disappeared and then reappeared with a little Styrofoam cup. I poured the water into Jake's bottle and he chugged it down.

"More," he said.

The medic disappeared again and came back, beaming, with the cup and a yellow plastic pitcher full of tap water.

Jake fell asleep on the way to the new hospital. When we got there, our room was already waiting for us. After the experience at the first hospital, I felt as if we'd arrived at a four-star hotel. They gave us a real bed and raised it halfway to keep Jake's head elevated. Our nurse puttered about efficiently, helped me remove my shoes, covered us up with blankets, and positioned a hose with cool mist under Jake's nose. She hooked up various sensors to Jake's body without waking him, then left. She returned a moment later with a full pitcher of water and a stack of cups. I didn't even ask for it. I loved this woman.

At ten thirty the next morning, they discharged us with oral steroids and a new inhaler. Brian came alone to pick us up; Ruby was already at kindergarten. When we got home, Jake and I lay down for a nap. Brian bustled about nervously, not wanting to leave us.

"Do you want to hold him?" I asked.

He nodded, and his eyes filled with tears.

Several minutes later, Brian wiped his eyes, handed Jake back to me, and went back out to his office. The show must go on.

AFTER JAKE'S BOUT WITH STRIDOR, I was shaken for days. I began to wonder how much longer I could keep going at this pace before something really bad happened.

Most of my friends had switched onto the Mommy Track by now. Jenny swore she was going to quit and look for part-time work as soon as she'd saved up a little more money. A colleague from another consulting agency told me she'd decided not to have a second child because she couldn't handle another child unless she worked part-time, but as it was, her family needed her full-time salary. Rebecca despaired that she was underpaid and over-qualified for her Mommy Track job doing health care research. "But I'm never going to get promoted if I don't publish, which would mean working at night instead of seeing my kids." My sister, Holly, solved her problems by getting a divorce: Now she had her weekends free and was training to be a firefighter/paramedic. Lee was still having enormous ups and downs trying to make it all work as a single mom. My friend Gillian had quit working altogether and was struggling mightily to make ends meet on her husband's income.

"We have good food on the table, and our children are clean and clothed, but Katrina, I feel *crushed* with the weight of financial debt," she said. "We have $30,000 on our credit cards and I don't see us paying it off anytime soon. Forget vacations. Forget home ownership. It ain't happening for us."

Stella was the only "dual-earner, multiple-child, middle-class" mom with a commute who seemed to be getting along just fine. How did she do it?

When I asked her, she confided that she'd had a panic attack several months ago.

"Being a mom, running my own business," she sighed heavily. "Sometimes it's too much."

"So what are you going to do?" I asked.

She brightened. "Oh, everything's better now," she said. "I hired a mother's helper! She comes at six and helps the kids with their homework. Makes a huge difference. You should really think about doing that, Katrina."

It was good, practical advice, but I couldn't see myself hiring a mother's helper. My kids were in school and day care all day long. Now I was supposed to have someone come to the house to take care of them in the evening, too? I was the *mommy*. That was *my* job. Maybe that worked for Stella, but the idea made me more upset. I would just have to try harder.

KEEP YOUR FOOT ON THE GAS?

The COO of Facebook, Sheryl Sandberg, gave a talk called "Why We Have Too Few Women Leaders" at the 2010 TEDWomen conference. When the video of the talk was released online, it quickly went viral. (Two years later, she published a book called *Lean In*, based on the themes of this talk.)

It was refreshing to hear a woman (with two children) who had achieved so much talk about how hard it was to work and raise children. Among the disturbing statistics Sandberg shared were these:

- Of 190 heads of state, 9 are women.
- Of all the people in parliament in the world, 13 percent are women.
- In the corporate sector, women in C-level jobs and board seats top out at only 15 to 16 percent.
- Even in the nonprofit world, women at the top equal only 20 percent.
- The numbers have not moved since 2002.

I watched the video, rapt. Until she started in with the advice.

Sandberg said she'd noticed that when women decide to have children, they check out mentally at work. They start "leaning back," letting themselves get passed over for promotions, and so on.

"Keep your foot on the gas pedal," she said. "Until the very day you need to leave to take a break for a child—and then you can make your decisions."

In other words, go as fast and far as you can, until you can't. Which is exactly what *I* did. But now I can see, in retrospect, I should have taken my foot off the gas pedal sooner, not later.

If there's one thing we need to do to make room for more women in leadership, it's not telling them to "keep their foot on the gas pedal." For many of us, that's the surest way to drive ourselves over the cliff. And it perpetuates the widely held belief that women are the source of their own problems, that if we're not getting ahead in our careers, it's our own damn fault. We're just not trying hard enough! Likewise, if we're overwhelmed with the competing demands on our time, that's our fault, too; we're simply not managing our time well!

Instead of "keeping your foot on the gas," women need to have more compassion for them-selves, and to know when to slow down. Which is

> very, very hard to do when the expectations for us to be supermoms are so great. And even harder when women like Sheryl Sandberg—accomplished, attractive, well-meaning—tell us they did it and we should, too.

CHAPTER 19.

IN FEBRUARY, A BUSINESS TRIP turned into a surprising respite from my daily worries, and Stella and I both found inspiration amid the palm trees and blue skies of Long Beach, California. We were attending the TED conference.

TED, which stands for Technology, Entertainment, and Design, was not just another conference. You couldn't just plunk down your credit card and reserve your spot—you had to fill out an application with essays and references, and if you were lucky enough to get accepted, it still cost a ridiculous sum to attend. Stella had been attending TED for almost a decade; she'd been hounding me for years to apply. Our most interesting projects had come through people she knew in the TED community, and she said it was a prime networking opportunity for us. It was most likely through her connections that my application was accepted. Dogstar paid my travel expenses and kicked in half of the conference fee.

The conference was only loosely connected to what I did for a living. We designed web sites. People at TED designed the *future*. The guy who created the one-laptop-per-child program was there, and so was the guy who designed robots that could carry on human-like conversations, and the woman who had written a "charter of compassion" to help spiritual leaders of different faiths find common cause. I wasn't in their league. It didn't seem to matter. If you made it here, you were in The Club. You were automatically interesting, and everyone wanted to meet you.

Standing in line for lunch my first day, I met the creator of *The Simpsons* and a man whose job at NASA involved planning how people could live on other planets. During the cocktail hour, I met a man who consulted to the British Parliament, and another who designed complex, *Fantasia*-like animations to give scientists a visual model of the inner workings of disease. While washing my hands in the ladies' room, I met Jill Bolte Taylor, the brain scientist who became famous when she spoke at TED the year before about the strangely beautiful experience of witnessing the left side of her brain shut down during a massive stroke.

Every conference session was a mindblower. A molecular biologist, Bonnie Bassler, explained how bacteria communicate with each other and talked about how we might be able to talk back to them. A researcher who studied trees, Nalini Nadkarni, told us how she recruited hip-hop artists to help her educate inner-city youth about the environment.

I could feel my mind expanding. The world was full of problems, and creative people everywhere were working tirelessly to solve them. Everyone I met seemed to glow from within, alive in a way that I had rarely seen.

Famous writers, comedians, business leaders, movie stars, and deep thinkers roamed the halls between sessions or sipped their complimentary cappuccinos, chatting animatedly with each other, or reclined on pillows while the current session was piped in to one of the themed viewing areas outside the main theater. Jeff Bezos. Bill Gates. Paul Simon. A slew of blond movie stars: Cameron Diaz, Meryl Streep, Meg Ryan. Tim Berners-Lee, the guy who invented the Internet. Steve Wozniak, the cofounder of Apple. Oliver Sacks, the doctor and writer. Arianna Huffington, creator of *The Huffington Post*. I was particularly starstruck when Al Gore sat almost directly behind me for one of the afternoon sessions.

There were far more men than women, and I briefly wondered why. The only benefit to this was that there was no line to the ladies' room, while the line to the men's room curved around the main hall.

ONE AFTERNOON, STELLA AND I lounged on one of the comfortable mezzanine couches, watching the conference on a large screen. Massage therapists were stationed near these lounges giving free massages, compliments of TED. On-screen, Elizabeth Gilbert took the stage. Everyone, including me, had heard of her international best seller, *Eat, Pray, Love,* although I hadn't read it. I didn't have time for "fun" reading anymore.

Instead of standing behind a podium, Gilbert roamed the stage as she told the story of her sudden and unexpected success and how frightened she became by other people's expectations.

"I should just put it bluntly because we're all friends here. It's exceedingly likely that my greatest success is behind me," she confessed to an audience of thousands. "That's the kind of thought that could lead a person to start drinking gin at nine o'clock in the morning." Everyone laughed.

Then she launched into a history of creativity. The ancient Greeks and Romans believed that creativity came from a source outside themselves, called "genius."

"If your work bombed," Gilbert explained, "it wasn't entirely your fault. Everyone knew your genius was just kind of lame." To live a creative life, you couldn't allow yourself to be swamped by other people's expectations.

I was riveted. It was so obvious, suddenly, that I had let my entire life, every moment of every day, be swamped by others' expectations—my coworkers', my clients', even my kids'. And I was so unhappy.

I thought Gilbert was terribly brave to tell this story while CEOs of Fortune 500 companies sat in the auditorium, scratching their smooth-shaven chins. It felt as if she were talking directly to me, to Stella, to all the women in the audience who had worked so hard to live up to what people thought we should do and who secretly felt like failures.

When she finished, I wiped a few tears from my eyes and looked around. Two other women were dabbing at their eyes with tissues.

"Wow," Stella breathed, eyes still on the screen. "I think that was the best talk of the whole conference!"

"Definitely," I said.

Then she turned to me suddenly, her smile burning its full one hundred watts.

"Katrina, I am so glad you're here. Now do you understand why I wanted you to come? You *belong* here."

I just smiled back at her. I was still overcome with emotion.

"I know things are hard right now with your kids being little," she continued. "Believe me, I've been there. But it's going to get better. You just have to *hang in there.* Think about how far the company's come since you've been working at Dogstar, how far *you've* come. This is just the beginning, Katrina. We're just getting started." She was luminescent. "I kept telling you, but you didn't get it. But now you get it. Don't you?"

I smiled. "I get it."

I so badly wanted her to be right. I wanted the magic TED dust to rub off on me. I wanted to do something with my life, something more than just wipe snotty noses and listen to spoiled designers gripe about their problems. I wanted to be part of something bigger than myself and my own petty problems. I wanted to be one of *these* people. I just had to hang in there.

WHEN I FIRST CAME HOME FROM TED, it was all I could talk about. Every time someone asked me a question at the office, the answer seemed to involve someone I met at TED or a talk I heard at TED. I became that annoying girl in *American Pie* who started every story with "This one time? At band camp?"

A week after I got home, Jake woke up crying at 12:45 AM, dried snot smeared across one cheek.

"Nose!" he said. "Nose!"

I stumbled to his room and dabbed at his nose with a clean diaper wipe while Brian set up the humidifier so the cool air pointed

toward his crib. Ever since the stridor incident, we took extra pre-
cautions to avoid another attack. I sat on the folded-up futon we
sometimes used as a guest bed and pulled Jake onto my lap. I mea-
sured grape-flavored Tylenol in a special medicine dropper, and
squirted it into his mouth. He took a sip of water from his plastic
cup, then settled himself on my chest.

"Go back to bed, honey. I've got him," I said to Brian.

"Aren't you going to put him back in his crib?"

"In a minute. Let's let the Tylenol kick in first."

Brian gave me a doubtful look but staggered back to bed. He
had more than a month to go with the grueling Dogstar project. He
needed every ounce of sleep he could squeeze in.

Jake and I cuddled on the futon while I smoothed his corn-silk
hair, enjoying the soft slip of it through my fingers. Time seemed to
stop, the way it can only in the middle of the night, when there is no
sound, no thought. Eventually, Jake drifted off to sleep. I gently set
him back in his crib. Immediately he sat up and started to cry.

"No! Mommy! Want Mommy!"

I paused to consider. I was awake enough to know that this was
a critical juncture, but I was still not thinking very clearly. What
did the book say to do at times like this? Which book were we using again? Ferber? Brazelton? Spock? Did *anyone* listen to poor Dr.
Spock anymore?

I didn't have the heart to leave, so I unfolded the futon and col-
lected sheets and a blanket from the hall closet. Jake stopped crying
and sat up in his crib to watch me make up the bed. When I lifted
him out of his crib again, he was positively ebullient, as if he'd won a
prize at the fair. *Mommy is going to lie down with me. We are breaking the rules!*

I set him down next to me on the futon and rubbed his back, but he wouldn't lie still. In between pointing to his nose, beckoning me to wipe the boogers off, he cooed to himself.

"Jake. It's nighttime. No singing."

He quieted down. I started to doze off, but soon he was thrashing around like a trout on the deck of a small boat.

"Jake. This isn't working. If you can't lie still and sleep, then you're going back to your bed."

"No! Mama!"

He wedged himself against my armpit and lay very still, like a turtle cooling himself in the shade of a stump. I started to doze off again, and then *thunk,* he flopped his head on my chest.

"Ow, Jake! Stop!" He lay still. He was totally playing me.

I looked at my watch, which I'd forgotten to take off when I first fell into bed: 2:47 AM. I had to get up in three hours for work.

I put him back in his crib, and he began to shriek.

"What's going on in here?" Brian loomed in the doorway, wearing a T-shirt and underwear. He had to get up in three hours, too.

"Nothing," I said. "I'm putting him back down."

"Why are you still in here?"

"Can we just talk about this in the morning?"

Jake kicked the bars of the crib, mixing horrible growls and grunts with his crying, like a creature from a Maurice Sendak book.

Ruby padded down the hall in her favorite fuzzy princess nightgown with the rip in the hem, her long brown hair hanging past her eyes.

"Jake won't let me sleep!"

"He'll stop in a minute, honey. Go back to bed."

"But I can't sleep!" She stomped her bare foot on the wood floor.

"C'mon, Ruby, let's go," Brian said in his most commanding Daddy Voice.

She stomped her foot again but followed obediently.

This was all my fault. This was not what the books, any of them, said you should do. Jake wasn't wet. He wasn't that sick. He'd had his Tylenol. When I first put him back in his crib, standard operating procedure was to say something soothing, walk out, and shut the door. You couldn't waver. You couldn't hesitate at the door. You couldn't show any weakness. You had to be committed, or kids would see right through you. Brian was good at this. He could be firm without showing any guilt or self-doubt, even if he felt it. But I sucked at it.

If I had followed standard procedure, Jake probably would have fallen back asleep within ten minutes. But it was late. I was tired. I wasn't thinking clearly. And you know what? I wanted to cuddle with my sick baby. I wanted something, anything, to be that simple.

THE NEXT MORNING, BRIAN AND I shuffled through our morning chores in silent defeat. When I said good morning in the kitchen, he pretended not to hear me. It wasn't entirely clear if he was angry about the night before or just so exhausted that he couldn't muster the energy it would take to form words.

The magic of TED had faded away. It was like something I'd dreamed, and now I was awake, and there were only snotty noses and piles of laundry and difficult clients awaiting me. I thought of Elizabeth Gilbert, how she'd warned us not to be swamped by others' expectations. What would she say to all this? Then I remembered that she didn't have kids.

THE "OPT-OUT" MYTH

For more than a decade, we've seen women graduate from college and rise up the career ladder, only to suddenly "opt out" of the workforce entirely after they have children. The media has covered this trend, often referring to it as the "Opt-Out Revolution" (a phrase coined by Lisa Belkin in a 2003 *New York Times* essay). The basic story line goes like this: "*Isn't it strange! Given the choice to have an exciting career or children, these educated women choose children. Well, go figure . . .*"

There was (and continues to be) much speculation about this phenomenon. These women were either noble (sacrificing ambition for the sake of their children) or backstabbers of feminism and a setback to the women's movement. (*They wasted a perfectly good college education!*). (Ironically, when the women "opting out" are uneducated single moms who can't afford the high cost of child care, they aren't depicted as "noble" for opting out; they are lazy moochers.)

What was lost in these discussions was that most of these college-educated women didn't want to give up their careers. In fact, they did everything they could to hang on to their careers and raise their children. Research shows 86 percent of these women would rather work but are pushed out by factors such as inflexible work schedules, which make their careers incompatible with family life. They didn't "opt out." They were shoved out the door.

The media reports tend to focus on the time right after these women "opt out." They fail to report on them ten or twenty years later, when many of them are divorced and struggling to support themselves. Research shows that when their children are older and women want to return to their careers, many cannot. So it should not come as a surprise that motherhood is now the single biggest risk factor for poverty in old age.

This "opt-out/pushed-out" problem hurts women and their families, but it also hurts our economy. Women are the better-educated half of the population now. We have more college degrees than men. Experts anticipate a looming talent shortage, and unless the workplace becomes friendlier to families, we will continue to see all that talent swirling down the drain. As Joan Williams reports, from the Center for WorkLife Law:

> *The United States cannot maintain its competitiveness if it continues to pay large sums to educate the many women who then find themselves "deskilled"—driven out of good jobs and into less good ones—by inflexible workplaces and family responsibilities discrimination.*

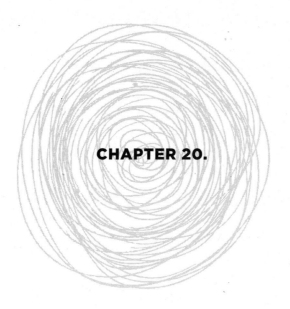

CHAPTER 20.

AROUND THE TIME I RETURNED from TED, Brian's late-night work sprints began to stretch even later. Each night, I went to bed alone. Often I woke up at 2:00 or 3:00 AM and found I was still alone, the light from Brian's office glowing softly through our bedroom window.

The more chores Brian dropped so he could focus on work, the more chores I picked up. There was no point in trying to plan anymore; I threw the complicated schedules in the trash. The only plan was to do what was in front of me.

It seems so obvious now, as I write this, that I was reaching the end of my physical and emotional limits. But I had no way of understanding that then. Like most able-bodied thirtysomethings who had never had to face crushing disappointment, *I didn't know I had limits*. I had lived my entire adult life under the naïve assumption that if I wasn't getting what I wanted, I just had to try harder. Very soon, I would be disabused of this notion.

The beginning of the end of my career at Dogstar came when I got my own difficult client: April.

April had been a Dogstar client on and off for years and had earned a reputation for being manipulative and demanding. When everyone on my team refused to work with her, I took over her latest project.

"April's not that bad when you get to know her," Stella enthused. "You'll know how to handle her."

I quickly learned that in addition to being manipulative and demanding, April was disorganized and moody. But she liked me, which made me automatically like her. She called me "sweetie" and "hon," as if we were college roommates. She was only a few years older than me but seemed more grown-up, maybe because she worked for a big insurance company and dressed the part: silk button-down blouses, straight skirts in solid colors or pressed slacks. Her makeup was always subdued: mauve lipstick, the right amount of mascara, and foundation that perfectly evened out her skin tone.

To work with April was to get on a roller coaster with April. On Tuesday, she told me she loved our thinking, she loved our presentation, she loved *me*. On Wednesday, I found my message light blinking red when I arrived at the office:

"Katrina! It's April. I've called you *four times* and I've called Kimberly *twice*. Why can't I get ahold of you guys? We really need to talk about your availability. I don't even have your cell phone number! So, okay. Bad news. Tracy hated the presentation you guys gave yesterday. Hated it! Call me when you get in."

I called her back, and before I knew it, she convinced me to put in an extra three days' work on a presentation that was never part of our original scope. In other words, I agreed to put in three extra days on a freebie.

I felt slimed. But I also felt perversely triumphant. Once again, April loved me, and the project was under control.

The next day, she asked for my cell phone number, and I cheerfully gave it to her. Almost immediately, she began calling in the morning as I drove my kids to school. Sometimes these calls were work-related ("I just have a quick question about the site map . . ."). Other times, not so much ("I just need to vent . . .").

Although her behavior was not always professional, I felt sorry for April and cut her a lot of slack. She was a working mom, too, with two boys in elementary school. She confided that her husband's company was in the midst of massive layoffs; he was expecting to lose his job any day. The insurance company where April worked was "reorganizing," which meant there would almost certainly be layoffs there, too. She felt enormous pressure to secure her position, as she could soon wind up the sole provider for her family. I let her vent.

A COUPLE OF WEEKS AFTER I STARTED working with April, Vlad came to town for his bimonthly visit. It was bad enough working with him over the nanny cam, but in person it was like having a dangerous animal roaming the office. During a meeting, Brian's laptop crashed and then wouldn't start up again. Our IT guy pronounced it dead. After the meeting, Brian told Vlad he was heading to the Apple Store to get it repaired.

"You're *what?* You can't leave!" Vlad blustered.

"My laptop's broken. I won't be able to get any work done until it's fixed."

"You *can't leave*," Vlad said again. "Tell Carol to do it. Or Stella."

Carol was a project manager, which is to say, she bore more responsibility for the project's success than anyone, even Brian. It was not her job to run errands. Brian found her at her desk and repeated the conversation. Her eyes grew wide.

"I have another meeting," she said helplessly.

"There's no way I'd ask you to go," Brian said. "I just want you to know what's going on."

Brian found me in the kitchen fixing myself a cup of tea. "Our client is holding me here against my will," he hissed.

"Oh, this is ridiculous," I said, and marched straight over to Stella's desk. At least she could step in and establish some ground rules.

But when I explained the situation to her, she shrank back into her chair. "Well, can Carol *go?*" she whispered.

"No, she's in meetings for the rest of the afternoon," I whispered back. "He wants to know if *you* can go."

Stella was the founder and CEO of our company. It was not her job to run errands, either. I knew better than to wait for an answer. Before she could ask, I added, "And *I'm* supposed to be running a workshop with April's group in five minutes."

"Well . . . can Eugene set Brian up with a spare computer until Vlad leaves?"

As we whispered, we darted glances at Vlad, who was pacing back and forth in the glassed-in conference room as he talked on his cell phone. He was like a Siberian tiger whose cage had been left open, and no one had the guts to bolt it shut. Including me.

Eugene, our IT guy, did set Brian up with a temporary desktop computer, but it was all for show—Brian couldn't get anything done with his work files trapped inside his dead laptop. When Vlad finally left for the airport several hours later, Brian slammed his real laptop into his bag and stalked off to the Apple Store, murder in his eyes. The client, the man-child we were working so hard to keep happy, had just cost him a precious afternoon's work.

WHILE VLAD WAS REDEFINING the phrase *demanding client*, April shot right past *demanding* and headed deep into *bizarre*.

Early one morning, she appeared in Dogstar's lobby, holding an odd-shaped box in her arms. As I approached, I realized it was a wooden dresser drawer filled with socks.

"Oh, good," she said, and shook her freshly trimmed shoulder-length brown hair out of her eyes. "You're here."

I glanced at my watch. It was a little before 9:00 AM. There were only a couple of people at their desks; the front door was still locked. No one had even turned on the kitchen lights yet. *How did she get in?* I wondered.

"Can I just leave this here for a minute?" She dropped the drawer on the rug with a small thud. The socks jumped silently.

"What's that?" I asked.

At a glance, they looked like little girls' socks, with bits of pink frills and scallops, maybe a girl Ruby's age. April had two boys. I got a creeping sensation that something was wrong.

"It's for a brainstorming activity for Friday! I just thought of it when I couldn't sleep last night." She flashed me a mischievous grin. Then she leaned in uncomfortably close and said in a loud whisper, "I'm having a *Magic Week*."

I took a step backward.

"What's happening Friday?" I hoped my voice sounded casual.

She ignored my question. "Let's go in here," she said, ducking into Conference Room B, which had been converted back into a regular conference room when I had weaned Jake several months before. The other two moms in the office had stopped pumping long before that, saying it was too difficult.

"We have to talk," April said, shutting the door. "I am so mad."

I could smell more free work coming.

"Aren't you supposed to be at usability testing?" I asked, as I cautiously took my seat.

"I'm supposed to. But that fucking Chauncey moved the location and I don't know where it is!"

"Chauncey?"

"That's the head of research, Katrina. I've told you that three times. He's the *head of research*." She stood abruptly and stabbed the whiteboard three times with the tip of a marker. I'd never seen her this irate. I couldn't tell if she was mad at me or Chauncey.

"Okay, slow down." I patted the seat next to me and she sat. "Start from the beginning."

"Chauncey stole my researcher away and convinced Tracy to put Felipe on his team and now they've hired Lofenberger's to do the usability study and Lofenberger's has totally and completely fucked up the recruiting . . ." Her voice started out low, but as she talked, it steadily rose in volume and pitch.

"Why don't we back up for a minute and   "

"No! I just need to vent for a second, okay? This is therapy. Just let me vent!"

I let her vent. For several minutes she described a half-baked plan to go to Chauncey's boss's boss and make a case for removing his position. April didn't have any gripe about us, or our work, which was a relief. Now I just needed to find a delicate way to escape.

"—I am going to get his ASS FIRED!" she continued. More pounding on the wall.

In the silence between rants, I heard murmurs in the adjacent conference room, where my next meeting had started. I wondered what they thought was going on in here. Maybe they were planning a rescue party. When April paused for breath, I made my move.

"April."

"Huh?"

"I'm sorry you're upset. Listen. I had a meeting that was sup- posed to start at nine." I was using my gentle-but-firm Mommy Voice.

"Oh my God, sweetie. I'm sorry! Should we talk about this later?"

"Sure. Or I can quickly tell you what I think now."

"Yes! That's why I'm here. What should I do?"

"The first thing I think you should do is get over to usability testing. Tracy will not be happy to find out you missed it. I'll ask Orlando to print you a map."

"Thank you. What about Chauncey?"

"If you're really going to have that meeting with Tracy's boss, I don't think you should even mention Chauncey's name. It will just make you look bad," I said.

"Right. But what do I say?"

"You bring it back to the business. It's all about what's best for the business. This is an organizational problem. It's about creating roles and processes that will make the web team more effective in their work."

"You're brilliant! Can you say that again?" She pulled out a pad of paper from her purse and started taking notes.

I was not brilliant. I was just calm. I went through it again. April was still taking notes when I left the room.

Norman and Roger were waiting, wide-eyed, in Conference Room C.

"What's going on in there?" Roger whispered.

"It's okay. She's not mad at us. She's calming down now."

Hearing my own voice, steady and sure, made me think of a surgeon who came out of the operating room to give the family an update. But I didn't feel steady and sure. I was light-headed and my hands were buzzing, as if I'd been holding a jackhammer.

THE NEXT FEW DAYS WERE punctuated with more "magic moments" like this one, pulling in an ever-growing number of distressed Dogstar staff. Kimberly, Thomas, Stella, and I conferred at length. Thomas, who happened to have a master's degree in psychology, was convinced that we were witnessing a bipolar manic episode.

I sometimes joked to people that I was more of a corporate therapist than a designer, and there was truth in that. But a professional therapist would have known what to do for April. A professional therapist would have been trained to let her clients' pain wash over her or through her. I, instead, absorbed other people's distress like a big fluffy cotton towel. I had no idea what to do. I was a consultant and April was my client. I couldn't risk offending her by addressing her behavior, even if she was having a serious mental health crisis.

A few days later, the drawer of socks mysteriously disappeared, and April sent our project team an email. "I need to take some time off," it said. "I've been under a lot of strain in my personal life."

April returned after a week off, looking a little more rested. She was still disorganized and demanding, manipulative and moody, but back within the bounds of normalcy.

Something broke inside me. Some invisible dam that had previously kept my work and personal life intact crumbled and washed away. I lost my ability to set a boundary with April. It seemed like too much work, so I just gave up. I attended every meeting with April that I could possibly attend. I continued to take her random phone calls and spend precious hours listening to her complaints about her job. The rest of my work piled up in a heap of unanswered emails and missed meetings.

"Why are you letting her take over your life like this?" Brian asked.

"Brian, this is my job," I said wearily. "What else can I do?"

"You could stand up for yourself," he said.

You're one to talk, I thought, but said nothing. Then my phone rang.

OUR EPIDEMIC LEVELS OF JOB STRESS

Americans today may experience more job stress than ever before. Long work hours, too much responsibility, job insecurity, tasks that have little inherent meaning, and, of course, a lack of family-friendly policies all contribute to our epidemic levels of stress.

Consider these facts:

- One-third of employees report high levels of work stress.
- One-quarter of employees view their jobs as the number one stressor in their lives.
- Three-quarters of employees believe today's worker has more on-the-job stress than those of a generation ago.
- The percentage of American workers who fear they'll lose their jobs in the next twelve months almost doubled from 2007 to 2010 (from 12 percent to 21 percent).

- Problems at work are more strongly associated with health complaints than any other life stressor, more than even financial or family problems.

Technology that was supposed to liberate us—first fax machines and pagers, then laptops, email, and smart phones—has, instead, given us more to do. Rather than being at home more, we're now at work no matter where we go.

Unfortunately, this stress disproportionately affects women. Globally, our job stress levels at work are 6 to 10 percent higher than men's stress levels, even when we have the same job position as men. This is true for middle and upper management jobs as well as for service and production jobs.

CHAPTER 21.

WHILE APRIL WAS TAKING her week off, we had a big pitch with a technology firm, and I found myself standing in front of twenty people in a windowless conference room.

"Can you explain more about the persona process, Katrina?"

"Sure." I straightened my shoulders and gazed out at the room. "How many of you have worked with personas before?"

Four people tentatively raised their hands.

"Okay, good. For those of you who haven't, personas are fictional characters we create as a stand-in for our target audience." I'd explained this a hundred times, maybe more. I could do this in my sleep. "They're a wonderful design tool because they help us think through the needs of the different types of people who come to your website . . ."

As always, I looked into people's faces as I spoke. Lots of pale, tired, middle-aged faces. I thought of chickens raised on factory farms. These people emanated an anemic, rubber-boned misery. I wanted to clap my hands and lead us outside for a quick jog. *C'mon, people! Knees up!*

"Another reason we do personas . . ." I began, and then—poof!— just like that the thought was gone.

Why *did* we do personas? Because the client read a design book and thought we were supposed to do them. No, wait. That wasn't it. Why did we do them again? I felt a jolt of panic.

"Another reason we do personas . . . is . . . they help the design team communicate." *Right! Nice save, Katrina.* "When we're reviewing a wireframe, instead of saying, 'What about users who are highly tech-savvy but have to report to a business colleague who is less tech-savvy,' we say, 'What about Jennifer?'"

My mouth kept moving, but my heart was pounding. *I* needed fresh air and a jog. "Any questions?"

"How do you create them?"

"Oh, right. I meant to explain that . . ."

More and more, I was losing my train of thought. More precisely, there were so many trains of thought they'd all piled into each other. Did I pack enough food in Ruby's lunch today? Did Brian remember to pay Thania? Thinking about Thania made me think about Jake, who was overdue for his annual physical. I had to remember to schedule that and also to figure out how far Jake was from catching up on his—shit—what's the word? *Injections?* No, *immunizations.*

That was happening a lot, too. Forgetting words. Or forgetting how to spell words, simple words that I'd spelled since second grade.

I'd recently written the word *view* and then stared at it for a long time. *V-I-E-W.* Was that really a word?

Too many trains.

My anxiety had resurfaced, too. It had been four years since I'd taken the panic class, and for four years I'd kept anxiety at bay. Now, suddenly, I was waking up in the middle of the night, worrying, unable to go back to sleep. *What if Brian had a heart attack from stress? What if I kept blanking out in presentations? What if the kids were suffering because they weren't getting enough attention from me? What if I started having panic attacks again? What if I got fired, because I couldn't do my job anymore?*

All this unproductive worry. I wanted to get my anxiety removed, like a wart. A worry wart. I wanted to cut it out and put it in a jar with some formaldehyde so scientists could study it and understand its origins and then explain it to me using Latin names for all the different parts.

What you're experiencing is a mixture of lamentacio *and* inquietar. *You need less* cogito, *more* lacrimar, *and lots of* requietum . . .

It wasn't just in my head. New, unpleasant things were happening in my body, too. I developed a twitch in my left eye that wouldn't go away. Every minute or so I felt it, like a moth adjusting a wing. My neck ached constantly, as if I'd slung a five-pound weight around the back of my head. My ribs felt as if they were wrapped too tightly around my lungs; sometimes it was hard to take a deep breath.

I started carrying an old pill bottle of Xanax in my purse like a talisman. The psychiatrist had prescribed the pills years ago; I rarely took one because they made me feel dopey when I needed to be alert. Now it gave me a little comfort knowing they were there, just in case.

At night, while the kids slept and Brian toiled away in his office, I pulled out the cognitive behavior therapy workbook I'd used, years ago, to try to manage my anxiety. I scanned through the affirmations (*I'm safe in body and mind*), but they seemed ridiculous. I *wasn't* safe in body and mind. I was a train wreck.

I flipped to the meditation exercises and decided to try one about lying on a beach. I set the book down on the bed, settled myself into a comfortable, cross-legged position, and closed my eyes. I took a few deep, relaxing breaths, and tried to imagine the sound of ocean waves. But instead of seeing sand and blue-green water, I saw something else that made my heart pound.

It was the recurring vision I'd started having recently. It wasn't exactly a hallucination; it was more like a thought that came and went, a waking dream over which I had no control. It came in flashes sometimes while I sat in meetings or at my computer, or now, while trying to meditate. In the vision, my mind appeared before me as a physical place, inviting me to explore. It was a dark and reddish landscape, like the surface of Mars, smooth in some places, pockmarked in others, with distant hills and vast open space. It was always nighttime there. I had a feeling the space went on forever. There were no limits. My mind was big and wide enough to include the most terrible places: Guantánamo, the New York City sewers, the killing fields of Cambodia, San Quentin. I felt acutely aware that I could go to any of these places, these different forms of hell on earth. I was afraid of losing myself in this vision, of turning a corner and finding myself in one of those places.

The other place I could go was madness. Madness didn't have a specific geography associated with it. It was like a dark moving storm or a black hole that I might stumble into by accident, and then I wouldn't be able to find my way out.

I quickly opened my eyes. Meditation had helped center me years ago, but now I was certain it would be the quickest road to madness. I finally understood what the writer Anne Lamott meant when she said, "My mind is a bad neighborhood I try not to go into alone."

BRIAN'S PROJECT FINALLY ENDED in late March. Vlad loved the design and praised the team for a job well done. We no longer cared. Brian had gained fifteen pounds from stress; he just wanted to put the project behind him as quickly as possible. Our birthdays, just four days apart, were coming up, and Brian suggested we throw a party to celebrate.

The day before the party, I ran errands while Brian stayed home with the kids.

I passed one gray warehouse after another on my way to Target. The black leather steering wheel grew sticky under my sweaty grip. I rolled down the window to let in some air, and sounds of freeway traffic rushed into the car, like the roar of a waterfall.

Suddenly, I knew the whole thing was wrong. The party was wrong. My attitude was wrong. Everything was wrong. The last few months had been a carnival ride of constant motion that left me dizzy and sick to my stomach. I wanted off. I wanted someone to pull the brake. I wanted to make it stop, but I didn't know how to make it stop. I didn't even know what stopping meant.

That's when I got the feeling that something horrible was about to happen. It was a feeling I knew all too well, a ghost pressing down on my chest. I pulled off the road onto the shoulder, kicking up pebbles and dust. Adrenaline shot through my body like an electric jolt.

The thing I'd been dreading was happening now. At least this time the kids weren't in the car.

My heart pounded in my chest. My head hurt. My hands shook. I heard a familiar sound in my head, the electric drone of cicadas.

This will be over soon, I thought. *This feeling will pass and you'll still be here.*

I took several slow, deep breaths.

The sun pounded through the windshield. A truck rumbled down the frontage road, piled high with stacks of cardboard held together with twine. I watched a crow the size of a large cat alight on a telephone wire. The drone in my ears slowly died to a faint hum.

I fumbled for my phone inside my purse. There was only one person I wanted to talk to in that moment. Brian picked up on the second ring.

I SHOWED UP FOR WORK MONDAY prepared to give my notice, but there was no one to give it *to*. Stella had just left for a vacation in Mexico. Vicente, too, was on vacation that week with his family. Norm and I were in charge.

I've been doing this for almost six years, I thought. *Surely I can get through ten more days.* I coasted through meetings that morning, cried through lunch, dried my eyes, then stepped back into the river of meetings. I cried silently on my commute home, dried my eyes, then picked up the kids.

That night, when the dinner dishes were put away and the children were tucked safely in bed, Brian slumped on a chair in the kitchen while I stood behind him, cutting his hair with the electric clippers. We were hollow shells of the people we once were. Silent, beaten. There was no point discussing it.

His dark hair, now turning salt and pepper, fell in big balls of fluff on the birch wood floor like small tumbleweeds. There was noticeably more white, silver, and gray than the last time I cut it, only a few months before.

We cleaned up again and fell into bed. I wanted to sleep, but my mind wouldn't let me. I started shaking, violently, as if I was standing naked on a glacier, floating in a dark sea. Was this a panic attack? It couldn't be. This wasn't how I experienced panic attacks. What was going on? Where were the cicadas? Now I *was* panicking. I had a terrible, detached feeling, as if I were not really in my body but just watching as some woman lay shaking uncontrollably in her bed.

She wakes her husband. She tells him something is wrong. Her mouth is dry and she can't drink enough water and now she has to go to the bathroom, as if someone has just administered an enema. Inside her brain and bowels, alarms are going off, red lights are flashing. EVACUATE! EVERYBODY! TIME TO BAIL OUT!

Now she is sitting on the toilet and her husband is talking softly to her. He is visibly frightened. He doesn't understand what is happening. Should he call someone? Who? He closes the bathroom door so the children won't wake up.

He starts running a bath. She climbs in with his help. She is so cold. The room starts to fill with steam. Her bones are cold. He holds her hand and murmurs reassurances.

"You're not going crazy . . . This is not how people go crazy . . . When people go crazy, they don't know they're doing it . . ." His voice purls with the sound of running water. "You just have anxiety . . . We're going to take care of you . . . You just need rest . . ."

As the water fills the tub, the shaking begins to subside.

"Okay," I said. Brian was Brian again, and I was me. "I'm here. I'm back."

I was sweating a little now from the hot water. He helped me out of the claw-foot tub as if he were supporting a frail old woman. He dried me off with a white towel, helped me into his comfy cotton pajamas that I often wore, and escorted me back to bed.

I lay down with my head on his shoulder and he rubbed my scalp gently with the pads of his fingers until I fell asleep.

At 2:45 AM I woke with a start, heart pounding.

It's just anxiety, I told my heart. *We're going to get rid of it. It's just anxiety.*

After a few minutes, my heart slowed to its normal rhythm. I curled up behind Brian and put my hand under his T-shirt. He was always warm, like a human-size potato just out of the oven. I drifted back to sleep.

ANOTHER WEEK WENT BY. To this day, I don't know how I managed to keep going to work. I continued to have panic attacks, crying attacks, and could barely keep food down, but I kept doing my job. No one seemed to notice anything different.

By the end of that week, I was jumping out of my skin. I had to tell someone I was quitting and be done with it, but Stella was still in Mexico. I couldn't just not show up, could I? If I was going to ever work again, I would need references. What would my coworkers say? *She couldn't take the stress. She abandoned us.*

I had to wait until Stella returned, and quit the normal way, the proper way. In the meantime, I needed to tell someone besides Brian that I was quitting. I wrote an email and sent it to my sister and a few other friends. Nine women in all.

Dear friends,

I need your help. This is going to sound crazy, but I'm feeling a little crazy right now.

As you probably know, I have been struggling for a long time to hold on to a pretty demanding full-time job in San Francisco and still be a mom.

Maybe some people can live this way and be happy, but it's always been uncomfortable for me. I've thought about quitting on and off for a long time, but my job pays well, people treat me well, it's a great company, and I haven't been able to make myself leave.

The last few months, things have become unbearable. It's alarming how bad I feel. I've finally reached the point where I need to make a big change. So I've decided to quit.

This is where you come in. My boss is on vacation and I need to tell someone I'm quitting, to hold me accountable so I don't chicken out when my boss comes back.

Will you be my witnesses?

I QUIT.

There. I did it.

Please send positive thoughts my way. I'll take prayers, whatever you got. Maybe we'll get to see each other more when I'm trying to live a sane life again.

Love,
Katrina

Over the next day, the emails came back. Alma was a full-time attorney with a boy a little older than Jake. We used to be close but hadn't talked in months.

I support you 100%. I too have felt exactly like you and I only have one child! You are an inspiration! Please, please let me know whatever you need in the weeks to come.

Rebecca also worked full-time and had two kids.

I believe in you completely. You are a clear thinker, a great decision-maker, and I trust that you need to leave that job. Your physical and mental well-being are essential for the health of those beautiful babies. It is not possible to "have it all" the way "it" is supposed to look. We all know it. The family bears the brunt. We crumble inside.

My friend Gillian left a full-time office job around the time we met to be a part-time dance instructor and massage therapist.

I wish for you to feel empowered by your decision, as you are taking back control over your time. I know it feels scary because it's a leap into the unknown, but it's your leap, directed by your own will, not because someone says "jump."

These women didn't think I was crazy at all. Everyone was so encouraging. I stored up the compliments and their offers to watch the kids like a squirrel with a pile of nuts. I didn't want to eat them yet; I just wanted to hold on to them, look at them every once in a while. They were small things, but they gave me brief moments of peace.

Stella made her grand return at ten thirty on Wednesday morning. Her voice floated up to my desk on the mezzanine, as she made her way from the back door, then down the stairs to the main floor, greeting people along the way. She dropped her laptop bag with a loud plop next to her desk.

People stopped by in ones and twos to welcome her back. I couldn't hear everything they said, but I could hear everything Stella said. She was always loud—when she was happy, when she was excited, when she was upset, or when she was just regular Stella. But when she got back from vacation, she seemed even larger and louder. It was as if, in her absence, the office had started to shrink in on itself, and when she returned, she immediately pushed the walls back out again.

"Stella! *Mumble mumble mumble mumble?*"

"Hi, guys! It was great!"

"*Mumble mumble mumble.*"

"Oh really? Do I look that tan? I used sunblock . . ."

I pulled up her calendar, found the first available time for that afternoon, and blocked out an hour.

"WHAT IS THIS ABOUT?" Stella asked, smiling. "I'm not in trouble, am I?"

I shut the door of Conference Room B (*B is for "Breakdown"!*) and sat down on a stool opposite her.

"No, but this isn't going to be a fun conversation."

Her face fell. "Uh oh."

"It's okay. Everything's okay. It's just that I'm quitting."

"You're quitting? Here?"

"Yes."

"What's going on?"

"I'm burned out, Stella. I can't do it anymore." This came off sounding casual, like when someone says, "I'm going to kill him" or "It makes me want to gag," but it was the literal truth.

A lot of emotions crossed Stella's face in quick succession, including a flash of anger. This was not what she wanted to hear on her first day back from vacation. She decided to lead with that one.

"You know, your timing is not great, Katrina."

"I'm sorry. I know. There's no good time to quit this job."

"But you haven't given me any warning! I didn't even know you were unhappy. Can't you give me some time?"

"Stella, I'm done. I'm really done. It's not you. It's not the company. I'm just done."

Wow, did this ever feel like a breakup. *It's not you, it's me . . . Can we still be friends?*

"C'mon. Let's go for a walk," she said.

"Don't you have another meeting at two?"

"This is more important."

I grabbed my sweater and keys and followed her out the door.

For the next hour, we plodded through the neighborhood while Stella laid on every ounce of charm and compassion she possessed. She said I couldn't quit. I was the personality of the company. I *was* Dogstar Studio. Then she wanted to know why. I tried to tell her, but it was difficult to talk about, because at a glance, her life looked a lot like mine. She had two kids. She had the same commute from Oakland. Her husband also worked full-time.

"But I'm doing it," she said, right on cue.

"I don't know how you do it," I said lamely. I just wanted to end the competition. She wins, I lose. Give her the trophy and let me go home.

She decided to switch gears, to invent a new job for me on the spot, something that I could do part-time, that didn't involve management. She begged me to give her more time. I was still wrapping up the April project, and Stella had some burning deadlines of her own. We just needed to get our work done, so we could figure this out.

"Just don't make a decision yet," she said. "You owe me a little time."

So I agreed. Yes, let's just get through these deadlines. We'll talk next week.

I *had* chickened out.

WHY WE'RE SADDER
THAN OUR MOTHERS

In the last few years, studies on human happiness have become all the rage. One study in particular caused quite a stir in 2009 when it showed that women's happiness has declined both absolutely and relative to that of men. In other words, we are less happy than our mothers were, and less happy than our husbands and boyfriends and brothers are.

How is this possible? We have more money than our mothers did. We have more independence. We're healthier and better educated, too. It doesn't make sense, right?

There has been much speculation about the cause of this disheartening trend: Maybe women feel too much pressure to achieve. Maybe we don't really want to work. Maybe we're unhappy because more of us are single mothers. Maybe we're trying too hard to be like men.

But none of those arguments sound right to

me. Here's what does: Our lives have changed dramatically since the '60s, but the institutions around us—government, workplace, and marriage—have not kept up. Mothers today are on the front lines of a deep dysfunction in society, trying to make up for the fact that there aren't enough hours in the day to do everything that is now expected of us. This, I believe, is a big reason why we are less happy than our mothers were.

But why do men in these studies appear to be getting *happier?* After all, men today are doing more housework and child care and experiencing more job stress than their fathers. On the other hand, men still aren't carrying their share of the load at home, and they still have more leisure time than women, time when they may work out at the gym or meet friends for a beer to watch the football game.

Meanwhile, women have so little leisure time that, according to Christine Carter, a well-regarded expert on happiness (yes, there is such a thing, and she has a PhD to prove it), we have "fewer strong and frequent social connections than women did forty years ago."

This is important. Studies show again and again that social ties are crucial to our sense of well-being. One of the many things we have lost, in our exhausting attempt to "have it all," is time to have friends.

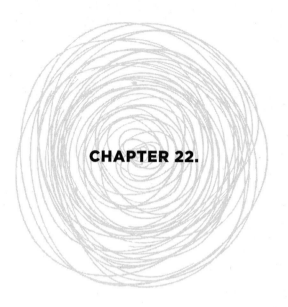

CHAPTER 22.

THE FOLLOWING MONDAY MORNING, I woke up sick. My body ached and it hurt to swallow. Jake had come down with something on Friday. On Saturday, Martha and Ruby got it, then Brian, too, one after the other, like a daisy chain of illness. Now, it was my turn.

It was an unusually hot morning for spring in the Bay Area. I picked out my green skirt, fresh from the dry cleaner, and a blousy short-sleeved top. I didn't know it, but I was getting dressed for my last day of work.

Stella and I had barely spoken since Wednesday; we'd both been too busy. In that time, the anxiety and depression I'd been feeling had faded from gray to black. Dread sat in my stomach like a ball of raw dough. No part of me wanted to go to the office, but we had yet another big pitch. I didn't know who else from the leadership team was going, and I didn't want to risk losing the project. Unemployment was now 9 percent. We needed every client we could get.

AFTER THE USUAL STRING OF MORNING meetings, Kimberly pulled her Prius into the alley behind the office. Stella climbed in front. I squeezed in back with Beth, one of my design directors. We headed down Second Street, toward Brannan, and parked in a lot next to the big flower market. It smelled like gardenias and car fumes.

It was almost ninety degrees by now. We weren't used to this heat and felt sticky and gross in our nice pitch clothes, like miserable little girls in their starchy new Easter dresses.

"Can you check my butt?" I said to Beth. "I feel like I'm sweating through my skirt."

She laughed. "You look fine. Can you check mine?"

The prospective client was a nonprofit organization that supported independent filmmakers. Their office was cool in both senses of the word. The large windows and exposed beams were a refreshing change from the soul-killing cubicle farms where some of our tech clients had their headquarters.

I couldn't shake the (now familiar) feeling that something bad was going to happen.

Nothing bad is going to happen, I told myself, just as I was taught to do, years before. *You can relax.*

Someone led us into a large conference room where framed movie posters hung from two walls. I recognized one of the films—a documentary about a Vietnamese girl who was adopted by Americans. I'd met the filmmaker when I was in grad school; in fact, she'd asked me to be her assistant editor. I'd turned her down to take my first Internet job. That was a lifetime ago. I was only thirty-seven years old, but I felt ancient, used up.

Everyone started settling—setting up the projector, exchanging names and business cards, smiles and handshakes.

"Hi, I'm Beth."

"Hi, Beth. I'm John."

"Hi, John. I'm Stella."

"Did you find parking okay?"

"How hot is it out there?"

I placed my notebook and cards on the conference table, hung a sweater I didn't need on the back of a chair, then wandered into the hall to look for a bathroom. In the stall, I fished around in my purse for the old bottle of Xanax, pried off the childproof top, shook out a small white pill, and bit off half. A whole one would make me sleepy. Bitter chalk taste. I drank from my cupped hand at the sink to wash it down.

Back in the conference room, more than a dozen people had gathered, seven or eight from the prospective client, our four, plus two more from our technology partner's company. We designed the websites and they built them.

"Let's get started!" Stella said. She stood up.

Someone dimmed the lights and someone else lowered the shade. Again I felt the pressure on my chest and then a tingling sensation down my arms and up the back of my neck.

It was our standard ninety-minute pitch. I had put most of it together the night before, after the kids went to bed, then sent it to Stella, who put in the finishing touches that morning.

"We're so happy you invited us here today," Stella said with genuine warmth. "Let me tell you a little bit about Dogstar. We're a user-centered design firm. Our job is to design things people love to use . . ."

Her Staten Island accent always got stronger at times like this, when she had something to prove.

"We're organized into four disciplines: user experience, visual design, technology, and project management . . ." Stella continued.

As she spoke, she clicked through slides of Dogstar employees working at our office. Huddled around a conference table. Waving our arms in animated discussion. Gazing thoughtfully at a diagram drawn in green marker on a whiteboard. We appeared earnest and enthusiastic, young and trendy.

Everything's fine. Everything's going to be just fine.

"Most of our work is for the web, but occasionally we design print pieces . . ."

She flipped through screenshots of our work. If you believe that a website can be beautiful, then these images were beautiful, each one a rectangular jewel. A home page for a sneaker company, a science museum, a nonprofit foundation, a brokerage, an online retailer. One after another, *click-click-click.*

"Oops. There I am wearing the same shirt," Stella said as she passed a picture of herself in the same short-sleeved checkered shirt that she was wearing today. "Now you know I only have one shirt!"

Everyone laughed. It was a genuine laugh, not an uptight Haha, now-please-move-on laugh.

Things are going well, I told myself.

What if you lose your train of thought again?

I won't. See? I'm making notes right now so that won't happen.

What if you really lose your shit?

That has never happened. I am always in control. I've done this a million times.

You're getting worse. What if you lose your train of thought? What if you make a total fool of yourself?

Why would I do that?

Because you're going crazy. What if you just burst into tears, or start yelling, or run out of the room?

I'm not getting worse. I'm just—

"Katrina, can you explain what your team does?" Stella said.

"Sure!"

I pushed back my chair, stood up, turned toward the full group, and smiled.

"The user experience group leads all research and strategy efforts for our projects. We interview people who represent your target audience and run usability tests of your current site . . ."

It's going to happen. It's going to happen RIGHT NOW.

My mouth kept emitting words, but I no longer heard what I was saying. Blood pounded in my ears. My head was filled with the electric hum of cicadas. I wondered if Beth, seated next to me, could see my hands shaking.

Why did this keep happening? And why wasn't the fucking Xanax kicking in?

"Then we translate these findings into a site map and schematics so that we can think through the architecture of your site. Our work is very iterative . . ."

One or two people nodded. Good. I was still making sense.

At some point, I'm not sure when, my mouth stopped moving. Was I done? Everyone turned toward Kimberly. It was her turn. I was done.

Quietly I grabbed my purse and slipped out to the bathroom again.

Some days it's just bad, I told myself as I swallowed the other half pill. *It doesn't mean anything. Just get through the next twenty minutes until the Xanax kicks in.*

But the Xanax didn't kick in. For the next hour, I could feel myself slowly unraveling, like a giant ball of thick green yarn, piling up on the floor. I wanted to scream. I wanted to scream so badly. If I could just scream, then the terrible thing I was so afraid of would be happening. It would be a relief. Staying in my seat felt almost, but not quite, impossible.

You're going to scream. You're going to scream RIGHT NOW.

Our tech partners gave their spiel. The client told us about their project, and Kimberly and Stella peppered them with questions to show how smart we were. I kept not screaming. I managed to present one of our case studies, looking down at my notes the whole time. Fuck eye contact.

At 3:00 PM sharp it was over.

"You feeling okay?" Stella asked on the way to the car.

"No," I croaked. "I'm not."

"Why don't you go home early? Take a sick day tomorrow," she said casually. "You probably need some rest."

"Yeah, that's a good idea. I might do that."

I did take the next day off. I lay on the couch in the living room and cried. Every once in a while I got up to go to the bathroom or drink a glass of water. Then I lay back down and cried some more.

At 5:00 PM, I dried my eyes and picked up Ruby from kindergarten. She doodled in her notebook while I drove to Jake's day care and picked him up. Back home, they watched PBS cartoons while I popped another Xanax, steamed some broccoli, and made organic mac and cheese from a box. It was the one dinner Ruby would eat without an argument, and I couldn't bear an argument.

At some point, Brian came home from a client meeting, dropped his laptop bag on the toy box in the family room, took one look at me, and said, "Oh, honey. I'm so sorry."

I didn't say anything. I just stared at him mournfully.

"Go upstairs and lie down," he said gently. "I'll do the kids."

I walked up the stairs and curled up on our bed. New tears started to flow.

An hour later, after tucking our two kids in bed and calling Martha at her mom's house to say good night, Brian came in to check on me.

"Do you want to talk about it?"

"No. I just want to cry. Will you sit here with me?"

"Of course," he said. He changed into a T-shirt and his light blue pajama bottoms, took a swig of cough syrup straight from the bottle, sat down, and leaned back against the headboard. I rested my head on his thigh and he smoothed my hair while I cried and cried and cried and he coughed and coughed and coughed, until we were both too tired to continue.

The next day was Wednesday. Earth Day. Brian took Ruby to school and Jake to day care. I took a deep breath and when I thought I could keep my voice steady, I called Stella on her cell phone. I told her I couldn't come in to work. Then I burst into tears again. Where were they all coming from?

"I'm melting down," I blurted out between sobs.

"Stay home, Katrina," she said quickly. She'd never heard me like this before. "Get some rest. Take a nap. Do some yoga." She went on this way, nervously giving me advice. I knew she couldn't bear to hear me cry. I felt sorry for her. "We can handle things. We're fine. You're just overtired. You should really do some yoga, Katrina. Or a bike ride. Go ride your bike. Or get a massage. Do you ever go to Piedmont Springs? You should get a massage . . ."

We agreed I should take a month off. I had some vacation and sick time left, and Stella kicked in an extra week of vacation. It sounded generous. In fact, it *was* generous. But I already knew it wasn't enough. I wouldn't be back in a month.

I hung up and immediately started thinking about my team, those eight people I had recruited and hired and managed over the past five and a half years. I was going to have to tell them something. And then there were the project managers. And my freelancers. And Norm, the head of the visual design group. I lay down on the couch with the phone and a staff list and methodically went through every name. It took the better part of the day.

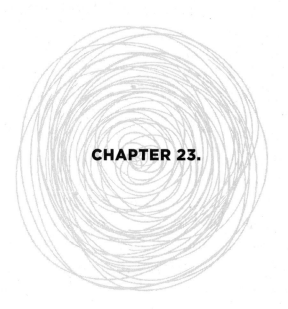

CHAPTER 23.

I WISH I COULD TELL YOU I QUIT my job, took a few weeks to recuperate, and emerged refreshed and ready to embrace a new chapter in my life. If I had quit seven months earlier, that might have happened. Maybe if I had hit the reset button then, before our ghastly winter, before Vlad and April, perhaps I'd have just quietly stepped away from my career, like so many other moms I knew.

This is what happened instead: The first few days after I stopped working, I cried constantly. I woke up in the middle of the night, shaking, heart pounding, unable to go back to sleep. I imagined myself as a car that had run out of gas. I just needed to refuel. But the days turned into weeks, and I wasn't getting any better. I hadn't run out of gas; I'd run out of *oil*. My internal machinery had ground against itself and fused. If you could have lifted my hood, acrid, thick smoke would have billowed out.

I continued to cry on the couch. Sometimes I would move from the couch to my bed, where I stared at the dark reddish purple leaves of the plum tree in our backyard. When the wind blew through the branches, the underside of the leaves looked silvery blue, like the bloom of a raisin. It was entrancing, like watching goldfish swimming in a bowl. Always moving but never going anywhere.

Brian had started a new project. Every few hours, he took a break from his work to come inside, stroke my hair, and say reassuring things.

"You're home. Everything's going to be okay. You just need a long rest," he said over and over.

He was remarkably upbeat, considering his wife had just lost her mind. The tension that had steadily grown between us since I started back full-time had evaporated. There was nothing to fight about anymore. It was as if Brian had been expecting this, and now that I'd finally collapsed, it was a relief to him. Now there was something he could do. For starters, he could take care of the kids.

Cruel irony. I had yearned for years to have more time with my children. Now that I finally had time, being around them was a torment. I felt as if my ears would bleed from their shrieks and happy squeals. I loved them, of course. I never stopped loving them and being their mother, but all I wanted was to lie down, alone, in profound silence. I wanted one of those sensory-deprivation tanks with no light and no sound, so quiet that silence itself became a noise. I would lie there until every thought stopped, until I was as relaxed as a boiled egg noodle. And still I would not move. I would stay until I was good and bored. I hadn't been bored in years. It sounded like such a luxury. I would go on lying there, in my dark, silent little tank, until the arid landscape of my bones grew moist, until it started to rain in the desert, until I felt the rustle of wildlife, until the birds began a new song, until I felt completely whole and human and alive again.

How long? I wondered. *How long would that take?*

I made an appointment with Dr. Lite, my psychiatrist, a few days after I stopped working. I hadn't seen her in five years, since Ruby was a baby. This time, I wasn't going to sign up for any classes. I longed to be fixed, once and for all. I wanted Dr. Lite to pull a high-tech vacuum cleaner out from underneath her desk and suck the misery right out of me. A Misery Removal Machine. Absent that, I was pretty sure I wanted drugs.

Dr. Lite looked exactly the same as I remembered her. Short, curly, brownish gray hair, no makeup, and that pleasantly asymmetrical gaze. After quickly listing my symptoms, like a truck stop waitress reciting the day's specials, I got to the point.

"I'm quitting my job," I said. I leaned back against the cool fabric of the couch. "That is . . . sort of. I'm on a leave of absence. I was planning to quit seven months ago, but then the economy tanked, so I stayed. I think I just got really burned out."

She narrowed her eyes and nodded almost imperceptibly. "Yes, that's what it sounds like."

I shifted forward again. "Dr. Lite, what's happening to me? Am I having a nervous breakdown?"

I hadn't said that phrase—*nervous breakdown*—out loud before, but as soon as I did, it sounded perfectly right, and strangely hopeful. Serious, yet temporary. Something I would get through, not something I had to live with. Reflecting on it much later, I could see that it also implied catharsis, an internal act of rebellion against the status quo. Like my spirit was going on strike to protest against the constant, mindless activity of my body.

"Well, we wouldn't call it a breakdown," Dr. Lite said. "That's not a medical term."

"What would you call it?"

She looked down at my file for several seconds, then back at me. "You may have a depression disorder and an anxiety disorder. Often people who are depressed have anxiety, but you may have both disorders."

"I have two *disorders?*" I said.

I didn't like the sound of this. I still don't. *Nervous breakdown* may not be an accepted medical term, but it neatly describes an *event*. Dr. Lite was describing a *pathology*.

She ran her index finger down a page of my file, then looked up again. "How do you feel about going on antidepressants?"

Now we were getting somewhere. She could call it whatever she liked as long as she made it go away.

"Will they make me feel better?" I asked.

"Many people find antidepressants are quite effective at relieving anxiety and depression."

Her tone reminded me of the disclaimers you hear at the end of drug commercials: *Individual results may vary*. She hadn't really answered my question, but then, what did I expect her to say? *Yes, they'll fix you right up, dear.*

"I'd like to start you on a new drug called Celexa," Dr. Lite continued. "It's a powerful drug that we use to treat both depression and anxiety. Unfortunately, it usually takes four to six weeks to start working."

Four to six weeks? I slumped back against the couch.

"There are some potential side effects," Dr. Lite continued, and then she began to list them. "Dry mouth, nausea, headaches, decreased sexual desire, night sweats, anxiety—"

Anxiety? Did she really just say that? It was like telling a drowning person to take one more big gulp of water.

My eyes filled with tears. Again.

"Dr. Lite, I don't know if I can do this. If I get any more anxious, I'll spontaneously combust."

"We can start you on a very low dose," she said, ignoring my hyperbole. Apparently, I was not her craziest patient. "You can work up to the *full therapeutic dose* slowly. That will minimize the side effects. But you won't get the benefits until you reach the *full therapeutic dose*." Each time she said the words *full therapeutic dose* she slowed down and enunciated each word with reverence, which made me think of a Catholic priest making the sign of the cross.

"I'll write you a prescription for Ativan as well." She swiveled back to her computer and started typing up the prescription, as if the matter were settled.

"You can take Ativan every four hours to minimize the anxiety symptoms," she said over her shoulder. "Once you've adjusted to the Celexa, we'll wean you off the Ativan."

Well, I thought, *I got what I came for.* I decided to trust Dr. Lite. She'd been right about the anxiety class. She obviously knew what she was doing, which made one of us.

When I got home that afternoon, I emptied my little white paper bag of medication on the kitchen table, as if I'd been out trick-or-treating.

"See?" I held up the two bottles to show Brian. "I've got my uppers, and I've got my downers."

"Just like Elvis," he observed. "All you're missing is the peanut butter and banana sandwich."

THREE WEEKS LATER, THE CELEXA began to kick in. In most respects, I felt the same—the crying, the loss of appetite, the insomnia. But now, in addition to my old, familiar anxiety, I had a sleek, new, pharmaceutical-grade brand of anxiety.

My old anxiety was like a horse I owned but had never broken in. Every once in a while I found myself astride his back. If I didn't hold on with everything I had, he would throw me to the ground and trample me with his thick muddy hooves. I'd learned to grip his mane, dig my knees in deep, and duck my head until he tired himself out. He always tired eventually. That wild, bucking, frothing-at-the-mouth energy could not be sustained.

This new anxiety was a whole other beast. It was more like a leopard that pounced with no warning. It made my heart race when it wouldn't normally race. If I had a panicky thought, a prickly heat immediately shot up my shoulders and then up the back of my neck. I tapped my hands on the table. I jiggled my foot whenever I sat down. I was jumping out of my skin.

I called Dr. Lite to tell her about these new symptoms.

"Believe it or not, Celexa is a powerful antianxiety drug, Katrina. You just need to give it time to work. How's the depression?"

I thought about it while I paced back and forth across the kitchen floor in my socks, occasionally crunching a stray Cheerio underfoot. "Maybe a little better. I feel really sad in the evenings, but I'm not crying as much."

"That's great! Have you raised the dose to twenty milligrams yet?"

I knew I was supposed to increase my dose the week before, but had decided to hold off. "Not yet," I said. Then, more brightly, "I'm almost there."

"Hmmm. Twenty milligrams is the *full therapeutic dose*. What are you at right now?"

"I'm still at fifteen."

"One and a half pills?"

"That's right."

She was silent. According to her instructions, I was supposed to be at two pills by now. And I would have been, if not for the fact that I wanted to climb the wall with my fingernails, perch on the curtain rod like a capuchin monkey, and leap onto people's heads when they walked by.

"I suppose you can give it a couple more days, but then you should *definitely* go up to twenty. If it bothers you, just take more Ativan until it evens out."

"I *am* taking the Ativan. I'm taking it three times a day." I expressed my concern that I'd get addicted to all this medication.

"You're overthinking this, Katrina. You'd have to be taking a much higher dose for many months before we'd worry about addiction."

"Oh," I said, embarrassed.

I got it now. I was a Pill Pussy. I should just take more of everything and stop overthinking.

After we hung up, I popped an Ativan, lay down on the bed, and went back to staring at the plum tree.

A MONTH LATER, DR. LITE CALLED at three o'clock sharp for our monthly check-in. I told her the depression was definitely improving, but the anxiety still came and went as it pleased, like an alcoholic ex-boyfriend with a house key. I couldn't sleep without Ativan.

"Have you quit your job yet?" she asked.

I'd *sort of* quit, except that Stella had talked me out of it again. She said there was no hurry to make a decision. So we were in limbo, waiting to see if I could get better and go back to work. But so far, I couldn't even bring myself to go in and clean off my desk. In fact, every time I thought about going back to the office, I literally felt I would vomit. I was waiting for that feeling to go away.

"It's a lot of pressure on us financially for me to just quit outright," I explained. "Who knows? Maybe I'll go back in a few months when I'm doing better."

Silence on the phone.

"Dr. Lite, are you still there?"

"I'm here."

I could imagine what she was thinking because I had thought the same things myself. If my job was so great, why couldn't I just go back to work? I had two arms and two legs. And if I couldn't go back to work, why didn't I just quit? Why was I being such a baby?

"Well," she said, "then we need to increase your meds. You should start taking thirty milligrams. I'll revise your prescription."

"Shouldn't we try twenty-five first?" I asked, trying not to sound alarmed. "I'm at twenty milligrams now. The full therapeutic dose." *The Father, the Son, and the Holy Ghost,* I thought.

Dr. Lite insisted I increase the dosage to thirty, and if I didn't feel better in two weeks, to forty. Now I was truly alarmed.

"Listen, I'm having a lot of trouble *sleeping* and I think it might be from these meds—"

She cut me off. "Usually when people take a leave of absence from work, they take a couple of weeks off and go back. You've been out more than *two months,* Katrina. I'm just trying to think of what else we can do." She paused for a moment, considering the options. "We have a clinic for people who come for daily treatment, but you know, that's for people who have one foot in the hospital. I think that's a little drastic for where you are. The only other thing we can do is get you in the boundary class."

"What boundary class?"

"It's for women who have trouble saying no, setting boundaries. It's very popular."

"You think I have a problem with boundaries?"

Dr. Lite sighed, then proceeded to list the facts with a tone of practiced patience. "You haven't quit your job yet. You tell me the symptoms are worse at night. I assume that's when you have your kids and they're asking you for things. What do you think?"

"I think it's hard to exercise your boundaries with a *two-year-old.*"

"Well, Katrina. Other people have two-year-olds, and they can function at work."

Ouch. She had me there. I took a deep breath. "You asked me what I think," I said. "I think I just tried to do too much for too long. I got way too stressed out, my nervous system short-circuited, and now I'm in a slow but steady recovery."

"I think you should take the boundary class," Dr. Lite said. Clearly, *she* didn't need a boundary class.

We arrived at a compromise of sorts. I agreed to call the number she gave me and she agreed to hold off on increasing my dosage.

As soon as we got off the phone, I popped another Ativan. Dr. Lite was stressing me out. I wasn't recovering on her timetable. I'd failed at being a working mom, now I was failing at my own cure.

I CALLED THE NUMBER for the boundary class, but the enrollment was full. It *was* very popular. I decided to crank up my own self-help regimen instead. I had already quit coffee, now I quit tea and all other forms of caffeine. I started a daily practice of yoga and meditation, which I did in the living room while the kids were at school and day care.

Summer came and went and my job was still in limbo. Things slowly started to get better. I began eating like a normal person. It became easier to be around the kids, and once in a while I ventured out to see friends. Still, when I thought about going to work, I felt physically ill. Finally, even I had to admit it—there was no salvaging this job. Luckily, Brian and I still had savings that we could use to supplement his income. I told Stella I wasn't going to come back.

Then, because I have issues with boundaries, I helped her find my replacement.

Life continued to improve in all respects save one: I still couldn't sleep without pills. Invariably, if I didn't take them, I woke up between 1:00 and 3:00 AM, heart pounding, and stared at the ceiling for two hours before I could fall sleep again. The circles under my eyes grew darker, and my chronic eye twitch returned, this time in my right eye.

Dr. Lite suggested I get analyzed in a sleep lab, so I packed up my pillow and spent a restless night at a nearby lab, with little white suction cups attached to my head and chest and legs.

The results came back a few weeks later, containing pages and pages of the most extraordinary, exotic, detailed findings. There was a problem with my "index of sleep arousals" and with something called RERAs, an intriguing acronym that was never spelled out. In sum, I had a "moderate" version of sleep apnea, a disorder that affects one's breathing and makes it difficult to get a restful night's sleep.

Dr. Lite received the results the same day I did and called me right away. She was exuberant.

"This could be what's causing your depression!" she said. "We need to get you an apnea machine so you can breathe at night. Katrina, if this works, all your problems may vanish!"

I'd never heard her sound like this before. She was positively triumphant. That's when I realized how much she cared. All her previous stubbornness had been born of frustration that she couldn't help me.

I started to get excited, too. Were all my problems really about to vanish? Was this why the last few years had been so hard? The more I thought about it, the more plausible it seemed. I'd always been a light sleeper. Even as a kid, I'd had bouts of insomnia, although never this bad. If it really was just sleep apnea, then the cure couldn't be more simple. I didn't need a pill. I needed an apnea machine. A Misery Removal Machine!

BACK AT MY HMO, a respiratory nurse patiently outfitted me with the very latest in artificial breathing technology, a CPAP (pronounced *SEE-pap*) machine.

"Our newest model," said the nurse. Her name tag read KAREN in gold letters.

The apparatus was a dark designer gray, slightly larger than a lunch box, with a corrugated hose that looped over my head. Three slim black straps held molded rubber nose plugs snug to my face.

"I gave you a medium," Karen said, looking critically at the fit of the nose plugs, which were plugged into my nose. "If those don't work, you can try the large."

The large? I thought. I knew I didn't have one of those cute button noses, but I'd never thought of myself as having a particularly *large* nose, either. Now, however, was not the time to be vain.

Karen snapped on the machine. Oxygen flowed up the vacuum-cleaner hose on top of my head and down through the nose plugs. When I opened my mouth, air whooshed out, as if I were a human leaf blower.

"Don't open your mouth," she said.

I closed my mouth and nodded.

I took the machine home for a two-week trial. I hated the Darth Vader breathing sounds, the itchy nose plugs, and sleeping with a hose on my head, but I used it faithfully. After all, if it worked, I was going to have to buy one—about $1,000. My insurance wasn't going to pay for it, so I had to be sure it worked for me.

After ten nights of this, I caught the worst head cold I've ever had. Eventually, I couldn't breathe through my nose at all, so I unplugged the machine and brought it back.

"I don't think it helped," I said. I could see Karen was disappointed. I sneezed. Not knowing what else to do about my breathing problem, she wrote me a referral to see a pulmonary doctor that same afternoon.

The pulmonary doctor was a middle-aged woman with kind

blue eyes who folded her hands on her lap while I explained my troubles. When I was done, she started asking questions.

"Are you sleepy during the day?"

"Tired? Yes. Sleepy . . . not really."

"Do you take naps?"

"I find it hard to nap," I told her.

"If you're not sleepy during the day, then you don't have sleep apnea."

I was flabbergasted. "What about the sleep test?"

"There are different ways to interpret the results," she said. "But the breathing issue that came up, that could be from the sleeping pills you're taking. They depress the central nervous system. They could definitely cause shallow breathing. Especially if you've been taking them for a while."

"I've been taking them for ten months."

"That could do it."

"But if I don't take them, I can't sleep!"

"Yes, well, the antidepressants you're on can cause insomnia in some individuals."

I waited a moment to let that sink in.

"And on top of it all, I got this horrible cold," I blurted out, for no other reason than I suddenly felt really sorry for myself.

"Oh, yes, that happens all the time," she said, without missing a beat. "The CPAP dries out your nasal passages and makes you more likely to catch a virus."

We smiled at each other. Because the whole thing was so stupid.

Let's recap here, shall we?

1. Trying to work full-time and raise young kids put my body under unendurable strain.

2. My body broke down.

3. The doctors decided that something was wrong with *me*, so they prescribed pills.

4. Those pills made it impossible to sleep, so they prescribed more pills.

5. The second pills screwed up my breathing and led to a diagnosis of sleep apnea.

6. The doctors gave me a machine to treat the sleep apnea I never had, which dried out my (medium-to-large) nose and made me sick.

I called Dr. Lite and told her the whole story.

"In conclusion," I said, as I kicked a stray Cheerio across the kitchen floor, "I don't think there's anything wrong with me. I just needed to quit my job, which I did. Finally. Now the only thing making me sick is the meds." I tried not to sound accusatory.

"There's a word for this," she said thoughtfully. "*Iatrogenic*. It means 'caused by the doctors.'"

At last, Dr. Lite and I could agree on something.

WOMEN ON THE VERGE OF A NERVOUS BREAKDOWN

When I stopped working at Dogstar, I was diagnosed with depression. As it turns out, I was in good company. Two years later, I posted a survey about working parents and stress on my blog. Of the hundreds of people who filled out the survey, 43 percent said they grappled with depression and 59 percent with anxiety *since becoming a working parent.*

The problem is not limited to people who happen to read my blog. Today, the number one prescription in the United States for adults under forty-four is antidepressants. More than 15 percent of American women are on them—making us two and a half times more likely than men to take them. Despite all our Happy Pills, studies show that women are less happy than men, and less happy than women of previous generations.

Around the time I was carting my Misery Removal Machine back to the HMO, *Newsweek* pub-

➤

lished a story called "The Depressing News about Antidepressants." It described some new studies that showed antidepressants may be no more effective than placebos, only worse because they come with a high price tag and a slew of side effects such as the ones I encountered.

This isn't to say that no one should take antidepressants. More than twenty-seven million Americans take them, and many (like my friend Lee) are certain that they need them. For all I know, they helped lift me out of the depths of my own depression. But they almost certainly made things worse during the period that will forever live in my memory as The Year I Couldn't Sleep.

I don't blame Dr. Lite for any of this, of course. By the time I dragged my sorry self into her office for the second time, I wasn't giving her much to work with. I was certifiably depressed, and she used the tools at her disposal to treat that depression, just as she was trained to do. And because I desperately wanted to believe in a miracle cure, I went along with it.

But now that years have passed, I'm certain that the root of my problem was not faulty brain chemistry. It was the chronic state of busyness, stress, and exhaustion that is all too common in families with young children and overworked parents. Here's *my* diagnosis: It is crazy to put working parents in impossible situations where they are bound to go crazy and then act as if there's something wrong with them for going crazy. This is not an individual pathology that can be solved with a pill (the effectiveness of which is now debatable). This is a massive cultural pathology.

Let me put it another way. Whether we have kids or not, Americans now work the longest hours of workers in any developed country. Surely, this is not good for our mental health.

But it does not have to be this way.

CHAPTER 24.

DURING THIS YEARLONG ADVENTURE with medication, other things were happening, of course. Soon after I went home sick from work, friends and family heard that I was in the midst of some sort of breakdown. They organically came together like atoms in a molecule, forming a support structure, so that no matter which way I fell, someone would be there to catch me.

The first week at home, my aunt Linda flew out from New Jersey. For seven days, she was a blur of cheerful activity. She cooked fragrant stews, roasted chicken, swept the floors, folded mountains of laundry, and thoroughly lavished the children with so much attention that they seemed completely unconcerned about the fact that Mommy barely ever got up from the couch.

After Linda left, Thania, who ran Jake's day care, offered to take the kids for a few hours on the weekend. Thania stood on our front porch after dropping off the kids and when I offered to pay, she shook her head emphatically and took a step backward.

"Oh, no, Katrina. We feel very lucky to have your family in our life," she said. "Let me do this for you. Your children are your heart. Let me take care of your heart."

My old housemate, Kat, came over one morning on the way to work and led me by the hand to our backyard. "Look at how beautiful your garden is, Katrina. This is what you worked so hard for," she said. I started to cry and she put an arm around my shoulders. "Now you can come home and enjoy it. You're in the perfect convalescent home!"

Gillian sometimes dropped by with food or little care packages of tea and bath salts, leaving them on the porch if I wasn't up to answering the door. Dinora started to leave meals in our fridge on Tuesdays when she came to clean. All kinds of Salvadoran delights: Tamales. Pupusas. Empanadas with salsa and cabbage salad. Like Thania, she refused to accept payment.

My friend David called once a week to check up on me. If I didn't answer, he left buoyant yet soulful messages that he was thinking about me and to call back if I wanted to, no pressure. My sister, too, called often. She usually skipped the preliminaries (*Are you eating? Are you sleeping?*) and went straight for the hardcore pep talk (*Katrina, this is a spiritual crisis. You are coming to terms with the meaning of your own life*). I found these talks incredibly reassuring.

My mother offered to be my own personal twenty-four-hour crisis hotline, saying I could call at any time, day or night. "You never have to worry about waking me," she said. "Just call."

Brian's parents offered to fly out to California, pick up all three kids, and take them back home with them to Detroit for a couple of weeks. It was a grand gesture, and although we didn't take them up on it, it was reassuring to know that they were there for us, too.

Brian was my biggest hero and champion through all of it. He kept up a relentlessly positive attitude, like a torch that never blew out. He took on the primary responsibility for the kids every evening for that first, hardest month so I didn't have to push through the dinner-to-bedtime routine alone. On weekends, he summoned all his strength to be the family clown, the activity director, the orchestrator of trips to the park and the beach. He never once showed resentment or impatience at my uselessness.

What an incredible feeling to be taken care of this way, after years of thinking the world would end without me.

Around the time I made the initial appointment with Dr. Lite, I also started seeing a wise and kind therapist named Randall, one-on-one. Randall insisted that I was not falling apart. I was falling into place.

"There is wisdom in your anxiety," he explained patiently. "It's been trying to talk to you all along, to tell you that this job wasn't working for you."

I suspected he was right.

ABOUT A MONTH AFTER I STOPPED working, I drove to Ruby's school to pick her up early. None of her friends went to her after-school program on Mondays, and although I was still at the stage when I'd rather be alone, staring at the leaves on the plum tree, it felt good to get her at 2:45 PM, instead of making her tough it out until almost dinnertime.

I arrived early and sat on a wooden bench to wait while other parents milled about the courtyard. I used to be so jealous of these parents, the ones who worked part-time, or not at all, who could pick up their kids when the bell rang instead of sending them to after-school care. *I guess I'm one of them now,* I thought ruefully.

Roma, another kindergarten mom, strode over, wearing elegant linen pants cut wide all the way to the ankle and pushing her three-year-old, Uma, in a stroller.

Roma had big brown eyes framed by long thick lashes and exuded an air of sultry competence. I met her on the first day of school—her oldest daughter, Tara, was in Ruby's kindergarten class. I instantly liked her and thought Roma and I would eventually become friends, but then it turned out I didn't have time for friends. She plopped herself down on the bench next to me and rummaged in her bag for Uma's sippy cup.

"So how are you?" she asked, as if we'd just spoken yesterday. It had probably been at least three months.

"Okay," I said. And then, because I couldn't think of anything else to say, I added, "Now that I'm not working."

She handed Uma her blue plastic cup and looked up sharply.

"Did you quit your job?"

"Uh, yeah, kind of."

"Did you get laid off?"

"No," I said, slightly embarrassed. "No, the truth is, I burned out."

"Oh," she said, with a solemn nod. Her eyes darted up and down me quickly, as if searching for physical signs of lunacy. I knew I didn't look good. There were circles under my eyes, and the lines around my mouth were more pronounced. Our bathroom scale said I weighed 112 pounds. I'd never been so thin; I barely recognized my body in the shower, the bony hips, the skeletal ribs.

"I'm not surprised," Roma said, leaning back on the bench. "I could tell you were headed that way."

"You *could?*"

"Yeah, I mean, you just had that *look*. I know because the same thing happened to me."

Roma, it turned out, had owned a successful food business. She published a cookbook and gave "cooking tours" in other countries. Her husband had a full-time job in advertising. They were a power couple.

"I was becoming so successful," she told me. "I was on The Path. Things were falling into place. Someone offered me my own TV show and I was planning for that but still hosting the tours. Tara was three, and Uma was still a baby, so I used to take them with me. But it got so I never stopped. I was always working, always with my kids, always trying to do too many things at once. My mind was always churning through my to-do list."

"It's awful, isn't it?" I said.

"It *is* awful. It was barbaric, trying to live that way. I went from being a fun-loving, cheerful supermom to being an irritable stress junkie. I stayed at my parents' house when we were on one of the tours and they watched me melt down right before their eyes. I was crying. I couldn't think clearly. I couldn't sleep. So I turned down the offer for the TV show, and I cut way back on work. I had to."

"That's so much like what happened to me," I said. "I'm probably going to take the summer off while I pull myself back together."

"Try a year," she said. "For me it's been *a year*. I'm still not ready to jump back into full-time work. It's hard for women like us who are ambitious. It's impossible, really. I think I aged more in these last couple years than I did in the previous ten."

Roma was blowing what was left of my mind. Up until that moment I had felt completely alone in my failure. How many other moms I knew had flamed out in their careers?

The bell rang. A moment later, Ruby came running out, minus the ponytails I put in that morning, messy hair tumbling over one eye. Her grin was as wide and open as a Kansas cornfield.

"Mommy! You're here!"

TWO MONTHS AFTER I STOPPED working, I started experiencing hours, then days, of feeling like myself. But always, the anxiety and depression would come back, like an unwanted guest, propping his dirty feet on the coffee table and cracking open a can of cheap beer. In between his visits, I wrote in my journal or took walks. I tried not to wonder what people were saying about my sudden disappearance at Dogstar or think about how I'd probably just ruined my career.

Often I had nightmares about work. Once, I dreamed that I went back to the office to clean off my desk. People approached me one by one, asking for things. ("Can you look at these schematics?" "Can you review this proposal?") I tried to answer their questions but they kept coming, one after another, without respite. Someone asked me to do a 4:00 PM meeting and I said I had to leave to get my kids. Everyone stood around my desk, staring at me blankly. Then I got angry.

"I don't even work here anymore!" I yelled. "Leave me alone! You're like paparazzi!"

"That's good, hon," Brian said the next morning when I told him about the dream. "You yelled at them. That's progress."

Another sign of progress: I began to want things. I wanted to eat meals, for example. As I regained my appetite, I began to want other things, too. I wanted to sit on the deck and feel the sun on my face. I wanted to read Jake a book. I wanted to draw cats with Ruby at the kitchen table. I wanted chocolate.

I began to cook again and do things around the house that needed to be done, like organizing the kids' clothes or washing the car. I tried to enjoy these chores, which I never enjoyed when I was rushing through them so I could get back to work. Now they became a moving meditation. It was satisfying to have an orderly closet, a clean car, a hot meal.

One day Thania called to say Jake was throwing up. Within minutes I was at her door. I lifted Jake up from where he was resting on the couch, and he slumped over my shoulder like a sack of rice. He was warm, but not alarmingly hot. He seemed to have gotten the vomiting out of his system.

When we got home, I stripped off Jake's smelly clothes, wiped him clean with a warm washcloth, and wrapped him in a fresh towel. He curled up on my chest. It felt so good to hold him on my lap, cuddly and limp. I didn't mind being home with a sick kid when that's all I had to do. It felt good and right, as if I were the sun shining down on him, as if just being in my arms was restoring all his vitamins.

I remembered a time when Ruby was about Jake's age and got strep throat. All she wanted was to lie on my chest in the rocking chair, but I had work to do and kept looking for opportunities to put her down. As soon as the antibiotics took hold, she was a wiggly, wriggly toddler again, and I was oddly disappointed. I didn't get enough time to hold her.

I refused to make the same mistake twice. I held Jake as long as he would let me, until eventually he scooched himself off my lap. I lay a towel down on the couch so he could lie on his tummy, and another one on top of him like a blanket. He was content to take occasional sips of apple juice and watch *Miss Spider* cartoons, with his feet partly tucked under my thigh. We sat that way for a long, long time.

AFTER I HAD THE ARGUMENT with Dr. Lite about my dosage, I ratcheted up the self-help. Every day I tried to meditate for at least a half hour. This was very difficult at first. I was still adjusting to the antidepressant and more restless than normal. When I closed my eyes, I saw the barren nighttime landscape of my mind stretching before me, and my heart started to pound.

Guided meditations helped. They gave my restless, grasping mind something more pleasant to hold on to. After a few weeks, I found I didn't need them anymore. I preferred to sit in silence.

Thoughts and questions and songs bubbled up randomly. When I noticed one of these bubbles rise up, I labeled it and let it go:

My shoulder hurts
Ruby's too young to have a fat obsession
Song: "Do You Know the Muffin Man"
What am I going to do with my life?
Jake—too much day care?
Does George Bush ever feel shame?

Thania—need to give her our extra toys
Song: "Forever Young"
I'm eating too much chocolate
Need to start dinner soon
What does my therapist think of me?

It would go on this way for a half hour. It was comforting to just let the thoughts go. Sitting still, I became aware that these thoughts did not own me. They were just thoughts.

One day while I was meditating, an idea came to me that was so powerful I had to open my eyes. I wanted to write about what had happened over these last few years. This was what I was going to do while I pulled myself back together. I began writing every day.

ONE SUNDAY IN LATE JUNE, I met my former coworker, Carol, at Lake Merritt for a walk in the early evening. This was a big deal for me—it was the first work friend I'd seen since my breakdown. I'd been half dreading getting together since she proposed it a few weeks before. I winced to think what rumors were being spread about me. But when I saw Carol waiting for me by her car, with her blond hair and lanky smile, arms outstretched to greet me in a hug, I knew it was the right thing to do.

We trotted down a small embankment to get to the path. The summer sun hung low in the sky, bathing the lake in golden light. All the birds were putting on a show: ducks and geese, a heron, an egret, and what Carol identified as a pair of grebes. People jogged and speed-walked past us, alone or in small groups, while others perched on benches staring out at the lake and listening to the music coming out of their white earbuds.

Carol began to fill me in on office happenings. Kimberly, the project manager I was working with before I left, had just abruptly taken her own leave of absence. She had sent a company-wide email saying she would be out for the next month.

"What happened?"

"Oh, she's just, you know . . . *maxed out,*" Carol said.

By now I knew this was working-mom code for "having some sort of a breakdown." Kimberly was a new mom with a son a bit younger than Jake; I had suspected for a while that she was feeling overwhelmed.

I felt a tingle of *schadenfreude,* that involuntary shiver of pleasure at another's misfortune. Kimberly was the least sympathetic of all the people I called that day in the spring to say I was taking a leave of absence. Almost immediately, I felt ashamed of my petty thoughts. What a hypocrite I was, so paranoid about what other people were thinking about me and at the same time so smug about another woman's crisis. In theory, Kimberly and I should have been friends, two working moms at the same company, managing the same over-the-edge client. But that never happened. Kimberly had one child and worked a four-day week. When she complained about the lack of sleep, the lack of personal time, instead of commiserating as a friend would, I only felt resentment—I had *three* kids to her *one* and worked *five* days, not *four.* And now here we were, the two of us, having our separate breakdowns.

Eventually, the conversation came around to me. I had planned to stick to my standard "just really maxed out" line, but when Carol looked straight at me and asked the magic question "How are you? I mean, *really,* how are you?" I told her the whole awful truth—how stressed I'd been for the last year, and how particularly painful the last few months had been.

"You did a great job hiding it, Katrina. No one had any idea. We were all shocked when you left."

"Really? No one had any idea?"

"*No one.* I mean, I think we could see you were under a lot of pressure, and we used to wonder how you did it all, but we didn't know it was so bad. After you left, Kimberly and I talked about how hard it is with just one kid, and you had three! Plus you were responsible for a team . . ."

"Yeah, I guess I didn't know it was that bad, either, until it was too late."

"Listen, Katrina, I haven't heard one person say anything bad about you. No one thinks you're weak because you had to leave. If you're worried about what other people are saying, you can just let that go."

I couldn't think of what to say, so I gave Carol a hug. It was exactly what I needed to hear.

SUMMER CAME AND WENT. I continued to argue with Dr. Lite about medication, struggle mightily with sleep, and wonder why I wasn't bouncing back more quickly. Just as Roma had forewarned, it was a full year before I felt able to work again.

You may be wondering how I could afford to stop working for a full year. In part, I got lucky. Despite the poor economy, Brian landed a full-time project that lasted that entire time, so we had steady income. By now we'd paid off all our debt except the house. We'd managed to save a cushion, not a huge one, but enough to supplement Brian's freelance income that year. Many times I thanked my lucky stars that we had not tried to buy a bigger house in a better neighborhood—a higher mortgage would have been unsustainable when I stopped working.

AS THE MONTHS WORE ON, more women came out of the woodwork with stories about burning out.

A mom from Jake's day care told me she had recently taken an extended disability leave for depression but couldn't afford to quit her job completely. Nor did she want to. She liked her job. She just didn't like the stress of working full-time while raising two young kids.

One of the moms from Ruby's school told me she developed a disturbing cough when her son was in preschool that plagued her for almost a year. None of the doctors could figure out what was wrong. She finally quit her full-time job in the software industry and enrolled in a graduate school program.

"How's your cough now?" I said.

"Gone," she said. "It was just stress. Stress is powerful stuff, isn't it?"

ONE EVENING, SOON AFTER I weaned myself off the medication and said good-bye to Dr. Lite, my friend Gillian came over with her kids for dinner. I bustled around the kitchen, boiling pasta and frying sausage I bought at the farmers' market that afternoon. Ruby and Gillian's older daughter, Maya, wandered upstairs to play, while Jake and Baby Tess did baby things on the floor. Even though her younger child was not yet sleeping through the night, Gillian looked radiant: voluptuous, oxytocin-mellow, her flawless complexion glowing with health. She sat on the floor, helping Jake fill a metal pot with wooden blocks.

"You know, I never really heard your story," I said. "Why you stopped working, I mean. Would you mind telling me?"

"When Maya was little?" she said. "Oh, God! I never *told* you?"

She told me the whole story. How she'd managed a billing department for an online directory, and how stressed she became after Maya was born and started full-time day care (at Thania's, which is where we eventually met).

This seemed wrong to her, to be away from Maya five days a week, but she couldn't discuss it with Maya's dad, Mateo, who had a completely different way of seeing the world.

"His ideas about child rearing are much simpler than mine," she said. "Make sure the kids are well fed and let them tag along while he works on his cars."

Often, Gillian felt alone in raising her child, alone in her job, alone in trying to save money or work toward any semblance of a good life. Soon after she returned to her job full-time, she planned a trip to North Carolina to visit family with her daughter. The night before the trip, she had her first panic attack. Mateo was already asleep when she finished packing. It was midnight, but Gillian wasn't ready to sleep. Her mind was racing.

Something is wrong, she thought. *Maybe we shouldn't fly.*

Then she started thinking about work. They would probably screw up the billing while she was gone. No one did it right but her. She'd probably come back from vacation to a big mess. Her heart started to pound. A prickly sensation crept up her hands and arms, neither warm nor cold. She heard a sound, like the sound she heard at the movies when the THX promo came on, a dissonant hum that started at eye level then dropped down to your gut.

I'm dying, she thought. *Some evil thing in me is coming out.*

"Mateo, wake up. Something's wrong."

She snapped on the light, then slid off the bed, and not knowing what to do, crouched on the wood floor on hands and knees, as she'd done in labor. She started crying. Mateo pulled himself out of bed and crouched on the floor with her, squinting out of one eye, sour sleep breath.

"I think I need you to take me to the hospital," she said.

"Gillian, *please.* Just come to bed. There's nothing wrong with you."

Gillian told me she doesn't remember what happened next, but eventually the terror must have subsided, because she fell asleep. The next day, she flew to North Carolina with Maya. It was a miserable visit; she was coming unraveled but trying to act as if she was fine. When she got home to Oakland, she called the office to say she couldn't come in.

"I'm sick," she said. Then, a few days later: "I'm *very* sick. I'll be out for a week."

As Gillian told me this story, I put the wooden spoon on the counter and listened, slack-jawed. It was so similar to mine. She stopped eating. She couldn't stand to be alone with her child. *What if it happens when I'm with her?* she worried.

Gillian's mother and Mateo disagreed about how to take care of her. Her mother thought Gillian needed around-the-clock pampering. Mateo insisted she was fine. There was nothing wrong. There were no broken bones. There was no blood. What could possibly be wrong?

Gillian kept having panic attacks, but she didn't know what they were. One night, she went to the emergency room. The doctors agreed with Mateo. Nothing wrong.

Gillian made an emergency appointment with a psychiatrist. He prescribed four kinds of pills. An antidepressant. Antianxiety medication. A third pill to help her sleep. And the fourth one?

"I want you to take this one for your husband," the psychiatrist said with a knowing smile. He was in his sixties or seventies. He had seen plenty of women like Gillian over the years. Hysterical women. "I call this the 'Be a Better Person Pill.' He'll like you more when you take this."

She took all the pills when he said to take them, even the one that was for Mateo, who frankly wasn't winning any awards for best partner at the time.

"When are you going back to work, baby?" Mateo asked impatiently.

After three weeks, Gillian did go back to work, finally, for one day. Just as she suspected, they'd screwed up the billing. It was an unholy mess.

"That's it," she said.

"What's it?" her boss asked.

"That's it. I'm not coming in anymore. It's over."

She drove away in her beat-up blue Volvo with no plan, no idea what to do next.

"All I knew is I wasn't going to have to go there anymore, and that made things seem a little more tolerable," she told me.

Dinner was on the table by this point in the story, and the kitchen was filled with the seductive scent of fried sausage. Gillian held Tess in her lap, who smacked her lips curiously at the food she was too young to eat.

"That's an incredible story," I said, as I spooned pasta onto Maya's plate. "I can't believe we never talked about it."

"Well, it took months to recover, and then I didn't *want* to talk about it," she said. "Mateo never understood what happened, and I stopped trying to explain it to him. I just wanted to move on with my life. That's when I started studying massage. In massage school we had to meditate every day, and of course, we practiced massage on each other. So I learned to relax in my body and I started a new life. And you know what?"

"What?"

"You're starting a new life, too."

MOMMY GUILT

As more mothers have entered the workforce, our level of guilt has increased. A 2009 survey by the Pew Research Center concluded:

> *Working mothers in particular are ambivalent about whether full-time work is the best thing for them or their children; they feel the tug of family much more acutely than do working fathers. As a result, most working mothers find themselves in a situation that they say is less than ideal.*

On my own website, I asked what was the hardest part about being a working parent. Not surprisingly, "guilt" was the top answer. Here is a ranked list of responses out of 554 people who answered the question (they were allowed to pick only one of the answers on the next page):

➤

- "Guilt that I can't do everything well" (41 percent)
- "Lack of time with kids" (24 percent)
- "Lack of time to myself" (16 percent)
- "Other (please specify)" (12 percent)
- "Lack of time with my partner" (5 percent)
- "N/A (It's not that hard)" (1 percent)

Of the 12 percent who answered "Other," the most common write-in answer was some version of "All of the above." One mom summed up the problem this way:

> I'm so tired of feeling like I don't measure up in every aspect of my life. Go to work? Miss time with kids. Work from home? Can't give undivided attention. House dirty, laundry piled up, kids sick. The thread is breaking.

CHAPTER 25.

THE HUMAN NERVOUS SYSTEM has evolved over millions of years in the struggle for survival. It includes two main divisions that work together in a delicate balance: the sympathetic and para-sympathetic nervous systems.

Your sympathetic nervous system mobilizes you for stressful situations—"fight or flight." When our ancestors were running away from bears, their sympathetic nervous systems would kick in, releasing hormones like adrenaline and cortisol to make their hearts beat faster and increase muscle strength. Very handy when you're running from a bear.

Your parasympathetic nervous system—sometimes known as "feed or breed"—has the opposite effect. It slows the body down, making it possible to digest our food, sleep, make babies, and do the other things that one does when not running for one's life.

The harmonious design of the nervous system is, in the parlance of my business, insanely great. (Unlike, say, the knee, which looks as if it were thrown together at the last minute after the budget ran out.) But here's the important part: These two complementary divisions are not meant to share the load equally. The fight-or-flight response is meant to be used occasionally. We are not designed to run from bear to bear, twelve hours a day.

Unfortunately, the juggling act of working and parenting can put you in a perpetual state of fight or flight. The adrenaline glands start producing stress hormones like mad. Chronic high levels of these hormones wreak havoc on our health. They can suppress thyroid function, decrease bone density and muscle tissue, raise our blood pressure, make it hard to think or sleep, lower our immunity, and create inflammation in the body, which is the basis for most disease. Eventually, the nervous system maxes out, and the body goes haywire. It can't stop even when it wants to.

This is what I've come to understand happened to me. I lived for six years with chronically high levels of adrenaline and cortisol. Gradually, but inevitably, it became impossible to think clearly, relax, sleep, or feel good in my body. I felt as if my actual nerves—those cables that run throughout our bodies like phone wires, carrying signals from the brain to our muscles and organs—had been fried. And they probably had.

It took a long time to work myself into that state, and it took a long time to come back. Trying to speed the healing process along only backfired. Impatience and hyperalertness, striving always to be in control—this is what gets so many of us in trouble in the first place.

Think of how we live: hunching over computers and smart phones, racing back and forth between the office and home, gulping down our food, using caffeine and sleeping pills to turn ourselves on and off at will. Many of us live almost *exclusively* in the realm of the mind. We're always thinking about what we've done or what we're about to do. We are never fully in our bodies. If anything, our bodies are an inconvenience. It takes time to eat, to wind down from the day, to go to the bathroom. Time when we should be working or picking up the kids from school.

Living in the realm of the mind gives us a false sense of control, as if we can merely *think* our way out of every problem. Headache? *Take a pill.* Neck hurts? *Buck up! It's not that bad.* Feeling anxious? *That's just your mind playing tricks on you. Ignore it!*

But the hard truth is that you are not an airy spirit. Nor are you a floating head with no body. You are an animal. I mean this kindly, the way the poet Mary Oliver does in her poem "Wild Geese":

> *You do not have to be good.*
> *You do not have to walk on your knees*
> *For a hundred miles through the desert, repenting.*
> *You only have to let the soft animal of your body love*
> *what it loves . . .*

Living in the "soft animal of your body" means you must respect the systems of that body. It doesn't work to say, "I shouldn't be this tired" or "I should stop being upset about this." You are tired. You are upset. When you ignore your body, it has ways of sending you messages: sore back, sore neck, a lingering cough, shortness of breath, insomnia, stomach trouble. Eventually, if we ignore the messages our bodies are sending us, there will be hell to pay. I didn't think I had time to take a sick day; instead, I ended up taking a whole sick year.

As the months went by, I learned to listen to my body, to slow down and accept healing on its own terms. When I did finally begin to relax, it felt as if the protective myelin sheath around my nerves began to thicken, like a down jacket, insulating me from harm. I could almost feel the nerves themselves regenerating, ever so slowly, like eyes budding on an old potato. The process was so gradual, and so riddled with setbacks, that it's impossible to pinpoint the exact day, week, or even month when it happened, but eventually I found I was better, meaning I could work and take care of my family and find enjoyment in my life. But I wasn't the same person I'd been. Some elasticity in me had disappeared, probably forever. Never again would I be able to take my body for granted.

THE ONE-YEAR MARK WAS an important milestone. That's when I started working again. Part-time at first, on the most boring, undemanding freelance projects I could dig up, but I was helping support my family, and that felt good. Around this same time, I started to write about my experiences on a blog, and I invited other women to share their stories of trying to work and raise children. At first, only my friends and relatives left comments, but as my readership grew, I began to hear from strangers around the country with stories eerily similar to mine.

I wrote about the humiliation of burning out. I wrote about the ways women judge each other and themselves. I wrote about guilt. More people left long comments about their experiences trying to work and raise kids. It was a relief to read these stories because they made me feel less crazy, less alone. They wrote from Connecticut, New York, Texas, Maryland, California, Tennessee. Many of them, like me, had tried to "have it all," then ended up "doing it all" and burning out. Women in other countries began to write in: the United Kingdom, Australia, Canada, France, Norway, and then more exotic places like Argentina and Indonesia. Life was not perfect for them, either, but more often than not, they pointed out how their situations were better, because they usually had more paid time off and didn't worry about losing their health insurance.

Some dads came out of the woodwork, too. One in particular, a dad from the Midwest, left an impression on me when he sent a long email detailing his experience as the primary parent when his wife went back to work. He maxed out trying to balance a part-time freelance career with full-time parenting, and chronicled his own saga with antidepressants and sleeping pills. What's more, he felt as if he wasn't living up to the role of traditional male breadwinner. In many ways, he and his wife had swapped gender stereotypes. She didn't appreciate how much he did at home and how his efforts made it possible for her to progress on her career path. He felt unappreciated and misunderstood. His story made me realize that men can be just as trapped by stereotypes as women.

It was amazing to me—all these people, all with variations on the same lament.

I began to immerse myself in research about parenting and work. It was worse than I could have possibly imagined. I found out that working and raising kids pretty much sucks across the board in America, for low- and high-income families alike. In Japan they have a word—*karoshi*—that means "death by overwork." Americans work longer hours than the Japanese. What word should we use to describe the physical and emotional impact this has on our health?

And yet, we need to work more than ever before. Low-income

families today earn 29 percent less than they did thirty years ago. Middle-income families earn 13 percent less. Only professional families are making more than they did in 1979 (7 percent more), but they're expected to work longer hours than ever.

So we keep working. The year I maxed out was the first year in history that half of all U.S. workers were women. Seventy percent of American children now live in households where all adults are employed.

SWEAT, EAT, SLEEP

On a very practical level, the key to managing extreme stress is understanding how to *calm* your sympathetic nervous system and *activate* your parasympathetic nervous system.

How?

I asked my sister, Holly, who knows a few things about stress. Not only is she a single mom with four kids, but she's also a firefighter and a paramedic trained to handle all kinds of medical emergencies. Holly is the closest thing I know to a real-life superhero. Her advice can be simplified into three words: Sweat, Eat, Sleep.

Sweat

"When people say to sweat it out, they mean sweat it out," Holly says. "You have to circulate those stress hormones out of your body." The best way to get rid of them is exercise.

➤

Now, I know that the last thing any exhausted parent wants to do is jump on the treadmill. But to get rid of those chemicals, you have to work out. Hard.

"Really push yourself," Holly says. "Run like you're running from a *bear.*"

If you can't run, bike or swim away from that bear. Aim for at least twenty or thirty minutes. If you belong to a gym, follow up with a few minutes in a hot tub or sauna to get a little extra sweating in.

Eat

After you've gotten rid of those stress hormones, the sympathetic nervous system is content. It has done its job. It can back off a little.

Now is the time to trigger your parasympathetic nervous system: You need to eat. Eating tells your body, *It's okay now. The bear is gone. You can come down from the tree, dear.* After all, you can't be in life-threatening danger if you're chewing.

Avoid the bad stuff: overprocessed foods, caffeine, sugar, and alcohol, because they put an unnecessary load on your nervous system. Raw food is good—perhaps because it requires more energy to digest, which is a nice, lazy way to absorb excess energy that you didn't sweat out at the gym.

And here's an extra-special trick that took me a lifetime to learn: Eat small amounts throughout the day. Every time you eat, you send another reassuring message to your parasympathetic nervous system: *Coast still clear . . . No bears!*

While you're at it, drink lots of water, which will help flush out any lingering stress hormones. Many people are dehydrated without realizing it, leading to more physical and mental stress. Most women need an average of 2.2 liters of water a day, according to experts at the Mayo Clinic. Men need 3.

Sleep

Sleep, essential during normal times, is even more important in times of extreme stress. Sleep helps mend your body at the cellular level, lowers your blood pressure, and enables your brain to process information from the day.

Hard exercise followed by strategic eating will help prepare your body for sleep. Sometimes that's not enough, and you need to try a more heavy-handed approach.

"When I'm having trouble winding down to sleep," Holly says, "I actually tell myself, 'There's no bear trying to eat your children. Everyone is safe. You can rest now.'"

➤

These three simple concepts—Sweat, Eat, Sleep—won't make you less busy. They won't make up for the fact that you have a demanding boss or that your husband doesn't do laundry. But they might help you back away from your edge in a particularly bad week.

CHAPTER 26.

AS I WRITE THIS, IT'S BEEN ALMOST four years since I burned out, and I think I finally understand what is happening all around me.

We are devastatingly overworked and simultaneously lack the government, workplace, and familial supports that exist in most other developed countries. The American Dream tells us if we just work hard enough, we'll get what we want. But the research shows that for working moms, hard work is not enough. The problem boils down to this: Most jobs do not accommodate people who have children.

Instead, we have this unwritten, unacknowledged, and unyielding expectation that working parents will make the accommodations necessary to do their jobs just as if they don't have children. If you don't like it, hire someone else to raise your children. And if you don't like that, then quit. Except, of course, you can't quit, because you can't get by on one income.

Well, then, if it's too much work, don't have babies!

And there you have it. America's delusion of rugged individualism, taken to its absurd conclusion: the end of the human race.

This may seem like a silly, made-up argument, but right now, more than ninety countries in Europe and Asia are experiencing a "global baby bust." The birthrate is so low in these countries that it has become a threat to their national security.

Why aren't women in these countries having more babies? Because the economics of family life have changed. Women are getting educated. They're joining the workforce. They're less inclined to voluntarily enslave themselves to caring for large families. You could say they're women who don't want to be on the verge of a nervous breakdown.

You don't want to help us out? they say. *Then raise your own future generation!*

Could this happen in America? Why not? Wouldn't you say that graduating more women from college than at any other time in history while simultaneously providing less support for working families than any industrialized nation in the world is practically *willing* it to happen?

In fact, it may already be happening. In 2009, the American birthrate slid to 2.0 (2.1 is considered replacement level). Then it continued to slide; in 2011, the U.S. birthrate hit 1.9, the lowest rate ever recorded. Some of this decline has been attributed to the global economic crisis that started in 2007, but the United States has seen a sharper decline over that same period than Europe. For the first time in recent memory, Americans are having fewer babies than the

French or the English. And there's no reason to believe the birthrate won't keep going down. As younger women see what's happening to the women like me, they may decide to stop at one child, or not to have any. And who could blame them?

Studies show that when women are given access to things like flexible work schedules and decent, affordable child care, the birthrate starts to inch closer to replacement levels again. It's not complicated. We just need a little helping hand.

THE POET WILLIAM BLAKE said, "What is now proved was once only imagined."

Let's take a moment to imagine a world where more people are involved in the work of caring for children. And by *people* I mean, specifically, er . . . *men*. How could this one fact change our government policies, the dynamics of the workplace, and our relationships with each other?

Recently I stumbled across a story in *The New York Times* by Katrin Bennhold that seemed to hold the answer. It described a quiet revolution that has been taking place in Sweden for the last two decades, affecting everything from the gender pay gap to workplace culture to relationships between parents and children. Here is the story in a nutshell:

Until quite recently, Sweden had many of the same problems with gender equality that we have in the United States; men and women were confined to traditional roles when it came to working and raising kids. Although the country offered more than a year of parental leave, mothers were traditionally the only ones who stayed home with the baby. Women made less money than men, and the 6 percent of fathers who did take time off were derided with a Swedish term that means "velvet dads" and stigmatized at work for being unmanly.

In 1995, in what turned out to be a bureaucratic stroke of genius, the Swedish government created financial incentives for men to take paternity leave. If the father didn't take time off, the family lost one month of subsidies. Suddenly it was like *Who cares if they call me a "velvet dad"? I'm not giving up free money!*

Soon it became the norm for dads to take off a month, two months, even longer. Men got a taste of what it was like to be the primary parent. They became more confident in their role at home, assuming those responsibilities traditionally left to the moms, such as clipping the children's fingernails. Dads started craving *more* time with their kids. Today, eight in ten fathers in Sweden now take a *third* of the total thirteen months of leave.

Those early months are a critical time for establishing bonds. Studies show that when fathers spend time taking care of infants, they are more likely to become involved parents as their children get older.

As everyone got used to the idea that dads would take time off, the culture at work began to change, with flextime becoming more common. The pay gap between men and women started to close. One study showed a mother's future earnings increased about 7 percent for every month the father took off.

And that's not all. Divorce rates started to go *down* in Sweden, at a time when they were rising in other countries. For the couples who did divorce, shared custody became more common. As the *Times* story explained, a "new definition of masculinity" began to emerge: Birgitta Ohlsson, European affairs minister, put it this way: "Machos with dinosaur values don't make the top-10 lists of attractive men in women's magazines anymore."

She continued, "Now men can have it all—a successful career and being a responsible daddy . . . It's a new kind of manly. It's more wholesome."

This simple little change—giving dads incentives to take parental leave—had a profound effect on employees, employers, women, men, and families.

And lest you think this could happen only in a little Scandinavian country, Germany (population eighty-two million) decided to try a similar experiment in 2007. In just two years, the number of fathers taking parental leave jumped from 3 percent to more than 20 percent.

Here in the United States we have a long way to go, of course. Among other things, we seem to have a life-threatening allergy to taxes. Many Americans choke and turn red in the face at the very mention of the word, even though our taxes are historically low and lower compared with most developed countries. We don't even have paid maternity leave for *mothers*. We scoff at comparisons with Sweden, presumably preferring the company of places like Papua New Guinea and Swaziland, which are among the few countries that do not provide some type of national paid parental leave. And the last few decades of "family values" have done nothing to create economic stability for families.

But the Swedish revolution gave me hope that change is possible, and solutions to these seemingly intractable problems may not be nearly as complicated as we expect. However we do it—whether it's through government incentives or some other type of intervention—*we need dads to get more actively involved as parents.*

ALMOST FOUR YEARS HAVE PASSED since that Saturday when I broke down on the way to Target. It's taken a lot of fine-tuning to get to this point, but I love my life as a working mom. For the last three years, I've maintained a steady stream of freelance work (which in this economy is something to be grateful for) and still get the time I need to be the kind of parent I want to be. And although I initially worried that writing so publicly about my experiences with burnout would ruin my future career prospects, it's had the opposite effect. Several leads for design work have come, not *in spite of* what I write, but *because* of it.

Writing about burnout has also improved some of my work relationships. Recently, a client asked me to collaborate with another design firm on a project. The lead designer from the other firm was less than friendly, and our first few meetings were strained. She seemed to feel threatened by my presence, as if I were going to steal business away from her company. So when she pulled me aside, a week later, to tell me she'd Googled me and found my blog, I felt my heart drop to my stomach.

"I just want to say thank you," she continued, with a meaningful look. "I was so moved by one of the posts you wrote. I sent it to everyone I know."

Career "experts" would tell you never to be as frank as I've been. They'd advise you to transform your nervous breakdown into a "sabbatical" or perhaps an ethnographic study of the behavioral health care system—anything to preserve the false narrative that you were in complete control of your life at all times. But I decided not to follow that advice, and here's what I learned instead: When you speak openheartedly, when you are true to your own experience, a lot of people will like you and want to work with you, even more than if you pretend to float sublimely above the messiness of your life.

I've worked with companies that spend ridiculous sums on corporate retreats and internal "messaging campaigns" to get people to work together better. But imagine how workplace culture would be transformed if everyone stopped posturing, fighting stupid turf wars, and trying to look like flawless mannequins and instead inhabited their own humanity.

Although I couldn't possibly have understood this at the time, it's obvious to me now that my breakdown has forced me to be a better person. Most important, I'm a better advocate for myself now, because I understand my limits. It's easier to set boundaries in my work, knowing that I don't have any other choice. And by making room for myself, I'm a more attentive mother, a less cranky wife, a more thoughtful friend, and a more engaged worker. I like to think that by making room for myself, I'm also giving others permission to do the same.

My relationship with my kids and with Brian is more relaxed, more spontaneous. When work is slow, I pick up the kids early, or Brian and I sneak out for a lunch date at a nearby restaurant.

There are trade-offs to this lifestyle, of course. Brian and I gave up on our dream of moving our family to a better neighborhood. And every once in a while, a client cancels a project suddenly, or pays late, and I get that quick jolt of adrenaline—*Will we be okay?* Then I remember we're fine; we live below our means, and we've proven time and time again that we can weather the ups and downs of self-employment.

The kids are blooming like plants that have exactly the right amount of water, soil, and sun. Martha is getting straight *As,* playing softball, and navigating the social waters of middle school with a maturity that often leaves the grown-ups who love her in awe. The other day, she was telling me about how much freedom some of her friends have. I asked if she thinks her dad and I are too strict.

"Oh, no," she said, with an emphatic shake of her head. "Actually, I think I have the four most reasonable parents on the planet."

That made my day.

After years of complaining about school, Ruby, who is now in fourth grade, has finally decided that she doesn't hate school after all. In fact, she loves it! She cries when she has to miss a day and begs me to let her stay late to be on "cleanup crew" with a few friends from her class. She's winning art awards and learning to play a complicated piece by the composer Leo Brouwer on her guitar.

Jake started kindergarten this fall, and the transition was shockingly easy. He's happy when I drop him off and happy when I pick him up. He's happy to play basketball on the play yard and happy to trace his letters at the kitchen table while I make dinner. He's happy when I organize a playdate with his friends and equally happy to stay home and play Uno with his sisters. He is, in a word, happy.

"Nothing like when Ruby started, is it?" Jake's teacher, Ms. Morrill, asked with a laugh at his first parent-teacher conference. Ms. Morrill and I mused about why the transition to kindergarten was so hard for Ruby four years earlier, and why it was so easy for Jake. Different personalities? Possibly. Or is it because Jake has a less stressed-out mom than Ruby did?

We'll never know.

AFTERWORD

YOU MAY FEEL TRAPPED. You may have gotten into this working-parent thing thinking, as so many of us do, that it would be different. Now you have kids, and you're too busy racing around to organize for economic or workplace reform. But doing *something*, no matter how small it may seem, will feel better than doing nothing. When a lot of people do a lot of little things, it can add up to real, lasting change.

As Brian often told me during the year I spent recovering from burnout: Sometimes you just have to point your feet in the right direction. Then let the walking take over.

Below is a list of ten things you can do right now. Each thing on this list is about simply pointing your feet in the right direction to create change in your home, in your heart, at your workplace, or in society at large. Pick one thing from this list and do it. It doesn't matter which one. Just pick the one that calls to you most. Then let the walking take over.

1. PRACTICE SAYING NO

Many working moms are allergic to the word *no*. We feel compromised that we're not able to give our all as workers or as moms, and so we feel obliged to say *yes,* again and again. But our energy is a precious resource. If we keep giving it all away, one day we'll find we have nothing left. We have to cultivate compassion for ourselves and find ways to say *no:* to our bosses, to our coworkers, to our kids, to *anyone who is claiming too much of our time.* It's not about letting other people down. Saying *no* to others is about saying *yes* to yourself.

Take action: I got this idea from Brian, who did this for a month and it really helped him. Write SAY NO TO SOMEONE on your to-do list. Do this every day for a week. See what happens.

2. BE AN ALLY TO OTHER WOMEN

We've all felt judged, at one time or another, about our choices to work or not work. Often we perpetuate this cycle by judging other women, even though we know better. All this judgment is, of course, a distraction. The real conflict we all feel, either directly or indirectly, is between *all parents* and the economic policies and social institutions that don't value the act of caregiving. This is what makes it so difficult to raise our children (or care for other family members), stay economically viable, and keep ourselves and our relationships intact. We have to find ways to cut each other slack.

Take action: This is such a small thing, but that's the point, and it will make a stressed-out mom in your life feel good. The next time you make dinner, like a soup, double the recipe, and drop off half at a friend's house. She will be so grateful to have a healthy meal she doesn't have to cook, and you may even find that meal swapping becomes a regular thing, one simple way to help each other stay sane.

3. TELL YOUR PARTNER WHAT YOU NEED

I get emails fairly often from women who feel alone in their parenting. They say their husbands may help a bit around the house but leave all the thinking work—planning the birthday parties, setting up dentist appointments, remembering to clip the kids' nails—to them. It's possible that these women married insensitive, hapless men. It's also possible that they're in relationships with men who love them deeply but aren't aware of how they're coming up short. Try stating, as clearly and evenly and with as much confidence as you can muster, exactly what you need from your partner, and see what happens. If you are a single parent, this exercise is about telling a friend or family member how they can make life a little more manageable, like taking the kids for a few hours on the weekend. It won't make you less busy, but it will make you feel less alone.

Take action: *Equally Shared Parenting,* by Marc and Amy Vachon, is a practical, how-to handbook for men and women who want to break out of traditional gender roles and share household chores and

the role of being a financial provider. More at www.equallyshared
parenting.com.

4. TELL YOUR BOSS YOU WANT TO WORK FROM HOME

The next time you're at work, look around. Are you sitting at a desk?
Do you see three walls, pictures of your kids, and a computer screen?
Congratulations! You should be able to work from home one day a
week, maybe more. Studies show that about 50 percent of jobs are
compatible with working from home at least part-time. Besides saving commute time, you may find the peace and quiet makes you more
productive and saner. (Also, you wouldn't believe how much laundry
you can fold while you're on one measly conference call.) The benefits
of telecommuting extend to your company, too, from boosting productivity and company morale to decreasing turnover. And if that's
not enough, it's good for the environment (fewer cars on the road).

Take action: Check out the Telework Research Network's interac-
tive calculator, which will allow you to calculate the potential savings to your employer. The site has fact sheets and other research to
help build your case for working from home. More at www.telework
researchnetwork.com.

5. TELL YOUR HR MANAGER ABOUT ROWE

Results-Only Work Environment (ROWE) is a management strategy gaining traction in corporate America. Its purpose is to make
the workplace more humane, not only for working parents but also

for anyone who wants to have meaningful work and a meaningful life. ROWE goes beyond flexible scheduling, emphasizing employee results over traditional measures like the number of hours you work. Rather than costing money, companies find that these practices save money and boost productivity.

Take action: CultureRx, the company behind ROWE, offers training for teams and managers to implement culture change. You can get started by booking a free "culture assessment" on their website: www.gorowe.com.

6. START A BABIES-AT-WORK PROGRAM

After I left Dogstar, the company started a formal "Babies at Work" program. My former coworkers tell me it was a big hit. According to the Parenting in the Workplace Institute, the program costs almost nothing to implement and has been shown to increase employee retention, improve workplace morale, and lower health care costs.

Take action: The Parenting in the Workplace Institute offers free assistance to parents who want to get their employers on board. Their contact information is available at www.parentingatwork.org.

7. SIGN UP FOR MOMSRISING

MomsRising is a leading advocacy organization for moms and the people who love them. With the help of more than a million members, they have lobbied for parental leave, flexible work, affordable child care, and other policies that improve the lives of families. I'm donating 10 percent of the proceeds of this book to MomsRising, because I believe they can make a significant impact on the issues I raise here.

Take action: Sign up for the MomsRising newsletter. Sign one petition. Better yet, give them $10. Just like that, you will become part of a movement to make America more family-friendly. This is the easiest thing on this list. It will take only five seconds, and you can do it after the kids go to bed. Join online at www.momsrising.org.

8. REGISTER FOR AN ABSENTEE BALLOT

Nothing changes in a democracy until people vote. Unfortunately, America has lower voter turnout rates than most European countries. If you're one of those people who intends to vote but gets too busy on Election Day, sign up for an absentee ballot. Save a trip to the polls and do your voting after hours.

Take action: To check the status of your voter registration, start here: www.canivote.org.

9. DONATE TO EMILY'S LIST

Half the population is women, yet we still hold about one-fifth of the positions in national government around the world. Moving more women into positions of power is an important step toward changing government policies to benefit women and families. Thanks in large part to groups like EMILY's List, the U.S. election in 2012 ushered a record number of women into Congress. Keep that trend going by giving a donation.

Take action: Learn more about EMILY's List and make your donation online at http://emilyslist.org.

10. CHANGE THE CONVERSATION

Far too often, the discussion about whether or not women can "have it all" devolves into a discussion of personal choices. (*You need to decide what's important to you: a career or a child!*) What often gets left out of the conversation is that our choices are profoundly influenced by the cultural and institutional forces around us. As Sharon Lerner writes in her 2010 book, *The War on Moms,* one of the most insidious lies we face is the idea that "women are to blame for their problems, that they are overwhelmed and overworked simply because they've individually taken on too much or done a bad job coping with their responsibilities." Until we understand the real problem—that we lack the social and systemic supports that we need in order to realize our potential and share our talents with the world—we won't ever be able to address it.

Take action: The next time you find yourself in one of these discussions, here are your talking points:

- It's not a coincidence that so many women struggle with working and raising kids. The **United States is the most hostile country** in the developed world for working parents.
- Women are now half the workforce, but we still do more than our share at home. As a consequence, a whole generation of women are becoming **psychically "maxed out."**

- Being maxed out is not only an individual problem, it's a **collective problem.**
- Being maxed out is **making us sick.** Women today are far more likely than men to suffer from depression and anxiety disorders, and studies show we are less happy than our mothers were.
- **We deserve better.** It's time to show that we value the hard work of caring for others; this means that we must change at every level of society—from our government and workplace policies to our very own homes (how we divide household labor) and hearts (how we value our own time and energy)—in order to bring our lives back into balance.
- **We need everyone to "lean in."**
  - We need **employers** to offer better part-time options, flexible schedules, and more forgiving career paths so we can take time off when our kids are young.
  - We need **government** policies that give us paid parental leave (for mothers *and* fathers), subsidized quality child care, guaranteed paid sick days, and universal health care so no one has to worry about losing benefits when they work part-time.
  - We need **men** to step up at home, so that we share all the joys and difficulties of raising families.

Find more talking points and join the discussion about what's wrong with the American workplace and how to fix it at my blog: www.workingmomsbreak.com.

NOTES

CHAPTER 2

13 Research shows 62 percent of working moms would prefer to work part-time Pew Research Center, *The Harried Life of the Working Mother* (Washington, D.C.: Pew Research Center, 2009), www.pewsocialtrends .org/2009/10/01/the-harried-life-of-the-working-mother.

14 People who work part-time earn as little as *58 cents on the dollar* Joint Economic Committee, *The Earnings Penalty for Part-Time Work: An Obstacle to Equal Pay*, April 20, 2010, www.jec.senate.gov/public/?a=Files .Serve&File_id=74203874-3821-44e4-b369-4efbe14d8745.

23 The Dutch . . . have made it possible for almost any worker to tailor her job to a part-time schedule and keep her benefits Sharon Lerner, *The War on Moms: On Life in a Family-Unfriendly Nation* (Hoboken, NJ: John Wiley & Sons, 2010), 154–55.

23 Today in the Netherlands there are part-time surgeons Katrin Bennhold, "Working (Part-Time) in the 21st Century," *New York Times*, December 29, 2010, www.nytimes.com/2010/12/30/world/europe/30iht-dutch30.html.

24 **working part-time may actually "increase employee effectiveness"**
U.S. Office of Personnel Management, "Overview," Hiring Authorities—
Part-Time & Job Sharing, www.opm.gov/policy-data-oversight/hiring-
authorities/part-time-and-job-sharing/#url=Overview.

CHAPTER 3

32 **parents of very young children incur a "sleep debt" . . . of five months or
more** Lisa Belkin, "Parents Losing Sleep," *Motherlode* (blog), *New York
Times*, July 23, 2010, http://parenting.blogs.nytimes.com/2010/07/23/
parents-losing-sleep/.

33 **CBS ran a story called "The Negative Effects of Childcare?"** Rome
Neal, "The Negative Effects of Childcare?" CBSNews, February 11, 2009,
www.cbsnews.com/stories/2003/07/16/earlyshow/living/parenting/
main563639.shtml.

38 **"Indeed most of the world's children are *not* cared for exclusively or
even primarily by the mother"** Christine Carter, PhD, *Raising Happiness: 10 Simple Steps for More Joyful Kids and Happier Parents* (New
York: Random House, 2010), 39.

39 **But most effects . . . disappear by the time children are in sixth grade**
Ibid., 158.

39 **mothers who take shorter maternity leaves . . . are at higher risk for
depression** Lerner, *War on Moms,* 111–12.

CHAPTER 5

65 **1979, the decade when divorce rates in the United States nearly dou-
bled** National Center for Health Statistics, "Advance Report of Final
Divorce Statistics, 1983," *NCHS Monthly Vital Statistics Report* 34, no. 9
(December 26, 1985): table 1.

72 **One-third of adults . . . will have an anxiety problem within their lifetime** Ronald C. Kessler et al., "Lifetime Prevalence and Age-of-Onset
Distributions of Mental Disorders in the World Health Organization's
World Mental Health Survey Initiative," *World Psychiatry* 6, no. 3 (October 2007): 168–76, www.ncbi.nlm.nih.gov/pmc/articles/PMC2174588/.

72 **forty-six million prescriptions for Xanax ... in 2010** Daniel Smith, "It's Still the 'Age of Anxiety.' Or Is It?" *Opinionator* (blog), *New York Times*, January 14, 2012. http://opinionator.blogs.nytimes.com/2012/01/14 /its-still-the-age-of-anxiety-or-is-it/.

72 **women are 60 percent more likely to suffer an anxiety disorder than men** National Institute of Mental Health, "Any Anxiety Disorder Among Adults," www.nimh.nih.gov/statistics/1anyanx_adult.shtml.

73 **a third said they take Xanax or another drug for anxiety** My own survey results: Katrina Alcorn, "What Are You On?" *Working Moms Break* (blog), January 19, 2012, www.workingmomsbreak.com/2012/01/19 /what-are-you-on/.

CHAPTER 6

95 **"If 'the conflict' continues to be framed as one between women"** Amy Allen, "'Mommy Wars' Redux: A False Conflict," *Opinionator* (blog), *New York Times*, May 27, 2012, http://opinionator.blogs.nytimes .com/2012/05/27/the-mommy-wars-redux-a-false-conflict/.

CHAPTER 7

111 **In one 2007 study, researchers at Cornell found** Shelly J. Correll, Stephen Benard, and In Paik, "Getting a Job: Is There a Motherhood Penalty?" *American Journal of Sociology* 112, no. 5 (March 2007): 1297–339.

CHAPTER 8

127 **Married couples in the United States spend, on average, 130 hours per week on paid and unpaid work** Barbara Schneider, "The Human Face of Workplace Flexibility," 6. Presented at the Alfred P. Sloan Foundation conference on Workplace Flexibility, Georgetown Law, November 29–30, 2010, http://workplaceflexibility.org/images/uploads/program_papers /schneider_-_the_human_face_of_workplace_flexibility.pdf.

127 **working parents "increasingly feel that they do not have enough time to get things done at their jobs"** Ibid.

127 **Hochschild painstakingly details this phenomenon in her book** *The Time Bind* Arlie Russell Hochschild, *The Time Bind: When Work Becomes Home and Home Becomes Work* (New York: Holt Paperbacks, 2001).

128 **Beck and Call** Beck and Call Errand Service, http://beckandcallnow .com. Business that markets its services in Middletown, Maryland.

128 **Here's how one such Boston-based company markets its service** Susan Ho, "How to Outsource Your Daily Tasks to Save Time and Money," *Boston Personal Concierge Services* (blog), Good Neighbor Concierge, April 19, 2012, www.bostonpersonalconcierge.com/_blog /Boston_Personal_Concierge_Services/post/How_to_Outsource _Your_Daily_Tasks_to_Save_Time_and_Money/.

CHAPTER 9

145 **long hours "kill profits, productivity, and employees"** Sara Robinson, "Bring Back the 40-Hour Work Week," *Salon,* March 14, 2012, www.salon .com/2012/03/14/bring_back_the_40_hour_work_week/. Originally published as "Why We Have to Go Back to a 40-Hour Work Week to Keep Our Sanity," *AlterNet,* March 13, 2012, www.alternet.org/story/154518/why _we_have_to_go_back_to_a_40-hour_work_week_to_keep_our_sanity/.

CHAPTER 11

164 **the "make it or break it" decade for our careers is . . . between ages thirty and forty** Mary Ann Mason and Eve Mason Ekman, *Mothers on the Fast Track: How a New Generation Can Balance Family and Careers* (Oxford: Oxford University Press, 2007), 110.

165 **Of women in the United States who take a couple of years off to be with their babies and then try to go back to work, about a quarter can't** Sylvia Ann Hewlett and Carolyn Buck Luce, "Off-Ramps and On-Ramps: Keeping Talented Women on the Road to Success," *Harvard Business Review,* March 1, 2005.

165 **mothers make *27 cents* less on the dollar than their male counterparts . . . Single mothers make *34 to 44 cents* less.** Joan Blades and

Kristin Rowe-Finkbeiner, "R: Realistic and Fair Wages," chap. 7 in *The Motherhood Manifesto: What America's Moms Want—and What to Do about It* (New York: Avalon, 2006). Available online on the MomsRising website: www.momsrising.org/page/moms/manifesto/chapter7.

166 The news media began to refer to this phenomenon as the "Mommy Track" in 1989 Tamar Lewin, "'Mommy Career Track' Sets Off a Furor," *New York Times,* March 8, 1989, www.nytimes.com/1989/03/08/us /mommy-career-track-sets-off-a-furor.

168 companies with more women in leadership roles outperform their competitors Sandrine Devillard, Georges Desvaux, and Pascal Baumgartner, *Women Matter: Gender Diversity a Corporate Performance Driver* (McKinsey & Company, 2007).

168 They do better on the stock exchange Claire Shipman and Katty Kay, *Womenomics: Work Less, Achieve More, Live Better* (New York: Harper Collins, 2009), 4.

168 they make higher profits Lois Joy, PhD; Nancy M. Carter, PhD; Harvey Wagner, PhD; and Sriram Narayanan, PhD, *The Bottom Line: Corporate Performance and Women's Representation on Boards* (Catalyst, 2007).

168 It could be that we're better listeners Indiana University, "Men Do Hear— But Differently Than Women, Brain Images Show," *Science Daily,* November 29, 2000, www.sciencedaily.com/releases/2000/11/001129075326.htm.

168 we have a more "open and inclusive style of management" Shipman and Kay, *Womenomics,* 7.

168 diverse groups (such as those that mix genders) tend to make better decisions James Surowiecki, *The Wisdom of Crowds* (New York: Anchor, 2005).

168 women may simply be better leaders Jack Zenger and Joseph Folkman, "Are Women Better Leaders Than Men?" *HBR Blog Network* (blog), *Harvard Business Review,* March 15, 2012, http://blogs.hbr.org /cs/2012/03/a_study_in_leadership_women_do.html.

168 Congresswoman Nancy Pelosi pointed out in a 2012 interview Laura Clawson, "Nancy Pelosi Swats Down Luke Russert's 'Offensive'

Question with a Lesson on Earning Your Job," *Daily Kos* (blog), November 14, 2012, www.dailykos.com/story/2012/11/14/1161570/-Nancy-Pelosi-swats-down-Luke-Russert-s-offensive-question-with-a-lesson-on-earning-your-job.

169 Congress passed the GI Bill *Wikipedia,* s.v. "G.I. Bill," last modified March 6, 2013, http://en.wikipedia.org/wiki/G.I._Bill.

169 For every $1 invested, the government and the economy received almost $7 in return William Triplett, "Treatment of Veterans: Is the Nation Keeping Its Promises to Veterans?" *CQ Research* 14 (November 19, 2004): 973–96, http://library.cqpress.com/cqresearcher/document.php?id=cqresrre2004111900. Calculated in 1952 dollars, factoring out inflation, from "A Cost-Benefit Analysis of Government Investment in Post-Secondary Education under the World War II GI Bill," Subcommittee on Education and Health of the Joint Economic Committee, December 14, 1988.

CHAPTER 12

172 fewer than half of working mothers . . . stay home for even *three* months 2002 U.S. Census.

179 "toxic culture" . . . was the main reason senior women leave corporate roles David Woods, "'Toxic Culture,' Not Glass Ceiling, Is the Reason for Senior Women Leaving Corporate Roles, Finds Corporate Crossovers," *HR,* June 12, 2012, www.hrmagazine.co.uk/hro/news/1073556/-toxic-culture-glass-ceiling-reason-senior-women-leaving-corporate-roles-corporate-cultures.

181 An essay . . . by the historian and *New Yorker* writer Jill Lepore Jill Lepore, "Baby Talk: The Fuss about Parenthood," *New Yorker,* June 29, 2009, www.newyorker.com/arts/critics/books/2009/06/29/090629crbo_books_lepore.

183 Having a baby is a leading cause of "poverty spells" MomsRising, "M: Maternity/Paternity Leave," MomsRising.org, www.momsrising.org/page/moms/maternity.

183 In a 2011 report called *Failing Its Families* Human Rights Watch, *Failing Its Families: Lack of Paid Leave and Work-Family Supports in* *the US*, February 23, 2011, http://www.hrw.org/reports/2011/02/23/failing-its-families-0.

CHAPTER 13

194 the United States could save $13 billion a year if women were able to breast-feed exclusively . . . for the doctor-recommended six months Melissa Bartick and Arnold Reinhold, "The Burden of Suboptimal Breastfeeding in the United States: A Pediatric Cost Analysis," *Pediatrics (The Official Journal of the American Academy of Pediatrics)*, April 5, 2010, doi:10.1542/peds.2009-1616.

194 only 14 percent of mothers are able to breast-feed that long Centers for Disease Control and Prevention, "Breastfeeding Report Card—United States, 2009," August 3, 2009.

195 your boss is *required by law* to accommodate your need to nurse Patient Protection and Affordable Care Act, Pub. L. No. 111-148, §4207, 124 Stat. 119, 318–319 (2010), www.usbreastfeeding.org/Workplace/WorkplaceSupport/WorkplaceSupportinHealthCareReform/tabid/175/Default.aspx.

CHAPTER 14

205 145 countries guarantee paid sick leave MomsRising, "S: Sick Days, Paid," MomsRising.org, www.momsrising.org/issues_and_resources/paid-sick-days-all.

205 In many countries, single people have even more days of paid sick leave Xenia Scheil-Adlung and Lydia Sandner, "The Case for Paid Sick Leave," *World Health Report*, Background Paper 9 (Geneva: World Health Organization, 2010).

205 in the United States, about half of us don't get any paid sick time "Quick Facts," Support Paid Sick Days: A Project of the National Partnership for Women & Families, http://paidsickdays.nationalpartnership.org/site/PageServer?pagename=psd_toolkit_quickfacts.

206 One of the core principles of a ROWE is that employees can have *unlimited paid time off* Jody Thompson, "Sick Time Sucks," *Cali & Jody*

Blog (blog), Results-Only Work Environment (ROWE), January 10, 2011, www.gorowe.com/blog/2011/01/10/face-time/sick-time-sucks/.

206 **Companies like Gap Inc. say ROWE has revolutionized their business** "Gap Inc. Case Study: Quality and Productivity through Trust," Results-Only Work Environment (ROWE), 2013, http://info.gorowe .com/case-study-gap-inc.

CHAPTER 15

216 **mother rats outsmart their childless counterparts at navigating mazes** Craig Howard Kinsley and Kelly G. Lambert, "The Maternal Brain," *Scientific American*, December 26, 2005, http://www.scientific american.com/article.cfm?id=the-maternal-brain.

216 **in pregnant and nursing mice, dendrites . . . are doubled** Ann Crittenden explains what happens to these mommy mouse brains in her book *If You've Raised Kids, You Can Manage Anything* (New York: Gotham, 2004).

217 **the amount of multitasking working parents do has doubled since the mid-'70s** Suzanne M. Bianchi, John P. Robinson, and Melissa Milkie, *Changing Rhythms of American Family Life* (New York: Russell Sage, 2007).

217 ***too much* multitasking has the same effect on our IQs as a bong hit** "'Infomania' Worse Than Marijuana," BBC News, April 22, 2005, http:// news.bbc.co.uk/2/hi/uk_news/4471607.stm.

217 **multitasking—something we do more than half our waking time** Shira Offer and Barbara Schneider, "Multitasking among Working Families: A Strategy for Dealing with the Time Squeeze," in *Workplace Flexibility: Realigning 20th-Century Jobs for a 21st-Century Workforce*, ed. Kathleen Christensen and Barbara Schneider (Ithaca, NY: Cornell University Press, 2010), 43–56.

CHAPTER 16

227 **In 1999, a researcher named Ellen Galinsky published a breakthrough study** Ellen Galinsky, "Ask the Children: The Breakthrough Study That

Reveals How to Succeed at Work and Parenting," Families and Work Institute, 1999.

CHAPTER 17

239 people who have children become less satisfied in their marriages Erica Lawrence et al., "Marital Satisfaction across the Transition to Parenthood," *Journal of Family Psychology* 22, no. 1 (February 2008): 41–50, doi:10.1037/0893-3200.22.1.41, www.ncbi.nlm.nih.gov/pmc /articles/PMC2367106/.

239 62 percent of working parents said they are too stressed from juggling work and family obligations to have sex Care.com, "New Study Finds Working Parents Are Too Stressed to Go to the Gym, Call a Friend, or Have Sex with Their Spouses," March 22, 2011, http://www .care.com/press-release-working-parents-are-too-stressed-p1186 -q5043318.html.

239 the balance of power has shifted and women are better equipped to negotiate for what they need Tara Parker-Pope, "She Works. They're Happy," *New York Times,* January 22, 2010, www.nytimes.com/2010/01 /24/fashion/24marriage.html.

240 researchers from UCLA videotaped thirty-two families Benedict Carey, "Families' Every Fuss, Archived and Analyzed," *New York Times,* May 22, 2010, www.nytimes.com/2010/05/23/science/23family.html.

CHAPTER 18

250 Sheryl Sandberg gave a talk called "Why We Have Too Few Women Leaders" Sheryl Sandberg, "Why We Have Too Few Women Leaders." Presented at TEDWomen conference, December 2010, http://www.ted. com/talks/sheryl_sandberg_why_we_have_too_few_women_leaders.html.

CHAPTER 19

261 "Opt-Out Revolution" (a phrase coined by Lisa Belkin) Lisa Belkin, "The Opt-Out Revolution," *The New York Times Magazine,* October 26, 2003, http://www.nytimes.com/2003/10/26/magazine/26WOMEN.html.

262 **86 percent of these women would rather work but are pushed out**
Joan C. Williams, Jessica Manvell, and Stephanie Bornstein, *"Opt Out"*
or Pushed Out? How the Press Covers Work/Family Conflict; The Untold
Story of Why Women Leave the Workforce (San Francisco: The Center
for WorkLife Law, UC Hastings College of the Law, 2006).

262 **motherhood is now the single biggest risk factor for poverty in old**
age   Ann Crittenden, *The Price of Motherhood: Why the Most Im-*
portant Job in the World Is Still the Least Valued (New York: Picador,
2010), xiii.

CHAPTER 20

274 **Long work hours, too much responsibility, job insecurity, tasks that**
have little inherent meaning, and, of course, a lack of family-friend-
ly policies all contribute to our epidemic levels of stress   Steven
Sauter et al., *Stress . . . at Work*, DHHS (NIOSH) Publication No. 99-101
(Washington, DC: National Institute for Occupational Safety and
Health, 1999), www.cdc.gov/niosh/docs/99-101/.

274 **One-third of employees report high levels of work stress**   Ibid.

274 **One-quarter of employees view their jobs as the number one stressor**
Northwestern National Life Insurance Company, *Employee Burnout:*
America's Newest Epidemic (Minneapolis, MN: Northwestern National
Life Insurance Company, 1991).

274 **Three-quarters of employees believe today's worker has more on-the-**
job stress   Princeton Survey Research Associates, *Labor Day Survey:*
State of Workers (Princeton, NJ: Princeton Survey Research Associates,
1997).

274 **percentage of American workers who fear they'll lose their jobs**
in the next twelve months almost doubled   Dennis Jacobe, "One
in Five Americans Fear Job Loss in Next 12 Months," Gallup, April
23, 2010, www.gallup.com/poll/127511/in-u.s.-fear-job-loss-double
-pre-recession-level.aspx.

275 **Problems at work are more strongly associated with health com-**
plaints   Stacey Kohler and John Kamp, *American Workers under Pres-*

sure: *Technical Report* (St. Paul, MN: St. Paul Fire and Marine Insurance Company, 1992).

275 **this stress disproportionately affects women** "Workplace Stress Greater for Women, *OfficePro* 70, no. 5 (August/September 2010): 8.

CHAPTER 21

290 **women's happiness has declined both absolutely and relative to that of men** Betsey Stevenson and Justin Wolfers, "The Paradox of Declining Female Happiness," *American Economic Journal: Economic Policy* 1, no. 2 (May 2009): 190–225.

290 **Maybe we're unhappy because more of us are single mothers** Ross Douthat, "Liberated and Unhappy," *New York Times,* May 25, 2009, www.nytimes.com/2009/05/26/opinion/26douthat.html?_r=0.

290 **Maybe we're trying too hard to be like men** Marcus Buckingham, "Women's Happiness: What We Know for Certain," *Huffington Post,* September 23, 2009, www.huffingtonpost.com/marcus-buckingham /womens-happiness-what-we_b_295876.html.

291 **we have . . . "fewer strong and frequent social connections than women did forty years ago"** Christine Carter, PhD, "Are You Sadder Than Your Mother?" *Greater Good* (blog), University of California, Berkeley, October 1, 2009, http://greatergood.berkeley.edu/raising_happiness /post/are_you_sadder_than_your_mother.

CHAPTER 23

315 **43 percent said they grappled with depression and 59 percent with anxiety *since becoming a working parent*** Katrina Alcorn, "Survey: 88% of Parents Suffer Stress-Related Health Problems," *Working Moms Break* (blog), June 20, 2011, www.workingmomsbreak .com/2011/06/20/survey-working-parents-health-problems/. Answers came from a total of 491 people who answered the question.

315 **the number one prescription in the United States for adults under forty-four is antidepressants** Laura A. Pratt, PhD, Debra J. Brody, MPH, and Qiuping Gu, MD, PhD, *Antidepressant Use in Persons Aged*

12 and Over: United States, 2005–2008, NCHS Data Brief 76 (Hyattsville, MD: National Center for Health Statistics, October 2011), www.cdc.gov/nchs/data/databriefs/db76.htm.

315 **women are less happy than men, and less happy than women of previous generations** Ibid.

315 *Newsweek* **published a story called "The Depressing News about Antidepressants"** Sharon Begley, "The Depressing News about Antidepressants," *Newsweek*, January 28, 2010, www.thedailybeast.com/newsweek/2010/01/28/the-depressing-news-about-antidepressants.html.

316 **More than twenty-seven million Americans take [antidepressants]** Mark Olfson, MD, MPH, and Steven C. Marcus, PhD, "National Patterns in Antidepressant Medication Treatment," *Arch Gen Psychiatry* 66, no. 8 (August 2009): 848–56, doi:10.1001/archgenpsychiatry.2009.81, http://archpsyc.jamanetwork.com/article.aspx?articleid=483159.

CHAPTER 24

335 **A 2009 survey by the Pew Research Center concluded** Pew Research Center, *The Harried Life of the Working Mother* (Washington, DC: Pew Research Center, 2009), www.pewsocialtrends.org/2009/10/01/the-harried-life-of-the-working-mother/.

335 **On my own website, I asked what was the *hardest* part about being a working parent** Katrina Alcorn, "Survey: 88% of Parents Suffer Stress-Related Health Problems," *Working Moms Break* (blog), June 20, 2011, www.workingmomsbreak.com/2011/06/20/survey-working-parents-health-problems/. Answers came from a total of 554 people who answered the question.

CHAPTER 25

341 **In Japan they have a word—*karoshi*—that means "death by overwork"** Joan C. Williams and Heather Boushey, *The Three Faces of Work-Family Conflict: The Poor, the Professionals, and the Missing Middle* (San Francisco: Center for WorkLife Law, and Washington, DC: Center for American Progress, January 2010).

342 Low-income families today earn 29 percent less than they did thirty years ago Ibid.

342 The year I maxed out was the first year in history that half of all U.S. workers were women Maria Shriver and the Center for American Progress, *The Shriver Report: A Woman's Nation Changes Everything,* ed. Heather Boushey and Ann O'Leary (Washington, DC: Center for American Progress, 2009).

345 Most women need an average of 2.2 liters of water a day . . . Men need 3 Mayo Clinic, "Water: How Much Should You Drink Every Day?" Mayo Clinic, October 12, 2011, www.mayoclinic.com/health/water/nu00283.

CHAPTER 26

348 in 2011, the U.S. birthrate hit 1.9 "Virility Symbols: American Fertility Is Now Lower Than That of France," *Economist,* August 11, 2012, www.economist.com/node/21560266.

348 the lowest rate ever recorded Gretchen Livingston and D'Vera Cohn, "U.S. Birth Rate Falls to a Record Low; Decline Is Greatest among Immigrants," Pew Research Center, November 29, 2012, www.pew socialtrends.org/2012/11/29/u-s-birth-rate-falls-to-a-record-low -decline-is-greatest-among-immigrants/.

349 a story in *The New York Times* by Katrin Bennhold Katrin Bennhold, "In Sweden, Men Can Have It All," *New York Times,* June 9, 2010, www .nytimes.com/2010/06/10/world/europe/10iht-sweden.html.

349 Here is the story in a nutshell Most of the facts about Swedish families came directly from the "Men Can Have It All" article cited above; however, I have since read several other articles about the same story:

> Erin Killian, "Parental Leave: The Swedes Are the Most Generous," *All Things Considered,* National Public Radio, August 8, 2011, radio broadcast, www.npr.org/blogs/babyproject/2011/08/09/139121410 /parental-leave-the-swedes-are-the-most-generous.

> Jens Hansegard, "For Paternity Leave, Sweden Asks If Two Months Is Enough," *Wall Street Journal,* July 31, 2012, http://online.wsj.com /article/SB10000872396390444226904577561100020336384.html.

Nathan Hegedus, "Snack Bags and a Regular Paycheck: The Happy Life of a Swedish Dad," *Slate,* August 31, 2010, www.slate.com /articles/double_x/doublex/2010/08/snack_bags_and_a_regular _paycheck_the_happy_life_of_a_swedish_dad.html.

350 **Studies show that when fathers spend time taking care of infants** Crittenden, *The Price of Motherhood,* 242 (see note for page 262).

351 **"family values" have done nothing to create economic stability for families** Jacob Hacker and Elisabeth Jacobs, *The Rising Instability of American Family Incomes, 1969–2004,* EPI Briefing Paper 213, Economic Policy Institute (May 28, 2008), www.epi.org/publication/bp213/.

AFTERWORD

357 *Equally Shared Parenting,* **by Marc and Amy Vachon is a practical, how-to handbook** Marc Vachon and Amy Vachon, *Equally Shared Parenting: Rewriting the Rules for a New Generation of Parents* (New York: Perigee Trade, 2010).

358 **50 percent of jobs are compatible with working from home at least part-time** "Latest Telecommuting Statistics," Telework Research Network, October 2012, www.teleworkresearchnetwork.com/telecommuting-statistics.

360 **America has lower voter turnout rates than most European countries** *Wikipedia,* s.v. "Voter turnout," s.v. "International differences," last modified March 11, 2013, http://en.wikipedia.org/wiki/Voter_turnout #International_differences.

361 **Sharon Lerner writes in her 2010 book,** *The War on Moms* Lerner, *The War on Moms,* 21 (see note for page 23).)

362 **Women today are far more likely than men to suffer from depression** One European study found that depression in middle-aged women has doubled in forty years because of the pressures of balancing work and children. More here: Nick Collins, "Women More Than Twice as Likely to Be Depressed," *Telegraph,* September 5, 2011, www.telegraph.co.uk /health/8740278/Women-more-than-twice-as-likely-to-be-depressed.html.

ACKNOWLEDGEMENTS

IT TAKES A VILLAGE TO RAISE A CHILD, and apparently it takes a village to write your first book, too. I am so grateful to so many people for being part of one or both of these villages that it's hard to know where to start.

With that said, I'll start with Brian Alcorn, who is always my first reader and editor. Without his unflagging encouragement (and many, many Sundays of taking the kids to the park), I would not have been brave enough (or had the time) to write this book. I seriously scored with this guy. Not only is he a loving husband, my best friend, and a devoted dad to our kids, he is my creative partner as well. (Darling, that pair of cape buffalo boots doesn't come *close* to expressing how grateful I am for you.)

Thanks to Angel H., Holly W., Dawn and Sherri K., Deborah W., Laura B., Liz W., Kim N., Aunt Linda, my sister Holly, Julia T., and all the moms who watched my kids and my book grow and continue to provide their support in myriad ways.

Thanks to Uncle Peter for sharing his knowledge of social science to help me make sense of the modern-day problem that has no name.

Thanks to the UC Berkeley J-School, which gave me a training ground to learn to write; Caroline Pincus, who shared valuable insights about writing a book proposal; the talented Adair Lara, who instructed me on the rules of memoir; and the ever generous and insightful Brooke Warner, who taught me to turn that memoir into a book. Thanks to Andy Couturier and his merry band of writers at The Opening (including Tobie, Chana, Bruce, Barry, Katrin, and Connie), who created a warm, inviting oasis to work on my first draft.

Thanks to Rachel Lehmann-Haupt, Phil Lapsley, Novella Carpenter, and Shoshanna Kirk, who wrote with me, took turns reading out loud in my living room, and made writing a book less lonely. (Note to self: Always make sure there is one food writer in every writers' group. The lunches are spectacular.)

Thanks to the moms and dads who read my blog and shared their stories. Without your letters and comments, I wouldn't have known if it was worth trying to tell this story.

Thanks to Randall Alifano for believing in me and in this book.

Thanks to Arlie Hochschild, Joan C. Williams, Ann Crittenden, and others who studied this topic in earnest and shared your wisdom with us all.

Thanks to Joan Blades and the folks at MomsRising for trying to make the world a better place for mothers and the people who love them.

Thanks to Krista Lyons, Laura Mazer, Donna Galassi, Natalie Nicolson, and the folks at Seal Press, for believing in this book and giving it a home.

Thanks, Mom and Dad, for always encouraging me to write, even if that means writing about you.

And thank you, finally, to Martha, Ruby, and Jake, who are turning into the most clever, funny, kind, delightful people I could possibly hope to know. You guys make me want to be my best self. I'm deeply grateful to be your mom/stepmom.

ABOUT THE AUTHOR

© Reenie Raschke

KATRINA ALCORN IS A WRITER and experience design consultant. She holds a master's degree in journalism and documentary filmmaking from UC Berkeley and is a regular blogger for *The Huffington Post*.

Since 1999, Alcorn's day job has been leading design projects with corporations in a variety of industries to help them put technology in the service of people (rather than the other way around). This work has given her an insider's glimpse at dozens of companies, from Fortune 500s to small start-ups. She has spoken at more than a dozen design conferences internationally.

She lives in Oakland, California, with her husband and three children.

Blogs

workingmomsbreak.com

huffingtonpost.com/katrina-alcorn/

Facebook

facebook.com/workingmomsbreak

Twitter

twitter.com/kalcorn

MomsRising.org

Join over a million moms and those who love them at MomsRising.org as we take on the most critical issues facing women, mothers, and families, by mobilizing massive grassroots actions to:

- Bring the voices and real world experiences of women and mothers straight to our nation's leaders;
- Amplify women's voices and issues in the national dialogue & in the media;
- Accelerate grassroots impact on Capitol Hill and at state capitols across the country;
- Hold corporations accountable for fair treatment of mothers and all workers & for ensuring the safety of their products.

We work together to increase family economic security, to decrease discrimination against women and mothers, and to build a nation where both businesses and families can thrive. Our priority issue areas include:

M Maternity and Paternity Leave (paid)

O Open Flexible & Healthy Workplace Practices

T Toxic Free Families

H Healthcare for All including Food Justice

E Early Care and Education

R Realistic and Fair Wages

S Sick Days

Together we're a powerful force for women and families!

MomsRising.org